Digital Transformation in Business
(theory/practice)

Ela Sibel Bayrak Meydanoğlu / Müge Klein /
Rıza Öztürk / Natalie Bartholomäus (eds.)

Digital Transformation in Business (theory/practice)

PETER LANG

Bibliographic Information published by the Deutsche Nationalbibliothek
The Deutsche Nationalbibliothek lists this publication in the Deutsche Nationalbibliografie; detailed bibliographic data is available online at http://dnb.d-nb.de.

Library of Congress Cataloging-in-Publication Data
A CIP catalog record for this book has been applied for at the Library of Congress.

Scientific, ethical and legal responsibility for the content of the book chapters belongs to the authors.

Printed by CPI books GmbH, Leck

ISBN 978-3-631-81718-6 (Print)
E-ISBN 978-3-631-82089-6 (E-PDF)
E-ISBN 978-3-631-82090-2 (EPUB)
E-ISBN 978-3-631-82091-9 (MOBI)
DOI 10.3726/b16910

Peter Lang – Berlin · Bern · Bruxelles · New York · Oxford · Warszawa · Wien

This publication has been peer reviewed.

www.peterlang.com

Preface

In today's increasingly digitalized world, digital transformation dramatically changes the way of doing business and reshapes business functions such as controlling, finance, human resources, marketing, logistics, etc. For companies that do not know how to implement digital transformation, it will be difficult to survive. Therefore, digital transformation is one of the most debated issues in today's business world. Being aware of this issue, Turkish-German University (TGU) hosted a conference on "Digital Transformation in Business" in cooperation with Bielefeld University of Applied Sciences on 15 November 2019 in Istanbul. The conference offered a platform where academicians as well as practitioners discussed current issues of digital transformation. The academic papers presented in the conference constitute the chapters of this book.

The chapter of Ela Sibel Bayrak Meydanoğlu, Müge Klein, Rıza Öztürk and Stephan Böhm with the title "The Role of Augmented Reality as an Experience Provider in Retail Marketing" is based on the growing importance of both experience economy and digital transformation in today's business environment. To realize pleasant and unique experiences for customers, new information technologies like Augmented Reality (AR) are used in retail marketing. Their study investigates what kind of consumer experiences retailers can generate by using AR technology and how these experiences provide benefit for retailers.

The chapter "Digital Marketing – an Empirical Study of Attitudes Toward Mobile Marketing Among Students from Different Cultures" by Rıza Öztürk and Ela Sibel Bayrak Meydanoğlu contains a study that aims to determine the effect of mobile marketing on consumer attitudes among comparable students at selected universities worldwide. The main interest was to find out about attitudes toward mobile marketing and to examine the influence of entertainment, information, irritation and credibility on the students` attitudes. And in addition, how they differ between countries and aspired degrees among the students.

Natalie Bartholomäus and Özlem Özdemir provide application-oriented recommendations for a digitally compliant target competence profile for leaders as well as initial indications for a new organizational positioning of HR in the digital age. Their contribution "The (New) Role of HR in the Digital Age: Changing Competences and Business Organization" refers to the new requirements for effective solutions for business organization, which meet the demands of the digital age.

In the chapter "Blockchains: Benefits and Problems for Applications Besides Cryptocurrencies", Ulrich Tamm analyzes the technical background and the infrastructure of blockchains in view of possible applications besides cryptocurrencies, with the aim, to yield a closer insight into benefits and problems beyond cryptography with an emphasis on the role of miners.

Using automated text analysis by applying natural language processing techniques in his contribution "Impact of Digital Transformation on the Role of Controlling", Felix Zeidler investigates if overall sentiment toward the future of Controlling has changed and if this change is driven by digitalization. There is qualitative indication that digitalization is associated with more risks than chances, whereas the main contribution is to show that natural language processing can be used in research to generate structured research data from text.

Daniel Antonius Hötte and Arthur Felk discuss in their chapter "Digital Transformation and the Law – The Impact of Information Technology on the Legal Business" how technologically charged new market entrants force changes that affect the nature of the legal business and expose it to profound challenges in an international context and in more and more of its traditional domains.

In the chapter "Enhancing Digital Reputation: New Tools for Monitoring Corporate Reputation in the Digital Age" Ela Sibel Bayrak Meydanoğlu, Margareta Teodorescu, Sevgin Batuk and Selin Karaca propose a review of the corporate reputation concept and its advantages, objectives, methods and process in the digital context. Furthermore, they analyze some of the most newly developed and frequently used tools for monitoring digital reputation and examine how these tools help organizations increase their digital and marketing capabilities.

Tolga Tuzcuoğlu examines in his chapter "Digital Transformation and the Changing Role of Controlling in Business Enterprises" the impact of digital transformation on controlling from a variety of perspectives: the changing role of controllers, organizational restructuring trends in finance and controlling, and recent instruments and concepts applied in controlling processes and practices.

The study of Lale Akarun, Necati Aras, Fatma Başak Aydemir, Ümit Bilge, Cemre Selcen, Aslı Sencer, Tuna Tuğcu, Sertaç Yerlikaya and Sedanur Yıldız, which is shown in the chapter "A Survey on Digital Maturity Models for SMEs", reviews the digital maturity models in the literature with a special focus on SMEs, by highlighting the special characteristics of SMEs and analyzing the development process considering that the maturity model is a design artifact.

Esin Bozyazı shows in her argumentative chapter, "Digital Transformation and Social Sustainability", the social dimension of challenges through digital transformation, by working out a roadmap based on previous research results.

The chapter tries to find the right questions for the next step in digital transformation, which can be used in decision processes.

The chapter of Çiydem Çatak is about so called "Robo-advisors", which are financial advisory tools that help investors make appropriate investment decisions. This study makes a comparison between robo and human advisors. While innovative robo-advisors are seen as competitors to traditional human advisors, this study shows that they are not suitable for dedicated, self-managed investors and for investors seeking a high level of personal service.

We would like to express our sincere gratitude to all authors who contributed to this book. Special thanks goes also to DAAD and Bosch Turkey for their financial support in order to realize and execute the conference. We hope that the different perspectives in this book lead to a wide range of knowledge about a topic, which will influence us in our business framework as also in our daily lives.

Istanbul, 15.11.2019

Ela Sibel Bayrak Meydanoğlu
Rıza Öztürk
Natalie Bartholomäus
Müge Klein

Table of Contents

List of Contributors

Turkish-German University, Istanbul, Turkey:

Prof. Dr. Ela Sibel Bayrak Meydanoğlu
Faculty of Economics and Business Administration, Department of Business Administration
Turkish-German University, Istanbul, Turkey
meydanoglu@tau.edu.tr

Assoc. Prof. Dr. Müge Klein
Faculty of Economics and Business Administration, Department of Business Administration
Turkish-German University, Istanbul, Turkey
klein@tau.edu.tr

Dr. Çiydem Çatak
Faculty of Economics and Business Administration, Department of Business Administration
Turkish-German University, Istanbul, Turkey
catak@tau.edu.tr

Dr. Sevgin Batuk
Faculty of Economics and Business Administration, Department of Business Administration
Turkish-German University, Istanbul, Turkey
sevgin.batuk@tau.edu.tr

Selin Karaca
Faculty of Economics and Business Administration, Department of Business Administration
Turkish-German University, Istanbul, Turkey
selin.karaca@tau.edu.tr

Bielefeld University of Applied Sciences, Bielefeld, Germany:

Prof. Dr. Natalie Bartholomäus
Faculty of Business and Health, Department of Business Administration
Bielefeld University of Applied Sciences, Bielefeld, Germany
natalie.bartholomaeus@fh-bielefeld.de

Prof. Dr. Daniel Antonius Hötte
Faculty of Business and Health, Department of Business Law
Bielefeld University of Applied Sciences, Bielefeld, Germany
daniel.hoette@fh-bielefeld.de

Prof. Dr. Rıza Öztürk
Faculty of Business and Health, Department of International Studies and Management
Bielefeld University of Applied Sciences, Bielefeld, Germany
riza.oeztuerk@fh-bielefeld.de

Prof. Dr. Felix Zeidler
Faculty of Business and Health, Department of Business Administration
Bielefeld University of Applied Sciences, Bielefeld, Germany
felix.zeidler@fh-bielefeld.de

Dr. habil. Ulrich Tamm
Faculty of Business and Health, Department of International Studies and Management
Bielefeld University of Applied Sciences, Bielefeld, Germany
ulrich.tamm@fh-bielefeld.de

Arthur Felk
Faculty of Business and Health, Department of Business Law
Bielefeld University of Applied Sciences, Bielefeld, Germany
arthur.felk@fh-bielefeld.de

Özlem Özdemir
Faculty of Business and Health, Department of Business Administration
Bielefeld University of Applied Sciences, Bielefeld, Germany
oezlem.oezdemir1@fh-bielefeld.de

Bogazici University, Istanbul, Turkey:

Prof. Dr. Lale Akarun
Faculty of Engineering, Department of Computer Engineering
Bogazici University, Istanbul, Turkey
akarun@boun.edu.tr

Prof. Dr. Necati Aras
Faculty of Engineering, Department of Industrial Engineering
Bogazici University, Istanbul, Turkey
arasn@boun.edu.tr

Prof. Dr. Ümit Bilge
Faculty of Engineering, Department of Industrial Engineering
Bogazici University, Istanbul, Turkey
bilge@boun.edu.tr

Prof. Dr. Aslı Sencer
School of Applied Disciplines, Department of Management Information Systems
Bogazici University, Istanbul, Turkey
asli.sencer@boun.edu.tr

Prof. Dr. Tuna Tuğcu
Faculty of Engineering, Department of Computer Engineering, NETLAB
Bogazici University, Istanbul, Turkey
tugcu@boun.edu.tr

Dr. Fatma Başak Aydemir
Faculty of Engineering, Department of Computer Engineering
Bogazici University, Istanbul, Turkey
basak.aydemir@boun.edu.tr

Cemre Selcen
Industry 4.0 Platform
Bogazici University, Istanbul, Turkey
cemre.selcen@boun.edu.tr

Sertaç Yerlikaya
Turkish Management Sciences Institute
Scientific and Technological Research Council of Turkey
sertac.yerlikaya@boun.edu.tr

Sedanur Yıldız
School of Applied Disciplines, Department of Management Information Systems
Bogazici University, Istanbul, Turkey
sedanur.yildiz@boun.edu.tr

RheinMain University of Applied Sciences, Wiesbaden, Germany:

Prof. Dr. Stephan Böhm
Faculty of Design, Computer Sciences and Media, Department of Media Management
RheinMain University of Applied Sciences, Wiesbaden, Germany
stephan.boehm@hs-rm.de

Koblenz University of Applied Sciences, Koblenz, Germany:

Prof. Dr. Margareta Teodorescu
Faculty of Economics
Koblenz University of Applied Sciences, Koblenz, Germany
teodorescu@hs-koblenz.de

Companies and Institutions:

Prof. Dr. Esin Bozyazı
Founder and Managing Partner of Crossover Projects GbR, Consulting and Collaboration for Sustainable Innovation & Entrepreneurship, Stuttgart, Deutschland and Co-Founder and Advisor of Institute for Social Sustainability (ifsn) in Mannheim, Deutschland.
esin.bozyazi@crossover-projects.com

Dr. Tolga Tuzcuoğlu
Controlling Section Manager
Bosch Sanayi ve Ticaret A.Ş., İstanbul, Turkey
tolga.tuzcuoglu@tr.bosch.com

Ela Sibel Bayrak Meydanoğlu, Müge Klein, Rıza Öztürk, and Stephan Böhm

The Role of Augmented Reality as an Experience Provider in Retail Marketing

Abstract: As a result of the growing importance of both experience economy and digital transformation in today's business environment, businesses tend to create pleasant and unique experiences for their customers. To realize this, new information technologies like Augmented Reality (AR) are used in retail marketing. This study investigates what kind of consumer experiences retailers can generate by using AR technology and how these experiences provide benefit for retailers. AR technology can generate pleasant sensory, affective, and relational experiences. It can support the buying decision of customers by product and service demonstrations, personalized pre-purchase offerings, and virtual trials. Moreover, it can generate a word-of-mouth effect and contribute to increasing customer satisfaction.

Keywords: Affective experience, augmented reality, experiential marketing, experience provider (ExPro), cognitive/intellectual experience, physical/behavioral experience, social/relational experience, retail marketing, sensory experience

Introduction

The rise of a new marketing approach called "experiential marketing" (Bulearca & Tamarjan, 2010; Kara & Çiçek, 2015) has been led by the rise of experience economy, where consumers focus on experiential consumption rather than the functional utility of products and services (under the assumption that the functionality is either taken for granted or seen as irrelevant). Unlike the traditional marketing approach where the selling of products and services is realized benefit-oriented, this approach aims to realize marketing goals such as increasing customer loyalty, repetitive purchasing, market share, and gaining competitive advantage by providing consumer experiences (Kara & Çiçek, 2015).

Any innovation in IT has a direct impact on business processes in the age of digital transformation. Marketing is also affected by this innovation. New technologies are being implemented rapidly in the marketing process. In this exploratory study, the role of the AR technology in generating consumer experiences is investigated based on the literature concerning experiential marketing, AR technology, and the usage of the AR technology, particularly in retail marketing. During the literature review, it was observed that the number of studies that directly deal with the usage of the AR technology for generating consumer experiences in retailing and their role for retailers is limited.

Bulearca and Tamarjan (2010) investigated in their exploratory and qualitative study whether the AR technology is convenient to use and how many functional aspects of a product consumers can experience through AR. Moreover, they analyzed whether AR leads to enjoyment and affects brand attitude. The primary objective of the study was to understand how AR experiential marketing (AREM) leads to the creation of a perceived experiential value that is accepted to increase customer satisfaction (Bulearca & Tamarjan, 2010). However, this objective cannot be understood from the results of the focus group interviews. The study primarily focuses on the investigation of the capability of AR to enhance the convenience and to contribute to consumers' enjoyment and attitude toward brands instead of explaining how this capability of AR creates consumer experiences that can lead to purchases. However, the relation among concepts such as "convenience," "enjoyment," "brand attitude," "consumer experience", and "consumer satisfaction" was not clearly expressed.

Based on the study of Bulearca and Tamarjan (2010), Eyüboğlu (2011) conducted an exploratory and qualitative study to investigate the understanding of the AR technology among Turkish consumers. It was observed that the understanding of consumers toward the AR technology could be used by Turkish brands. The objective of the study was not to explain how the AR technology can be used for generating experiences and analyzing the impact of generated experiences on retail marketing. But, in a similar manner, like Bulearca and Tamarjan (2010) the study by Eyüboğlu (2011) investigated how many functional features of a product consumers can experience through the AR technology, whether the application is easy to implement and interact. Unlike Bulearca and Tamarjan (2010), Eyüboğlu (2011) investigated whether the AR technology is useful compared to other promotional activities, time and cost-efficient, enjoyable, relevant for the applied product, and if the AR app entails a WOM factor. The relation between the concepts above—convenience, enjoyment, relevancy of idea, and WOM factor—and their connection to generate consumer experience was also not discussed in the study of Eyüboğlu (2011).

Küçüksaraç and Sayımer (2016) conducted an exploratory and qualitative study to explore whether AR apps meet the physical and psychological needs of Turkish consumers with the purchased product or service. Moreover, they investigated the emotional reactions of Turkish consumers toward purchased products and services, and the impact of the physical and nonphysical price paid (e.g., time and effort) during the purchase process. Primarily, they focused on explaining the reasons for using AR apps in marketing campaigns and not directly to investigate how AR apps generate consumer experiences and what the impacts of these experiences on retail marketing are.

Dacko (2017), in his study, investigated the experiential value of mobile AR (MAR) shopping apps for customers. The aspects they analyzed are the benefits MAR apps provide to retailers, the user profile of MAR apps, how users of MAR apps learned about these apps, the drawbacks of using MAR apps from the viewpoint of consumers, and users' view about the future of MAR apps. Moreover, they studied the impacts of MAR shopping apps on retail preferences of users, the purpose of consumers for using MAR apps, and how MAR apps change the shopping behavior of consumers. Different from other existing studies, where experiences of consumers generated by AR apps and their role in retail marketing are discussed more extensively, the study of Dacko (2017) deals with different issues related to MAR apps simultaneously.

As a result of the literature research, it can be stated that there is no systematic approach concerning the use of the AR technology to generate consumer experiences in retail. Furthermore, there is no research that defines the type of experiences generated through AR apps and explains the role of these experiences in retail marketing. This study aims to close this gap. The study is organized as follows: first, the concepts "AR technology" and "experiential marketing" are introduced. Then, it is explained how AR technology generates consumer experiences based on some sample applications in retailing. Next, the role of experiences generated by the AR technology in retail marketing is explained. Finally, in the conclusion section, the findings are summarized, limitations are discussed, and future research areas are proposed.

Augmented Reality

Augmented reality is an interactive technology that modifies physical objects (e.g., a product or a person) or surrounding space with superimposed virtual (computer-generated) objects such as textual information, images, videos, etc., in real-time (Javornik, 2016). Real and virtual objects are combined with AR technology (Azuma et al., 2001). This feature enables a user to see virtual objects superimposed in the real world. AR is applied in a real environment unlike the virtual reality (VR) technology, which enables users to immerse inside a synthetic, artificial environment (virtual environment) (De Paolis & Aloisio, 2010). Augmentation is the special characteristic of the AR technology that differentiates this technology from other interactive technologies. AR apps can be classified into three groups based on the entities they augment (Javornik, 2016):

- **AR apps that augment a surrounding place:** For example, on a smart device a virtual element (e.g., virtual furniture) can be superimposed on a physical room base by an AR app on a smart device (Javornik, 2016).
- **AR apps that augment a product:** An additional digital content can be obtained with AR apps by scanning a related image. For instance, reviews or a video of a product can be displayed on the screen of a smart device by scanning a magazine ad about the product (Javornik, 2016).
- **AR apps that enable self-augmentation:** Screens of smart devices convey a reflection of your body or its part (e.g., head and face) by using these apps. Users can make a trial on this reflection with virtual add-ons, such as glasses, make-up, and clothes (Javornik, 2016).

The AR technology can be applied in various areas, such as medicine, gaming, entertainment, education, tourism, military, real estate, aviation, architecture, and industry. One of the application areas is marketing (Schart & Tschanz, 2015).

Experiential Marketing

According to Pine and Gilmore (2017), economic evolution is defined as a process in which the agrarian economy (based on commodities) was superseded by the industrial economy (based on goods), which in turn was superseded by the service economy (based on service provision), which is now being replaced by the experience economy (based on experiences).

In the agrarian economy, the commodities that were extracted from nature were sold after they were processed. In the industrial economy, the commodities that were used as raw materials were processed and transformed into goods. In the service economy, companies were differentiated from each other by offering services added to their goods. Companies wanted to create an added value for consumers and increase customer satisfaction by offering these services. Moreover, it was believed that the identification of goods in the market could be eliminated or decreased by the offered services. However, services also became identical and lost the potential for differentiation over time. In the experience economy, experiences were defined as a distinctive economic value (Bahçecioğlu, 2014). Companies try to provide unique experiences for their consumers and differentiate among their competitors through staged experiences (Günay, 2008).

The progression of the economic value and the differences between the experience economy and former stages as reported by Pine and Gilmore (2017) are illustrated in Figure 1.

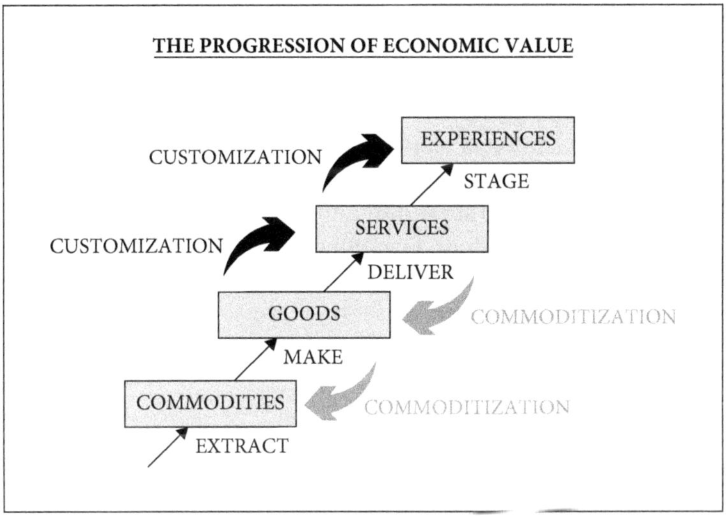

Figure 1: The Progression of Economic Value (Pine & Gilmore, 2017).

The progression of economic value is explained by Pine and Gilmore (1998) based on a coffee example, wherein coffee beans are defined as a commodity. Coffee beans that are packaged and sold in a grocery store are defined as goods, whereas a cup of coffee served at a coffee shop is defined as a service. A cup of coffee served in the lobby of a five-star luxury hotel can be considered an example of an experience (Pine & Gilmore, 1998). Furthermore, as a result of the increasing role of experiences, companies try to differentiate from their competitors and create loyal customers by unique experiences (Bahçecioğlu, 2014). Marketing also took its share from the defined progression of economic value. Experience plays an important role in the marketing and the sale of products by influencing consumers' behaviors. This significance of experience in marketing produced the term "experiential marketing".

Schmitt (1999a) defines traditional marketing based on the following features:

1. Traditional marketing focuses on functional features and benefits of products or services: Marketing practitioners think that consumers decide to buy a product or service considering only its functions and benefits for them. For instance, according to this approach, a consumer who wants to buy a laptop decides to buy it considering its basic functions, such as speed, portability, connectivity, etc. (Schmitt, 1999a).

2. Product category and competition are narrowly defined: According to traditional marketing, competition takes place only among narrowly defined product categories. For instance, McDonald's and Burger King have the same product category, and they are considered as competitors to each other, and for both of them, Pizza Hut or Starbucks are not defined as competitors although they operate in the same sector.
3. Customers are considered as rational rather than emotional decision-makers.
4. Methods and tools used in marketing are analytical, quantitative, and verbal: For instance, inputs of regression analysis usually consist of verbal ratings collected in interviews or surveys. Moreover, purchase or choice is predicted, and relative importance weights are assessed based on several predictors.

Experiential marketing differs from traditional marketing, considering the following characteristics (Schmitt, 1999a):

1. Experiential marketing focuses on customer experiences instead of functional features and benefits. Experiences replace functional values and provide sensory, emotional, cognitive, behavioral, and relational values to consumers.
2. Consumption is defined as a holistic experience: "*Experiential marketing approach diversifies the concept of a product/service category and examines the meaning of the specific consumption situation in a broader sociocultural context* (Schmitt, 1999a, p. 58)."
3. Experiential marketing practitioners consider customers not only as rational but also as emotional human beings.
4. In experiential marketing, not only analytical, quantitative, and verbal methods but also intuitive and qualitative methods (e.g., focus group interview, brainstorming, in-depth interview) are used. According to this approach, methods and tools used in marketing are eclectic.

Experiences are considered as memorable events (Pine & Gilmore, 2017) that "*occur as a result of encountering, undergoing, or living through things*" (Schmitt, 1999a, p. 57) and are based on direct or indirect consumer engagement (Brakus, Schmitt & Zarantonello, 2009). Direct experiences are gained directly at the point of product purchase or consumption, whereas indirect experiences are felt when consumers encounter advertising or any marketing communication (Brakus et al., 2009).

Five types of experiences are defined by Schmitt (1999a), which are called strategic experiential modules (SEMs). Managers can apply them to create different types of customer experiences: sensory experiences (SENSE), affective

Table 1: Strategic Experiential Modules

Module	Consumer Experience
SENSE (Sensory Experience)	Experiences for five senses
FEEL (Affective Experience)	Experiences for feelings
THINK (Cognitive/Intellectual Experience)	Experiences for cognitive functions
ACT (Physical/Behavioral Experience)	Experiences for behaviors, physical activities
RELATE (Social/Relational Experience)	Experiences for social groups, interaction

Note. Adapted from "Customer experience management: Influencing on human Kansei to management of technology" by S. Y. Nagasawa, 2008, *The TQM Journal, 20*, p. 314.

experiences (FEEL), cognitive/intellectual experiences (THINK), physical/behavioral experiences (ACT), and social identity and relation to a reference group or culture (RELATE).

- **SENSE - Sensory Experiences:** These experiences appeal to the five senses of consumers "seeing, hearing, touching, tasting, and smelling" (Schmitt, 1999a). For instance, with the smell of coffee that diffuses in the environment as well as with posters on the walls, which describe different coffee types and the exhibition of coffee beans in a Starbucks store, Starbucks aims to create an experience on customers by appealing to their smell and sight senses (Uygur & Doğan, 2013).
- **FEEL - Affective Experiences:** These experiences appeal to the inner feelings and emotions of consumers (Schmitt, 1999a). For instance, a sparkling beverage brand aims to create affective experiences on consumers by placing products on iftar tables within its advertising campaign during Ramadan, which has a high value in the Turkish society (Güney & Karakadılar, 2015).
- **THINK - Cognitive/Intellectual Experiences:** These experiences appeal to the intellects of consumers to sustain customers with a cognitive and problem-solving experience. Generally, they are used for new technology products (Schmitt, 1999a). For instance, a smartphone brand that launches a new app sustains its consumers who are interested in this app with a cognitive experience by this new app, if consumers need to spend a cognitive effort to use the app.
- **ACT - Physical/Behavioral Experiences:** These experiences are related to physical behaviors and lifestyles of consumers. In this approach, alternative ways of doing things and alternative ways of living and interactions are offered to customers (Schmitt, 1999a). Generally, famous people, inspiring role models, are used in marketing campaigns to create behavioral changes in consumers. For instance, in a milk advertising campaign, famous people can be used to

encourage people to drink milk and to make consuming milk a lifestyle. These types of campaigns focus on creating physical experiences (Schmitt, 1999b).

- **RELATE - Social/Relational Experiences:** These experiences appeal to consumers' senses of belonging. It makes consumers feel that they belong to a social group in which they think they belong or wish to belong (Schmitt, 1999a). For instance, a brand in a luxury automotive segment can create a relational experience on its consumers by organizing a party for the launch of its new model wherein consumers share common pleasure and those belonging to the same socioeconomic class come together (Güney & Karakadılar, 2015).

Tools that are used to create experiences are called experience providers (ExPro) (Schmitt, 1999a). The defined experiences can be implemented with the ExPros listed as follows:

- **Communications:** Communication media such as advertising, public relations, brochures, annual reports, etc. (Kotler & Keller, 2006; Schmitt, 1999a).
- **Visual and Verbal Identity, and Signage:** Tools related to corporate identity such as brand, logo, etc. (Kotler & Keller, 2006).
- **Product Presence:** Tools related to product presence such as product design, product packaging, etc. (Kotler & Keller, 2006; Schmitt, 1999a).
- **Branding:** Tools such as sponsoring, product placement in films, etc. (Kotler & Keller, 2006; Schmitt, 1999a).
- **Spatial Environment:** Tools related to visuality, such as being located on retailers' shelves, trade fairs, etc. (Kotler & Keller, 2006; Schmitt, 1999a).
- **People:** such as managers, salespersons, customer representatives, etc. (Kotler & Keller, 2006; Schmitt, 1999a).
- **Electronic Media** (Schmitt, 1999a).

In the study of Schmitt (1999a), the scope of the ExPro "electronic media" was not defined. Different types of digital technologies and tools such as websites, e-mails, social media, video portals, mobile applications (Kotler & Keller, 2006), AR apps, and VR technology are considered as ExPros in today's world where digital transformation is used frequently. In this study, the term *digital tools* instead of electronic media is recommended, which is thought to have a wider scope.

AR Technology: Is It an Experience Provider?

The widespread application use of various digital technologies led to the usage of some of these technologies to create consumer experiences. Various terms are used for these types of experiences such as "online experience" (e.g., Zhou et al., 2007), "web experience" (e.g., Constantinides et al., 2010), "online customer experience" (e.g., Chen & Jin, 2012), and "virtual experience" (e.g., Li et al., 2001) based on the used digital technology. The term "digital experience" can be used as an upper term to be more inclusive. Since the AR technology is discussed in this study, the study focuses on the term "virtual experience" that indicates the experience provided via the technologies such as AR technology, VR technology, or 3D technology used in online platforms (Bahçecioğlu, 2014). Below, based on some examples, the uses of AR technology to generate virtual experiences in retail marketing campaigns are discussed. In this context, it is also investigated which type of experience (sensory, affective, cognitive/intellectual, physical/behavioral, or social/relational) can be generated via AR apps.

AR apps create sensory experiences directly by appealing to senses of seeing and hearing of consumers as well as affective experiences by arousing emotions such as entertainment and curiosity in customers. For instance, Pepsi Co. UK surprised and delighted Londoners by its so-called "unbelievable bus shelter" AR advertising campaign (Figures 2–4). In this case, a special real-time display was placed on the exterior face of the glass billboard wall of a bus shelter which projects the illusion of the street ahead and visualizes an augmented live stream of exaggerated events (including an alien invasion, a robot attack, a racing tiger, and a crashing meteor) from the inside (Caula, 2014; Göçmen, 2018).

Figure 2: AR Advertising Campaign for Pepsi Max (Digital Marketing Group 48, 2015).

Figure 3: AR Advertising Campaign for Pepsi Max (Büsser, 2014).

As a result, people waiting at the bus shelter are surprised with unusual scenarios on the street and required to look at the exterior side of the glass wall so that they could see the advertisement of Pepsi Max (Figure 4).

Figure 4: AR Advertising Campaign for Pepsi Max (Digital Marketing Group 48, 2015).

Similarly, the AR technology is used by the clothing brand American Apparel to enhance the in-store customer experience. Shoppers can scan a picture of signage by using a mobile AR app that shows product details, including customer reviews, color variants, and pricing (Figure 5). The app also enables shoppers to share product photos or their views about the products by using e-mail or social media (Sheehan, 2018). The AR app contributes indirectly to relational experiences by enabling consumers to share views and information on social media. Getting likes or comments concerning his shares makes consumer feel that he belongs to the social network in which he shared views, information or can show him that his thoughts are well accepted in the social network.

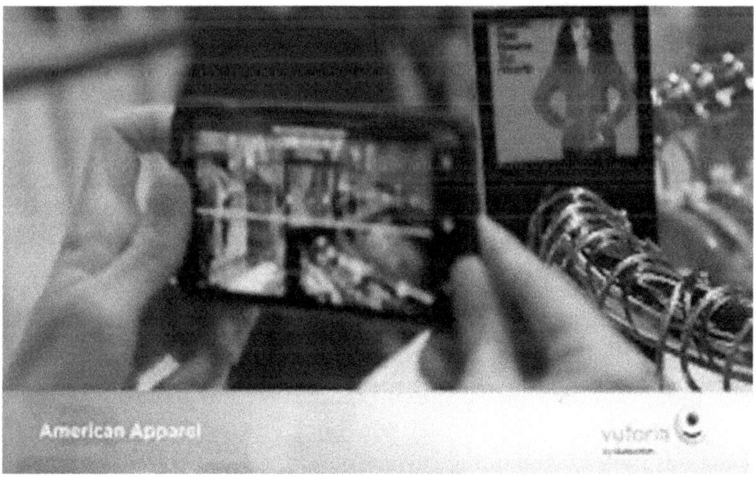

Figure 5: AR App of American Apparel (Sheehan, 2018).

Another example that shows how AR apps generate sensory experiences concerning the seeing sense is the AR app of the brand Timberland. By using a large screen and camera, Timberland created a virtual fitting room and used this room as one of the main window displays (Figure 6). Shoppers passing by could stand in front of the camera and see a virtual version of themselves on the screen. They could try different products without even entering the store (Sheehan, 2018). Hence, such a fitting room experience can let consumers decide to buy a product.

No AR app or add examples were encountered in the existing literature, which could generate physical/behavioral or cognitive/intellectual experiences. In this context, although it is not possible to say something certain about the contribution of AR technology in generating physical/behavioral and cognitive/

Figure 6: AR App of Timberland (Sheehan, 2018).

intellectual experiences, it is important not to ignore the possibility of benefiting from the AR technology directly or indirectly in creating such experiences in future as a result of rapid developments in the field of IT.

The Role of the AR Technology in Retail Marketing

In the 1960s, postmodernism primarily affected art and architecture, and then it affected various areas (Odabaşı, 2006). Though the primary objective of consumption has not changed in the current period, where postmodern trends are being applied, there has been a difference in the style of consumption. It is important to note that today's consumer is interested in whether an interesting product or service leads to an unforgettable experience instead of the functional characteristics of the interesting offering. This understanding of consumers results in the concepts of "experience economy" and "experiential marketing" as described above. In line with the concept of postmodern marketing, customer-oriented companies benefit from strategic and creative marketing approaches to create customer satisfaction. Experiential marketing is one of these strategic and creative marketing approaches (Genç, 2009). The literature on traditional consumer behaviors states that consumption is an activity that aims to meet the needs and the buying decision of consumers, which relies on the cost-benefit analysis of consumption. It was observed that changing consumer characteristics brought different perspectives to consumer behavior. Among one of these perspectives is the experiential perspective (Altunışık, 2007). The experiential dimension of consumption is emphasized in the experiential perspective. According to this perspective, consumers give importance not only to the rational and functional benefits while purchasing products or services, but also to the interesting, unique, and emotional experiences that come along during the purchasing process.

Nowadays, it is inevitable for companies to benefit from new information technologies in generating consumer experiences as digital transformation is being discussed intensively. The AR technology can generate unique and pleasant sensory, affective, and relational experiences for consumers in the retail sector as clearly explained and understood in the above examples. These experiences affect conversion rates, store footfall, application of personalization in the pre-purchase phase (Dacko, 2017) and buying decisions of consumers, and they also exhibit the WOM effect.

AR technology can "*put the product in the hand of users*" (Woods, 2009, p. 37). It enables consumers "*to test the product as they would already own it and can trigger a purchase*" (Bulearca & Tamarjan, 2010, p. 241). For instance, a mobile AR make-up mirror enables the screen of your smart device to reflect your face. You can then make a trial on this reflection with an add-on "virtual make-up" (Javornik, 2016). As a result of this trial, you can buy the product though you did not think of buying it before trial. Therefore, AR apps have the potential to convert consumers into customers.

Some AR apps enable personalization, which is an important aspect for consumers. For instance, based on the skin color of consumers, Shiseido introduced an app for its consumers to try different cosmetic products (Dacko, 2017). Personalization and opportunity for trial can convert consumers who use the app into customers.

An interesting and entertaining AR app, such as an app of Timberland as defined above, can arouse curiosity among consumers, or consumers can find such an app entertaining. This can drive store footfall that can also increase conversation rates. Entertaining AR apps also exhibit a WOM effect (Eyüboğlu, 2011) related to the marketed product or service, which is the subject of the app. Consumers who observed an interesting experience with an AR app are more likely to communicate with others about the app and the retailer, as well as his products and services. Hence, consumers can be attracted, who are likely to convert into customers after using the app.

The AR technology can support the subprocesses such as "information search," "evaluation of alternatives," and "postpurchase behavior" of the buying decision process. Consumers can receive information about products as well as services and share information or read views on social media about the relevant offerings by using AR apps (Küçüksaraç & Sayımer, 2016). These are also important factors that help in attracting consumers.

The benefits of using the AR technology, which include opportunity for trial, personalization, entertaining demonstrations, and support of the buying decision process, essentially increase customer satisfaction which plays an important role in increasing customer loyalty, repetitive purchasing, market share, and gaining competitive advantage as the satisfied consumer will ignore competing brands' ads and refrain from buying products or services of competitors (Bulearca & Tamarjan, 2010; Yuan & Wu, 2008). Moreover, satisfied customers also promote the offerings that they have purchased (Yuan & Wu, 2008).

Conclusion

In this study, the following conclusions have been drawn based on previous studies in the relevant literature:

- "*Along with the experience economy, the strategy of marketing world has been transformed for providing emotion-oriented consumer experience instead of traditionally selling benefit-oriented products and services.*" (Kara & Çiçek, 2015, p. 177).
- AR technology can generate unique and pleasant sensory, affective, and relational experiences for consumers (Dacko, 2017).
- Consumer experiences (such as opportunity for trial, personalization in the pre-purchase phase, and entertaining demonstrations) generated by AR technology
    - enable consumers to get information about products and services.
    - can contribute to increase store footfall.
    - can generate WOM effect.
    - can contribute to increases customer satisfaction.

The AR technology—one of the enabling automation technologies of digital transformation—is likely to be used more widely in marketing shortly as a result of the increasing importance of digital transformation. The findings of this study shed light on the role of generated consumer experiences in retail marketing by using AR technology. In this perspective, it is considered informative for retailers who can use the AR technology in their marketing campaigns.

This study is conceptual. Therefore, the findings require validation by using convenient quantitative and qualitative methods in future research. Also, in future research, it can be investigated whether the consumer experiences generated with the AR technology affect the purchasing decision of consumers, and if so, then to what extent experiences are decisive. The present study provides preliminary information to conduct future research. To evaluate whether generated experiences have a value for consumers, future quantitative research can also be conducted for measuring the perceived experiential value of consumers.

References

Altunışık, R. (2007). Yeni Tüketicilerin Tüketime Yansıyan Farklılıkları. In Ö. Torlak, R. Altunışık, & S. Özdemir (Eds.), *Yeni Tüketici* (pp. 111–131). İstanbul: Hayat Yayınları.

Azuma, R., Baillot, Y., Behringer, R., Feiner, S., Julier, S., & Macintyre, B. (2001). Recent advances in augmented reality. *IEEE Computer Graphics and Applications, 21*(6), 34–47.

Bahçecioğlu, A. (2014). *Sanal Deneyimsel Pazarlamanın Tüketici Tutumuna Etkisi* (Yüksek lisans tezi). Ege Üniversitesi Sosyal Bilimler Enstitüsü, İzmir.

Brakus, J. J., Schmitt, B. H., & Zarantonello, L. (2009). Brand experience: what is it? How is it measured? Does it affect loyalty? *Journal of Marketing, 73*(3), 52–68.

Bulearca, M., & Tamarjan, D. (2010). Augmented reality: A sustainable marketing tool. *Global Business and Management Research: An International Journal, 2*(2), 237–252.

Büsser, M. (2014, April 14). *Augmented reality bites as Pepsi max bus stop advert stuns Londoners* [Image]. Retrieved April 26, 2019, from https://www.mbandf.com/en/parallel-world/augmented-reality-bites-as-pepsi-max-bus-stop-advert-stuns-londoners.

Caula, R. (2014, March 25). *Augmented reality bus shelter by Pepsi max creates unbelievable scenarios* [Video file]. Retrieved April 26, 2019, from https://www.designboom.com/technology/augmented-reality-bus-shelter-pepsi-max-03-24-2014.

Chen, B., & Jin, Y. (2012). Online customer experience and its determinants in e-Retailing. *International Review on Computers and Software, 7*(5), 2353–2360.

Constantinides, E., Lorenzo-Romero, C., & Gómez, M. A. (2010). Effects of web experience on consumer choice: a multicultural approach. *Internet Research, 20*(2), 188–209.

Dacko, S. G. (2017). Enabling smart retail settings via mobile augmented reality shopping apps. *Technological Forecasting and Social Change, 124*, 243–256.

De Paolis, L. T., & Aloisio, G. (2010). Augmented Reality in Minimally Invasive Surgery. In S. C. Mukhopadhyay & A. Lay-Ekuakille (Eds.), *Advances in*

Biomedical Sensing, Measurements, Instrumentation and Systems (pp. 305–320). Berlin, Heidelberg: Springer.

Digital Marketing Group 48. (2015, April 6). *Pepsi Max "Unbelievable" campaign* [Image]. Retrieved April 26, 2019, from https://bs2dm48.wordpress.com/2015/04/06/pepsi-max-unbelievable-campaign/.

Eyüboğlu, E. (2011). Augmented reality as an exciting online experience: Is it really beneficial for brands?. *International Journal of Social Sciences and Humanity Studies*, *3*(1), 113–123.

Genç, B. (2009). *Deneyimsel Pazarlamanın Tüketici Satın Alma Kararlarına Etkisi* (Yüksek lisans tezi). Ege Üniversitesi Sosyal Bilimler Enstitüsü, İzmir.

Göçmen, P. Ö. (2018). Artırılmış Gerçeklik Uygulamaları ile Yeni Medya Reklam Tasarımı. *Sanat ve Tasarım Dergisi*, Aralık, 175–191.

Günay, G. N. (2008). Hizmet pazarlamasından deneyimsel pazarlamaya: bir güzellik merkezinde uygulama. In M. Ş. Akdoğan (Ed.), *13. Ulusal Pazarlama Kongresi (2008) "Pazarlamada Yeni Yaklaşımlar" Bildiriler Kitabı* (pp. 64–72). Nevşehir: Nevşehir Üniversitesi İktisadi ve İdari Bilimler Fakültesi Yayınları.

Güney, H., & Karakadılar, İ. S. (2015). Starbucks firmasının deneyimsel pazarlama uygulamalarının incelenmesi. *İÜ İşletme Fakültesi İşletme İktisadı Enstitüsü Yönetim Dergisi*, *26*(79), 131–155.

Javornik, A. (2016). Augmented reality: Research agenda for studying the impact of its media characteristics on consumer behaviour. *Journal of Retailing and Consumer Services*, *30*, 252–261.

Kara, M., & Çiçek, B. (2015). Deneyimsel Pazarlama ve Satın Alma Karar Sürecine Etkisi: Termal Turizm Sektöründe Bir Uygulama. *Gümüşhane Üniversitesi Sosyal Bilimler Enstitüsü Elektronik Dergisi*, *6*(13), 177–200.

Kotler, P., & Keller, K. L. (2006). *Marketing Management* (12th ed.). Upper Saddle River: Prentice Hall.

Küçüksaraç, B., & Sayımer, İ. (2016). Deneyimsel Pazarlama Aracı Olarak Artırılmış Gerçeklik: Türkiye'deki Marka Deneyimlerinin Etkileri Üzerine Bir Araştırma. *İstanbul Üniversitesi İletişim Fakültesi Dergisi*, *51*(2), 73–95.

Li, H., Daugherty, T., & Biocca, F. (2001). Characteristics of virtual experience in electronic commerce: A protocol analysis. *Journal of Interactive Marketing*, *15*(3), 13–30.

Nagasawa, S. Y. (2008). Customer experience management: Influencing on human Kansei to management of technology. *The TQM Journal*, *20*(4), 312–323.

Odabaşı, Y. (2006). *Postmodern Pazarlama* (2nd ed.). İstanbul: Mediacat Yayıncılık.

Pine, J., & Gilmore, J. (1998). *The Experience Economy*. Cambridge: Harvard Business Review Press.

Pine, J., & Gilmore, J. (2017). Distinctive experiences. *Journal of Shopper Research*, *1*(1), 60–65.

Schart, D., & Tschanz, N. (2015). *Praxishandbuch Augmented Reality für Marketing, Medien und Public Relations*. Konstanz: UVK Verlagsgesellschaft.

Schmitt, B. (1999a). Experiential marketing. *Journal of Marketing Management*, *15*(1-3), 53–67.

Schmitt, B. (1999b). *Experiential Marketing: How to Get Customers to Sense, Feel, Think, Act, Relate*. New York: The Free Press.

Sheehan, A. (2018, February 21). *How These Retailers Use Augmented Reality to Enhance the Customer Experience* [Video file]. Retrieved April 26, 2019, from https://www.shopify.com/retail/how-these-retailers-are-using-augmented-reality-to-enhance-the-customer-experience.

Uygur, S. M., & Doğan, S. (2013). Deneyimsel Pazarlamanın Müşteri Memnuniyeti Üzerine Etkisi: Restoranlar Üzerine Bir Araştırma. *Dumlupınar Üniversitesi Sosyal Bilimler Dergisi*, *37*, 33–48.

Woods, A. (2009). Augmented reality: reality check. *Revolution Magazine*, April, 36–39.

Yuan, Y. H. E., & Wu, C. K. (2008). Relationships among experiential marketing, experiential value, and customer satisfaction. *Journal of Hospitality & Tourism Research*, *32*(3), 387–410.

Zhou, L., Dai, L., & Zhang, D. (2007). Online shopping acceptance model–A critical survey of consumer factors in online shopping. *Journal of Electronic Commerce Research*, *8*(1), 41–62.

Rıza Öztürk, and Ela Sibel Bayrak Meydanoğlu

Digital Marketing – an Empirical Study of Attitudes Toward Mobile Marketing Among Students from Different Cultures

Abstract: Today's era of internet has opened a gate of a vast variety of opportunities for businesses. As we live in a super-connected world these days, marketing is no longer as it once was. This is especially true due to the rise of social media, which has changed how businesses communicate with potential and existing clients. Nowadays, it is important to have a strong online presence, coupled with a great brand that is presented uniformly across all mediums. Digitalization using Mobile Marketing is an essential part of this for companies who want to utilize the power of the internet in order to boost business. The study aims to determine the effect of mobile marketing on consumer attitudes among comparable students at ten selected worldwide universities. The main interest of this chapter is to find out about attitudes toward mobile marketing and to examine the influence of entertainment, information, irritation and credibility on consumer (students) attitudes. And, in addition, how they differ between different (selected) countries and aspired degrees among students. A questionnaire was used as data collection method, and a logistic regression analysis was computed to test the stated hypothesis. The result of this analysis is that entertainment, credibility and permission have a significant positive influence on the consumer attitude – Irritation, a negative significant influence along with it and Credibility, without a significant influence. Regarding the countries, the study shows a positive significance for South Korea, Turkey and USA and a negative influence for France, Germany and Czech Republic. The aspired degrees do not play a significant role. The study recommends: For companies who use this marketing strategy and want to go for a mobile marketing campaign need to better understand which kind of keys they have to be aware, if they want to sell, inform or just communicate with customers.

Keywords: Mobile marketing, mobile advertising, permission marketing, entertainment, informativeness, credibility, irritation, consumer attitude, logistic regression, IBSEN

Introduction

Mobile marketing is the result of steadily evolving marketing opportunities. It is not a new thing, but within the last years, mobile marketing strongly gained application areas and popularity. Nonetheless, mobile marketing still is not familiar to majority of the general public. Apart from professionals who work in the area of digital marketing, the knowledge about what mobile marketing is and which instruments go along with it is limited. The research on mobile marketing is also limited. While a lot of work is being done on digital marketing and other forms of marketing, mobile marketing is very less explored. An additional international interest exists, as mobile marketing is becoming more and more transnational. Social media serves as a stage for campaigns from all around the world. Taking a look on most users' Instagram or Facebook threads, a large part of the content is not native. This applies not only for private, but also for advertising content. Additionally, the extension of mobile networks worldwide increasingly connects people and ideas. But it also gives insights into a diverse marketing landscape. Does this diverse landscape bring along different attitudes toward mobile marketing? Is there an impact of the national affiliation on the formation of these attitudes?

For these purposes, a research in the form of a quantitative study with business students as target group takes the center stage. Business students are chosen, as they have basic knowledge about marketing and are considered as digitally versed. Furthermore, the study is executed in ten countries, with the aim to get an insight of attitudes toward mobile marketing in different countries and find out about their differences. For this purpose, the research is executed in cooperation with the members of the International Business Studies Exchange Network (IBSEN). This network unites ten universities in Canada, Czech Republic, Finland, France, Germany, Italy, Netherlands, South Korea, Turkey and the United States of America (USA)[1].

Mobile Marketing

Mobile marketing is a comparatively young phenomenon. Its main embossment can be traced back to the year 2003, when the first commercial SMS launched. In 2005, the first SMS campaigns were created by major brands like Nike and Pontiac (EZ Texting Feb 2019). The implementation of mobile internet is another important aspect of mobile marketing, as it opens up a wide range of possibilities far beyond SMS-marketing. In 1998, mobile internet in the form of technologies like the Wireless Application Protocol (WAP) developed. WAP is a transmission standard that enables the access to simplified websites via mobile

1 Many thanks to: Carol Steinhaus, Michel Labour, Gülin Vardar, Veronique Sangetti, Alessandro Mura, Alessandro Spano, Patrizio Monfardinio, Amber Pohl, David Stangeland, Martin Pelikan, Karel Tomsik, Jana Melezinkova, Armand von Ostrom, Rob Laas, Maria Kangasniemi-Haapala, and Mikhael Nemilentsev.

devices. Smartphones and their toned down version, the feature phones, evolved. The first smartphone was launched in 1994 by the company IBM and initially targeted only wealthy business people. Its main special features were a calendar, an e-mail and a fax function as well as software applications available for download. Feature phones are web-enabled mobile phones with less functions than smartphones but more functions than regular mobile phones. They are not only used for calls like the previous units, but are equipped with features such as cameras, music players, SMS and internet browsers. Despite the fascination for the new mobile internet, the implementation was characterized by long loading times that were connected to waiting times and high costs. Additionally, phones at that time were not created for a user-friendly utilization of internet with their small displays and restricted operational options.

Now, the question for the classification of mobile marketing in the construct of marketing comes up. Defining mobile marketing in clear terms is difficult, because it includes a wide range of activities and is still a developing marketing channel, performed on quick developing technologies. Mobile marketing includes all marketing political measures, a company executes under the use of mobile devices to influence the consumer's behavior. Kreutzer (2014) differentiates between four main application areas of mobile marketing: mobile transmission of information, mobile extraction of information, mobile sale of mobile products and services, and mobile sale of real products and services.

Andreas Kaplan, Dean of the ESCP Europe Berlin and renowned Professor of marketing (ESCP Europe Mar 2019), defines mobile marketing as *"any marketing activity conducted through a ubiquitous network to which consumers are constantly connecting using a personal mobile device"* (Kaplan, 2012, p. 231).

According to a publication of Bauer, Reichardt and Neumann (2008), there is a range of five main performance characteristics of (permission-based) mobile marketing. These characteristics show the inevitability of mobile marketing for contemporary and successful marketing. Firstly, mobile marketing is featured by its independence in location. Getting in contact with a consumer is independent from his or her geological location as long as there is an intact mobile network or any other internet connection. Additionally, mobile marketing is time independent, what is stated by the almost constant availability of users as smartphones are quasi uninterruptedly in operation and close at hand. Another performance characteristic of mobile marketing is its personalization. Smartphones are considered to be the most personal technological devices. They are usually used only by one person who carries them around almost all the time. Therefore, the mobile marketing message can be individually adapted to its receiver. A smartphone serves as a medium for calendars, address books, and photo galleries. Furthermore, smartphones give information about calls, texts, and safe browser history; application downloads; and application usage characteristics. Smartphones count as status symbols, which tell much about their owner's personality: the choice of brand and model with size, color and special features like a high-resolution camera, water resistance, etc., and the choice of operator. With this last point, there comes another aspect: through the subscriber identity module (SIM-card), every smartphone can be individually allocated to one user. Fourthly, mobile marketing is distinguished by its interactivity. A smartphone is an interactive medium, which enables the receiver of a (advertising) message to immediately react on this message. The opportunity of a bi-directional communication intensifies the integration of the receiver or consumer in the advertising process, and direct feedback helps to optimize this process. Lastly, localizability is one of mobile marketing's performance characteristics. The localization of users is made possible by technologies like global positioning system (GPS), cell of origin (COO), and enhanced observed time difference (E-OTD). These technologies allow several marketing activities that will be shown in the next part. Even though the initial features of mobile marketing like SMS and later mobile websites or also QR codes still are significant, mobile marketing nowadays is much more than that.

Mobile marketing instruments

There exists a high variety of mobile marketing instruments, and new ones are constantly emerging. Figure 1 shows an overview of mobile marketing instruments according to Daniel Rieber (2017), author of the book "Mobile Marketing".

Mobile Web	Mobile App	Mobile Advertising	Proximity Marketing	Social Media & Content	Messaging & Chatbots
Mobile Website	Mobile App	Banner Ads	Location-Based Marketing	Social Media	SMS / MMS
Mobile Shop	Mobile Shop	Interstitial Ads	QR Codes	Mobile Content	Messenger
Mobile Search	Push Benachrichtigung	Rich-Media Ads	Beacon		Chatbots
E-mail		Video Ads	NFC		Personal Assistants
		Native Ads	Mobile Payment		

Figure 1: Mobile Marketing Instruments Described in Rieber (2017).

International Status/Statistical Data for the Relevant Countries

Of course, mobile marketing is an international issue. Due to high penetration of mobile devices and convergence of content and services, mobile marketing has a significant international development. It is well described in the next figure, where we can see the market power of mobile marketing, which exceeds the desktop marketing if we compare the revenues.

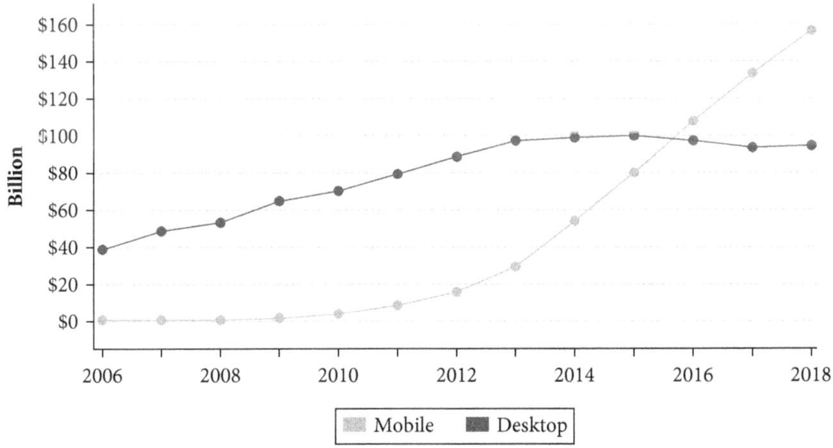

Figure 2: Revenues Mobile and Desktop Marketing.

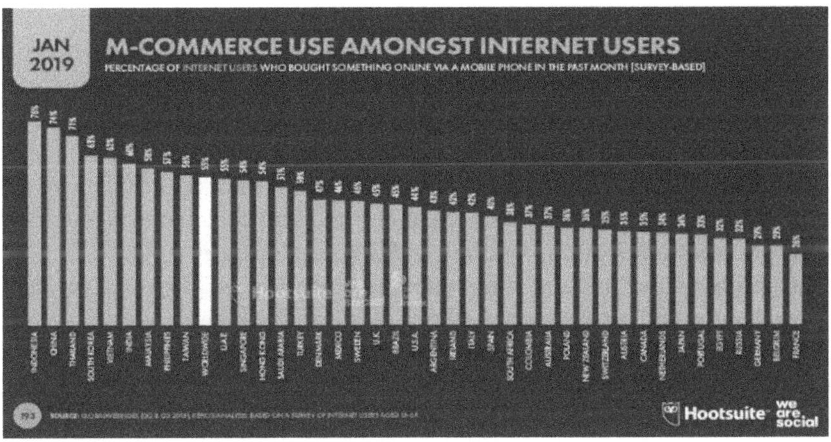

Figure 3: M-Commerce Use Among Internet Users.

This can be explained, if we take a look at some numbers which describe the "mobile world". In 2018, the total world population counts 7.593 billion people with an urbanization rate of 55 percent. A total 53 percent of the total world population are internet users, the global unique mobile user penetration is 68 percent. In comparison to 2017, a growth of seven percent of internet users and a growth of four percent of unique mobile users have been reported. Worldwide, there are 8.485 billion mobile connections, which make up 112 percent of the total population (we are social 2019). There are on average 1.65 mobile connections per unique mobile user. The following analysis points out the digital and especially the mobile status of the ten countries, which are relevant for the later research and where the survey results came from. In the direct contrast between the countries, which are relevant for this study, several differences can be highlighted. Looking at the percentage of internet users, who bought something online via mobile phones (figure 3), shows us a clear trend. It is interesting to see that most of the European countries are not at the top. The Asian countries have the lead. So, South Korea with 63% are on the top level, and surprisingly only Turkey and USA can show relative high numbers, comparing with the other countries of interest in our chapter.

Mobile phone usage experiences the strongest quotes in Finland (99 percent) and Czech Republic, South Korea, and Turkey (98 percent). The lowest quotes are in the USA (90 percent) and Canada (86 percent). All quotes are closely settled around the average of 95 percent. Smartphones have the highest usage rate in South Korea with 92 percent and in the Netherlands with 87 percent. France and Czech Republic are found to have the lowest smartphone usage rates of 71 percent and 65 percent. Laptop and desktop computer usage are the highest in the Netherlands (87 percent) and in Finland (85 percent), the lowest usage rates amount to 62 percent in Italy and 48 percent in Turkey. Tablet computers are mostly used in the Netherlands with a quote of 61 percent and in Finland with 49 percent usage. At the very end, Turkey (25 percent) and South Korea (19 percent) are settled. All in all, the most used devices are mobile phones, followed by smartphones, laptops, and desktop computers. South Korea especially stands out in terms of mobile phones and smartphones, and Finland and the Netherlands stand out regarding laptops, desktop-, and laptop computers.

In terms of the share of web traffic by devices, several trends are illustrated. Laptop and desktop web traffic share is still the highest with an average of 56 percent; yet, there is a negative development of minus eight percent on average. The highest shares are found in Czech Republic (79 percent) and France and Italy (both 59 percent); the lowest shares are in the USA (51 percent) and Turkey (36 percent). Strongest declining laptop and desktop web traffic is spot in France (-14 percent) and South Korea (-17 percent). In second

Table 1: Device Usage in Person for Relevant Countries

	Mobile phone	*Smartphone*	*Laptop or desktop*	*Tablet*
Canada	86%	76%	83%	47%
Czech Rep.	98%	65%	76%	29%
Finland	99%	79%	85%	49%
France	93%	71%	81%	41%
Germany	92%	75%	76%	39%
Italy	97%	76%	62%	31%
S. Korea	98%	92%	71%	19%
Netherlands	97%	87%	87%	61%
Turkey	98%	77%	48%	25%
USA	90%	78%	77%	46%
Average	*95%*	*78%*	*75%*	*39%*

Table 2: Share of Web Traffic in 2018 Comparison to 2017

	Laptops and desktops	*Development*	*Mobile phones*	*Development*	*Tablet devices*	*Development*
Canada	55%	-7%	33%	16%	11%	-5%
Czech Rep.	79%	-8%	18%	65%	3%	-2%
Finland	57%	-12%	36%	34%	7%	-12%
France	59%	-14%	34%	49%	7%	-13%
Germany	55%	-12%	37%	27%	7%	-3%
Italy	59%	-6%	35%	16%	5%	-15%
S. Korea	52%	-17%	47%	32%	1%	-30%
Netherlands	58%	-0.1%	33%	2%	9%	-8%
Turkey	36%	-1%	62%	1%	3%	-14%
USA	51%	-4%	41%	10%	8%	-15%
Average	*56%*	*-8%*	*38%*	*25%*	*6%*	*-12%*

place after laptop and desktop comes the mobile phone with an average share of 38 percent and a growth of 25 percent on average. In terms of share of mobile phone traffic, the strongest countries are Turkey (62 percent) and South Korea (47 percent), and the Netherlands and Canada (both 33 percent) and Czech Republic (18 percent) are in the last place. Regarding the strongest increasing shares, Czech Republic is on top with a growth rate of 65 percent, and France follows with an increase of 49 percent. Weakest developing shares are observed in the Netherlands with a growth of 2 percent and in Turkey with a growth of 1 percent. Tablet computers show an average web traffic share of 6 percent with an average decrease of 12 percent. Canada is the country with the highest share, 11 percent, of tablet computer web traffic. The second strongest share of 9 percent is found in the Netherlands. Czech Republic and Turkey (both 3 percent) and South Korea (1 percent) are recorded to have the weakest tablet computer shares. Highest decreasing tablet web traffic is in the USA (-15 percent) and South Korea (-30 percent). As this data is only based on traffic in web browsers and latest data shows that the usage time of mobile applications is seven times higher compared to mobile web browsers, mobile internet share is likely to be higher than indicated in the table above.

Theoretical Framework and Research Model

Since the research on the attitude of students toward mobile marketing is a main part of this chapter, a closer look will be taken on the concept of attitude, including the definition of attitudes in general, the formation of attitudes and reviews on attitudes toward advertising in general, as well as on mobile advertising. As the existing literature largely is limited on advertising, but not on marketing as a whole, this chapter reflects this fact.

Murphy, Pratkanis and Turner (2018, p. 178) describe the concept of attitude and its formation in their article for the Salem Press Encyclopedia of Health as the following: *"An attitude is a person's positive or negative evaluation of an object or thought…Much research finds that attitudes can influence a broad range of cognitive processes, such as social inference, reasoning, perception, and interpretation, and can thereby influence behavior…Given that attitudes can have pervasive effects on social behavior, it is important to understand how they are formed and changed"*.

The formation of attitudes plays a major role in the research of this study, more precisely the formation of attitude of consumers toward (mobile) marketing. There exists a wide range of models that explain this process. In the following, the model of Lana K. Brackett and Benjamin N. Carr (2001) serves as base for attitude formation. Brackett and Carr generate their model on the basis of the advertising value model by Robert H. Ducoffe (1996) and influences of the MacKenzie and Lutz (1989). Ducoffe defines three perceptual antecedents for attitudes toward web advertising and advertising value variables: entertainment, informativeness and irritation.

Entertainment is understood as an advertisement's ability to *"fulfill audience needs for escapism, diversion, aesthetic enjoyment, or emotional release"* (Ducoffe, 1996, p. 178). Advertisings considered as being likeable or pleasant are thought to have a positive effect on the attitude toward advertising. Informativeness is another positive influencing factor on the attitude toward advertising. It describes the ability to inform about product features and alternatives in order to maximize the consumer's purchase satisfaction.

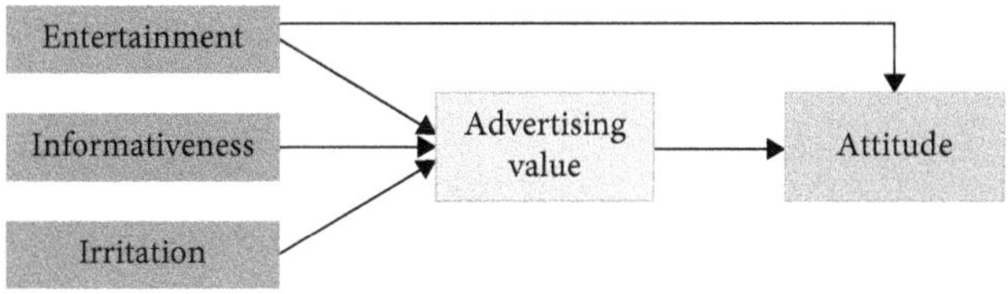

Figure 4: Ducoffe (1996) Model on Advertising Value and Attitudes Toward Web Advertising.

According to Ducoffe, with reference to former studies, informativeness is considered as main function of advertising and as major driver of acceptance of advertising from consumers' point of view. Besides these two content-based factors, Ducoffe adds another perceptual antecedent – Irritation, which is triggered by the employment of methods that "*annoy, offend, insult, or are overly manipulative*" (Ducoffe, 1996, p. 178). As a result of these techniques, the advertising is perceived by the consumer as irritating and unwanted occurrence. Irritation is thought to have a negative impact on the attitude toward advertising. As Figure 3 shows, the three antecedents determine the perceived value of advertising. This advertising value then defines the attitude toward the advertising. Ducoffe interposes at this point that advertising that is perceived as likeable is not automatically valuable and vice versa. Based on this construct, Brackett and Carr add another two antecedents. Firstly, there is credibility, which is adopted from MacKenzie and Lutz (1989) and several other models. Credibility is directly related to advertising value and attitude toward advertising. This antecedent describes "*the extent to which the consumer perceives claims made about the brand in the ad to be truthful and believable*" (Mackenzie & Lutz, 1989, p. 326). Secondly, relevant demographic variables are added as influencing factors on the attitude toward advertising. As pointed out, the relevance of these demographic variables depends on the target audience and the extent of respondents. Furthermore, Brackett and Carr determine informativeness as a direct influencing factor on attitude in addition to its direct influence on advertising value. This model is illustrated in Figure 7.

General attitude toward advertising was found to have changed over time. Before the 1970s, attitude toward advertising generally was rather positive as it was experienced to be informative as revealed by Gallup in 1959. The respondents also indicated that they preferred advertised products over unadvertised products, but feel advertising to increase the price of the corresponding products. After the 1970s, Zanot found a negative change in attitude. This trend

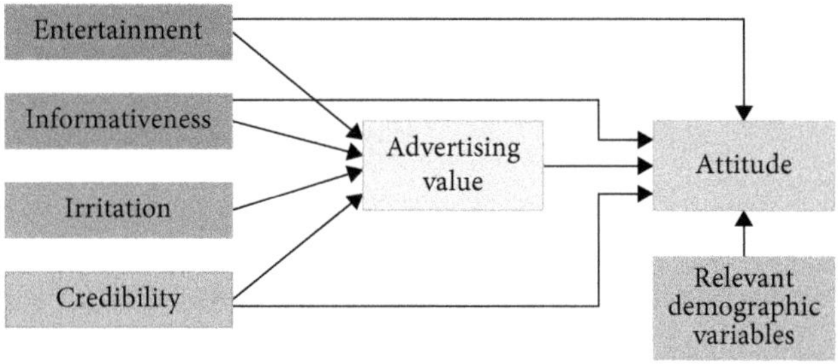

Figure 5: Brackett and Carr (2011) Model on Attitudes Toward Web Advertising.

was supported by Harris (1998) and Associated who found that TV advertising was experienced by most interviewees as misleading. According to a study by Shavitt, Lowrey and Haefner (1989), the attitude of US-Americans have gotten more positive compared to earlier research. Despite a general positive attitude, the respondents reported mixed feelings with associations like distrust, offense and enjoyment.

Several previous researches described different findings about the attitude toward mobile advertising and the influencing factors on the attitude toward mobile advertising. Tsang, Ho and Liang (2004) found out about the general negative attitude toward mobile advertising in their study from 2004 in Taiwan. It is experienced as irritating, whereas the grant of a permission is favorable for the attitude. Entertainment presents the most significant factor followed by credibility and irritation. Chowdhury, Parvin, Weitenberner and Becker (2006) identify credibility to be the only direct positive and significant influencing factor on consumers' attitude toward mobile advertising. Neither informativeness nor entertainment or irritation represent significant influencing factors on the attitude toward advertising. The study was conducted in 2006 in Bangladesh with a student sample and shows a contradictory result to previous research on this topic. Sethi (2017) and Singh found a mainly positive attitude toward mobile advertising in their research at Manipur University in India in 2017. Informativeness is identified as the most significant factor on the attitude toward mobile advertising. Additionally, a significant positive relationship between consumer attitude and behavioral intentions was worked out. These three recent studies show very different findings on the attitudes toward mobile advertising. Thus, further research in this area becomes important and necessary. This is where this chapter comes in and has its justification.

Research framework

Based on existing literature about consumer behavior models and researches on the attitude toward mobile marketing, a research framework is constructed to find out about the attitude of students toward mobile marketing and, thereby, the associated attributes. Additionally, the effects of this attitude are regarded. Mainly, the research construct is based on Ho, Tsang and Liang's publication "Consumer Attitudes Toward Mobile Advertising: An Empirical Study" from 2004. This construct is based on two models. Firstly, Ho Tsang and Liang adopt Brackett and Carr's extrapolation of the Ducoffe model from the article "Advertising value and advertising on the web" from 1996 with influences from MacKenzie and Lutz. Furthermore, this base is added by the theory of reasoned action (TRA) by Fishbein and Ajzen (1975) from 1980. It focusses on the three constructs: attitude, intention and behavior. The psychological model aims to explain the relation of attitude to behavior. Its main notion is that attitudes influence intention and intention influences behavior. The theory will be applied rather superficially with special regard on the attitude component.

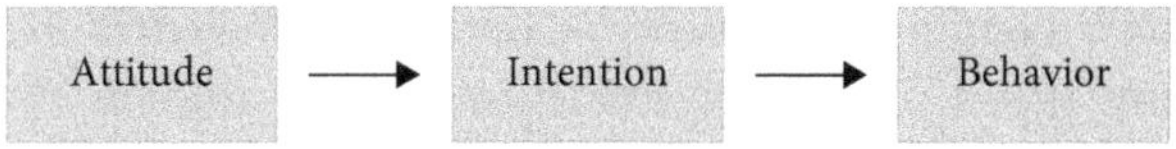

Figure 6: Theory of Reasoned Action by Fishbein and Ajzen (1975), Found in: Tsang (2004).

The theory of reasoned action will be accomplished by the model on attitude toward advertising by Brackett and Carr on the basis of the Ducoffe model. Ducoffe determines three perceptual antecedents for web-advertising value: entertainment, informativeness and irritation. These three are complemented by two additional antecedents in the Brackett and Carr model. Firstly, there is credibility, and secondly, there are relevant demographic variables. As the major is presupposed for the focus group, this does not present a relevant variable. The focus will be set on class rank (bachelor, master, PhD) and university. Age is secondary, as it is assumed that the age range will be rather small within the target group. In addition, there will be added permission as influencing factor on attitude and incentives as influencing factor on intention according to Tsang, Ho and Liang. The final research model is pictured in Figure 7.

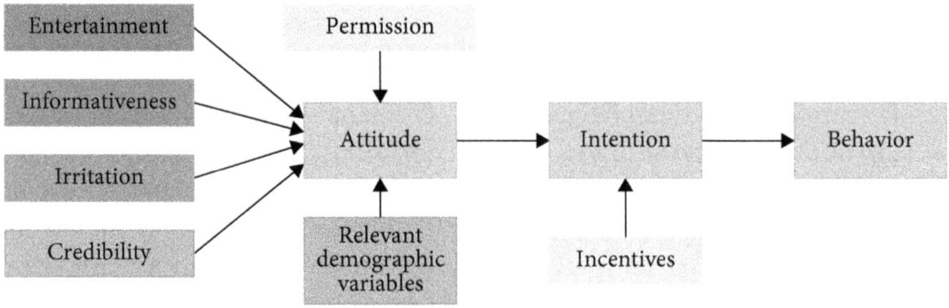

Figure 7: Research Model (own illustration).

Research hypotheses

The following research hypotheses are proposed according to the research model:

H1: Entertainment has a significant influence on the attitude toward mobile marketing.
H2: Informativeness has a significant influence on the attitude toward mobile marketing.
H3: Irritation has a significant influence on the attitude toward mobile marketing.
H4: Credibility has a significant influence on the attitude toward mobile marketing.
H5: Permission has a significant influence on the attitude toward mobile marketing
H6: Relevant demographic variables (Nationality, aspired degree) have a significant influence on the attitude toward mobile marketing.
H7: Incentives have a significant influence on the intention.

The volume of this chapter is limited; therefore, the focus is set on the Hypotheses H1 to H6, as they refer to the main question on the attitude toward mobile marketing. The topic "incentives" is a larger impact with several complicated characteristics. Therefore, the research results are only analyzed regarding the first six hypotheses.

Research objective and data collection

The study aims to find out about the general attitude of business students toward mobile marketing and how this attitude is formed. Business students have been chosen as target group for several reasons. On the one hand, they get in touch with related topics and, therefore, are able to express their attitudes and thoughts on mobile marketing rather than students who are unfamiliar with the topic. On the other hand, these students are considered as digital versed. Nevertheless, this target group does not consist of professionals who work in direct proximity to mobile marketing and thus largely have an outside view on mobile marketing. Furthermore, the study aims to find out about attitudes toward mobile marketing on an international level, as the location of university is considered as relevant demographic variable. Therefore, students from ten countries are consulted. Besides the general attitude toward mobile marketing and its formation, international differences are spot, with a special regard toward cultural factors.

A field survey has been conducted from October 25, 2018 to January 5, 2019. An online questionnaire has been created and virtually conducted at the ten universities, as the target group are students from ten countries. The specific universities, which participated at the questionnaire are part of the International Business Studies Network (IBSEN), through which the survey is distributed. The questionnaire is accessible via QR code and web link and is mostly published and executed in class, as it is announced by the lecturers. The questionnaire consists of five parts. Firstly, questions on the mobile affinity are asked. Secondly, questions on the attitude part of the research framework (except relevant demographic variables), according to Tsang, Ho and Liang arise. This part includes questions on the general attitude toward mobile marketing, permission-related questions and questions concerning the impacting attributes (entertainment, informativeness, irritation and credibility). Thirdly, questions on the influence of incentives on the intention follow. Fourthly, questions about mobile purchasing and payment behavior arise. Lastly, the questionnaire ends with questions on (relevant) demographic variables. In total, the questionnaire includes 26 questions, with 19 five-point Likert scales, with "strongly agree" on the top and "strongly disagree" on the bottom, in the first, second, third and fourth part. Two semantic differentials are embedded in the second part. The demographic questions' part consists of two alternative questions (university, degree), two bipolar questions (sex, exchange student) and one open question (age). Twenty-five out of the total of 26 questions are mandatory, except the question for the sex. According to international differences in standards, the unitary inclusion of a third response "gender X" was inappropriate; therefore, the decision to make this indication voluntary was made. A pretest with 25 participants was executed on October 17, until October 20, 2018. Based on feedback, the questionnaire was revised and prepared for its actual distribution beginning October 25, 2018 at the 10 previously descripted countries. A total of 1488 questionnaires were answered, 1353 of them in the full extent (all mandatory questions answered). As the study concentrates on country-specific differences and cultural causes, questionnaires answered "yes" to the question "I am an exchange student" are excluded. This ensures that the participant can be understood as representative of his or her university's national affiliation, independent from his or her citizenship. As a result of his filtration, 1246 questionnaires remain. After eliminating questionnaires with obvious misrepresentations of age, a total of 1220 usable questionnaire sums up, which is a good number for such an analysis. The used statistical software is R with his last version of. 3.6.1.

Logistic Regression

The logistic regression tests the influence and its extent of entertainment, informativeness, irritation, credibility, permission and relevant demographic variables on the participants' general attitude toward mobile marketing. As dependent variable, the general attitude toward mobile marketing, expressed in the question "In general, I like mobile marketing", is chosen. Independent variables count a total of 24, including 13 dummy variables. The independent variables are tested on their influence on the attitude toward mobile marketing, including the two questions on permission, two questions on entertainment, three questions on informativeness, three questions on credibility, two questions on irritation and two questions on relevant demographic variables: location of university and aspired degree, which are split up in 13 dummy variables (10 for location of university and three for aspired degree). The variables use the enter method described in Backhaus (2011); therefore, all variables were entered in one single step.

$$p_k\left(y=1\right)=\frac{1}{1+e^{-z_k}}\text{ with : } z_k=\beta_{0+}\sum_{j=1}^{J}\beta_j\times x_{jk}+u_k$$

Applied to this case: $p_k\left(\textit{positive attitude}\right)=\frac{1}{1+e^{-z_k}}$
with

$$\begin{aligned}z_k = {} & \beta_0+\beta_1\times permission1_k+\beta_2\times permission2_k+\beta_3\times entertainement1_k\\ & +\beta_4\times entertainment2_k+\beta_5\times informativeness1_k+\beta_6\\ & \times informativeness2_k+\beta_7\times informativeness3_k+\beta_8\times credibility1_k\\ & +\beta_9\times credibility2_k+\beta_{10}\times credibility3_k+\beta_{11}\times irritation1_k+\beta_{12}\\ & \times irritation2_k+\beta_{13}\times location\ of\ university_k+\beta_{14}\times aspired\ degree_k\end{aligned}$$

To determine the fit of the model, there is a variety of quality criteria to find out about the how good the independent variables as a whole fit to the characteristic categories (0 or 1) of die dependent variable y. The three following criteria of fit will be applied:

- Likelihood ratio test described in Backhaus (2011)
- Pseudo R^2-measures: Nagelkerke-R^2 described in Nagelkerke (1991), Schäfer (2012)
- Assessment of the classification results Hosmer-Lemeshow-test described in Morrison (1969)

Table 3 shows that the regression coefficients of the second variable on permission "I ignore mobile marketing I did not permit", both variables concerning entertainment, all three variables that are related to informativeness and both variables on irritation are significant. Additionally, the regression country variables as S. Korea, Turkey, USA, France, Germany and Czech Republic have significant coefficients. The Wald statistics indicates the significance of these variables as the values are superior to the reference value from the χ^2-table. The reference value is 3.84. The remaining coefficients offer Wald statistics below the reference χ^2-value of 3.84, as shown in tables. Hence, these coefficients and their appendant variables are insignificant. Subsequently, the related variable to the significant coefficients are examined regarding their influence on the probability of a positive attitude toward mobile marketing. This analyses is executed on the basis of the odd ratios.

The likelihood-ratio-test, illustrated in Table 19, delivers a chi-square (χ^2) of 402.637 at a degree of freedom of 23 and a significance level of 0. The reference value from the χ^2-table is 35.17, which is smaller than the likelihood-ratio value of 402.637. Therefore, the null-hypothesis is rejected, and the significant influence of the independent variables is proved. The model is significant for the collected data. The Nagelkerke-R^2 value, as indicated in table 20, is 0.479. This value is understood as an almost very good indicator for a good explanatory power of the model. According to the classification table in Table 21, the model classifies 1067 out of 1220 results correctly; therefore, the quote is 87.5 percent. A negative attitude toward mobile marketing ($y = 0$) was classified correctly in 46.7 percent of the cases, whereas in 95.3 percent of the cases, a positive attitude toward mobile marketing ($y = 1$) was classified correctly. This hit rate is above the maximum chance probability of 83.85 percent and above the proportional chance probability of 72.92 percent. As the hit rate is above the probability of the principle of chance, the logistic regression function is useful. The Hosmer and Lemeshow test, displayed in Table 22, offers a χ^2-value of 7.047 at a significance level of 0.532. As the level of significance is below 0.70, the null-hypothesis is not rejected. Therefore, it is assumed that variances between the empirically observed and the calculated frequencies for the result $y = 1$ (positive attitude) do not appear more frequently than by chance (Backhaus, 2011).

Table 3: Result Logistic Regression - General Attitude Toward Mobile Marketing

	B	S.E.	Wald	df	Sig.	Exp(B)	95% C.I.for EXP(B)	
							Lower	Upper
Permission 1	-0,039	0,214	2,122	1	0,141	0,962	0,632	1,464
Permission 2	-0,674	0,258	6,837	1	0,009	0,51	0,308	0,845
Entertainment 1	0,934	0,296	9,945	1	0,002	2,545	1,424	4,549
Entertainment 2	0,832	0,346	5,79	1	0,016	2,297	1,167	4,524
Informativeness 1	0,991	0,248	15,899	1	0	2,693	1,655	4,382
Informativeness 2	0,788	0,29	7,352	1	0,007	2,198	1,244	3,884
Informativeness 3	0,568	0,217	6,834	1	0,009	1,765	1,153	2,703
Credibility 1	0,35	0,338	1,073	1	0,3	1,419	0,732	2,75
Credibility 2	0,222	0,244	0,832	1	0,362	1,249	0,775	2,014
Credibility 3	-0,062	0,265	0,054	1	0,816	0,94	0,56	1,579
Irritation 1	-0,479	0,245	5,921	1	0,012	0,62	0,383	1,002
Irritation 2	-0,843	0,253	11,071	1	0,001	0,43	0,262	0,707
Loc of University			32,726	9	0			
Canada	-0,071	0,337	0,045	1	0,832	0,931	0,481	1,802
Czech Republic	-0,988	0,252	15,353	1	0	0,372	0,227	0,61
USA	0,142	0,295	4,325	1	0,021	1,153	0,558	1,776
Finland	-0,06	0,302	0,04	1	0,841	0,941	0,521	1,7
France	-0,774	0,285	7,39	1	0,007	0,461	0,264	0,806
Germany	-0,481	0,318	5,874	1	0,011	0,618	0,866	3,013
Italy	0,178	0,406	1,293	1	0,255	1,194	0,285	1,396
Netherlands	0,144	0,323	0,199	1	0,656	1,155	0,613	2,175
South Korea	1,565	0,29	13,455	1	0	4,785	0,672	2,091
Turkey	0,17	0,478	10,744	1	0,001	1,185	1,876	12,201
Aspired degree			1,181	2	0,275			
Bachelor	0,7	0,235	2,422	1	0,1012	2,013	1,269	3,192
Master	0,021	0,265	0,006	1	0,938	1,021	0,607	1,716
PhD	-0,72	0,391	1,398	1	0,254	0,487	0,226	1,047
Constant	0,958	0,337	8,1	1	0,004	2,607		

Table 4 and 5: Likelihood-Ratio-test and Pseundo R^2 Measures

Likelihood-Ratio-Test

	Chi-square	df	Sig.
Step	402,637	23	0
Block	402,637	23	0
Model	402,637	23	0

Pseudo-R^2 measures

-2 Log likelihood	Cox & Snell R Square	Nagelkerke R Square
676,108[a]	0,281	0,479

Table 6 and 7: Classification Table and Hosmer/Lemeshow Test

Classification table

Observed		Predicted: In general, I like mobile marketing 0	Predicted: In general, I like mobile marketing 1	Percentage Correct
In general, I like mobile marketing	0	92	105	46,7
	1	48	975	95,3
Overall Percentage				87,5

Hosmer and Lemeshow test

Chi-square	df	Sig.
7,047	8	0,532

The regression analysis shows that the model as a whole is significant, as well as a part of the coefficients of the variables. Permission partly has a significant influence on the probability of a positive attitude toward marketing, as the non-permission issuance decreases the probability of a positive attitude by 49 percent. Entertainment is the attribute with the strongest positive influence on the probability of a positive attitude toward mobile marketing. Its recognition as entertaining increases the probability by 154.5 percent and its perception as pleasant enhances the probability by 129.7 percent. Informativeness also has a significant positive influence on the probability of a positive attitude toward mobile marketing. Mobile marketing as informative experience boosts the probability by 169.3 percent and the agreement on the usefulness of information it delivers increases the probability by 119.8 percent. The percipience that mobile marketing keeps one updated about products of interest or need raises the probability of a positive attitude toward mobile marketing by 76.5 percent. Credibility is found to have no significant influence on the probability of a positive attitude toward mobile marketing. Whereas both irritation variables have a negative influence of 38 percent (its irritating me) and 57 percent (it annoys me) on the probability. Regarding the country groups, it appears that the location of university in general has influence on the probability. The indications of locations which have negative influences are Czech Republic with a decreasing effect of 62.8 percent, France with a influence of 53.9 percent and Germany with a influence of 38.2. On the list with countries with positive influences, we can find at the first place South Korea with an increasing influence of 378.5 percent. The affiliation to this group almost quadruples the probability of liking mobile marketing. The countries Turkey with a influence of 18.5 percent and USA 15.3 percent are also significant. The other four countries are not showing significant values. Also, in context of the aspired degrees, it is neither in general nor in specific degrees. At this point, it has to be remarked that the bachelor group with a size of 945 members delivers more representative results than the other groups with sizes of 247 and 28 members.

Conclusion

After all, this final chapter concludes and reflects the gained findings and connects them with the prior theory. By now, another research in the field of attitudes toward mobile marketing has been conducted, and it is aimed to be an impulse for further research. Coming back to our research hypotheses:

H1: Entertainment has a significant influence on the attitude toward mobile marketing. – confirmed
H2: Informativeness has a significant influence on the attitude toward mobile marketing. – confirmed
H3: Irritation has a significant influence on the attitude toward mobile marketing. – confirmed
H4: Credibility has a significant influence on the attitude toward mobile marketing. – not confirmed
H5: Permission has a significant influence on the attitude toward mobile marketing – partly confirmed

The research framework approves for entertainment and informativeness as influencing factors on the attitude toward mobile marketing. On average, entertainment is the strongest significant perceptual antecedent. Irritation is found to have significant influence, and credibility has no significant influence. Permission also shows to have a partial influence on the attitude toward mobile marketing. These results are in line with the findings in the literature. In addition, the facet for the variable permission was analyzed, and it is detected that this variable is also very important for the attitude. At the level of relevant demographic variables, only the country variables (six of ten) are showing influences on the attitude toward mobile marketing; the aspired degrees have not any influences. Coming back to our research hypotheses:

H6: Relevant demographic variables (Nationality, aspired degree) have a significant influence on the attitude toward mobile marketing. – partly confirmed

Looking more detailed on the country variables: As the regression results show, the model indicates an influence for some of the country groups on a positive or negative influence for the attitude toward mobile marketing. These influences account for South Korea, Turkey, USA as a positive and France, Germany and Czech Republic for a negative manner. This investigation is superficial and does not aim to execute a detailed cultural analysis. Instead, a short excursion is started on this aspect and may stimulate further occupation with this topic applied on the present results. The actual results differ only partly from the expected outcome, based on the insights in part "International Status and Statistical data for relevant countries" of this paper. Mainly South Korea and Turkey were presumed to be locations, which significantly influence the formation of attitudes toward mobile marketing in a positive way. As significant location indicators toward a negative attitude, Czech Rep, France and Germany came into consideration. As the in-depth study of all ten countries' cultures goes beyond the scope of this thesis, nonetheless, the actual results are on hand. So further research can be executed to examine the validity of the theory of reasoned action for mobile marketing. Another potential is a research with an enlarged target group. This may not concentrate on a suchlike special audience, but on a more representative group for all students, all mobile users or even the whole society. In this next step, the results of this thesis could take the role of a comparison group. In this frame, the above-mentioned validity of the country-specific differences may be retested. The occurrence of suchlike characteristics may be unique for this study, or it approves for other research. By increasing the number of studies in the field of attitude research toward mobile marketing, the comparability and, therefore, the explanatory power augments.

To catch up with the beginning of this chapter, it can finally be said that the presence of mobile marketing in the daily life steadily increases. This fast evolution of technologies and approaches is an evidence for the need of insights. Researches on how people experience the very technologies and approaches are an important indicator for their dissemination and adaption in practice. Mobile marketing has an increased international component compared to other forms of (digital) marketing, which turns up due to social media platforms and worldwide mobile network expansion, as only two examples. With this regard, this international research gives a more complex insight, compared to a large part of existing research.

References

American Marketing Association. *Definitions of Marketing*, Retrieved February 22, 2019, from https://www.ama.org/AboutAMA/Pages/Definition-of-Marketing.aspx.

Backhaus, K., Erichson, B., Plinke, W., Weiber, R. (2011). *Multivariate Analysemethoden*, 13th ed., Heidelberg.

Bauer, H. H., Reichardt, T., Neumann, M. M. (2008). Erfolgreiches Marketing im Mobilfunknetz. In Bauer, H. H., Dirks, T., Bryant, M. D.: *Erfolgsfaktoren des Mobile Marketing*, 1st ed., Heidelberg/Berlin.

Brackett, L. K., Carr, B. N. (2001). Cyberspace advertising vs. other media: consumer vs. mature student attitudes. In *Journal of Advertising Research*, Vol. 41, 23–32.

Chowdhury, H. K., Parvin, N., Weitenberner, C., Becker, M. (2006). Consumer attitude toward mobile advertising in an emerging market: an empirical study. In *International Journal of Mobile Marketing*, Vol. 1 No. 2, 33–42.

Ducoffe, R. (1996). Advertising value and advertising on the web. In *Journal of Advertising Research*, Vol. 36, 21–35.

ESCP Europe Business School. *Kaplan Andreas Biography*, Retrieved March 21, 2019, from https://www.escpeurope.eu/kaplan-andrea.

EZ Texting. *A Brief History of Mobile Marketing*, Retrieved February 22, 2019, from https://www.eztexting.com/sms-marketing-resources/history-of-mobile-marketing.

Kaplan, A. M. (2012). If you love something, let it go mobile: mobile marketing and mobile social media 4x4. In *Business horizons*, Vol. 55, No. 2, 129–139.

Kotler Marketing Group. *Dr. Philip Kotler Answers Your Questions on Marketing*, Retrieved March 09, 2019, from https://kotlermarketing.com/phil_questions.shtml.

Kreutzer, R. T. (2014). *Praxisorientiertes Online-Marketing*, 2nd ed., Wiesbaden.

MacKenzie, S. B., Lutz, R. J. (1989). An empirical examination of the structural antecedents of attitude toward the ad in an advertising pretesting context. In *Journal of Marketing*, Vol. 53, 48–65.

Morrison, D. G. (1969). On the interpretation of discriminant analysis. In *Journal of Marketing Research*, Vol. 6, 157–163.

Nagelkerke, N. J. D. (1991). A note on a general definition of the coefficient of determination. In *Biometrica*, Vol. 78, No. 3, 691–692.

Pratkanis, A. R., Turner, M. E., Murphy, M. (2018). Attitude formation and change. In *Salem Press Encyclopedia of Health*, 5.

Rieber, D. (2017). *Mobile Marketing*, 1st ed., Wiesbaden.

Schäfer, T. (2012). TU Chemnitz. *Logistische Regression*.

Sethi, G., Singh, I. (2017). The impact of mobile advertisment on the students of Manipur University. In *International Journal of Science and Research*, Vol. 6, No. 6, 755–765.

Shavitt, S., Lowrey, P., Haefner, J. (1998, July/August). Public attitudes toward advertising: more favorable than you might think. In *Journal of Advertising Research*, Vol. 38, 7–22.

Statista. Digital Advertising Canada, Czech Republic, Finland, France, Germany, Italy, Netherlands, South Korea, Turkey, United States https://www.statista.com/outlook/216/108/digital-advertising/.

Tsang, M. M., Ho, S.-C., Liang, T.-P. (2004). Consumer attitudes toward mobile advertising: an empirical study. In *International Journal of Electronic Commerce*, Vol. 8, No.3, 65–78.

We are social (S. Kemp). *Global digital report 2018*, 01/30/2018, Retrieved February 25, 2019, from https://wearesocial.com/blog/ 2018/01/ global-digital-report-2018.

We are social (a). *Global Digital Report 2018*, Retrieved February 24, 2019, from https://digitalreport.wearesocial.com/.

Natalie Bartholomäus, and Özlem Özdemir

The (New) Role of HR in the Digital Age: Changing Competences and Business Organization

Abstract: Digitalization as contemporary megatrend challenges HR departments in many respects. The impact of a digital transformation requires effective solutions for target competences and business organization that meet the new demands of the digital age. Despite an increasingly differentiated treatment of the digitalization's impact on business in scientific literature, precise transfer solutions in competency-based and organizational approaches are just beginning. The following conference contribution aims at providing application-oriented recommendations for a digitally compliant target competence profile for leaders as well as initial indications for a new organizational positioning of HR in the digital age.

Keywords: Digital transformation, cultural change, digital competence, new target competence profiles in the digital age, Chief Human Resources Officer (CHRO), HR as strategic driver and member of the executive board

Introduction

Digitalization, with its essential implications for business and society, is making further progress. In order to remain competitive in the long term, an effective digital transformation seems to be indispensable. Thereby, a digital transformation should not be conceived as paper solution that expresses a strategic intent; all the more, it has to be driven by top-level management and brought to life in an organization-specific way.

Despite an increasingly differentiated treatment of the digitalization's impact, the transfer in concrete management-, leadership- and organizational approaches for the digital age seems to be at the very beginning. Among others, the following questions seem to be insufficiently answered:

- **Which (new) target competences are relevant in the digital age?**
- **Which organizational framework supports the digital transformation?**
- **Which (new) role does HR play in the digital age?**

According to Armutat and Grebe (2018), the following digitalization is understood as the combination of data technologies with the overall entrepreneurial system. These junctions lead to significant changes for business. New working environments are arising. Due to their global connection and local independence, new business opportunities occur. At the same time, new challenges meet employees` competences and forms of business organization for an effective collaboration (Hammermann & Stettes, 2016).

Despite new possibilities, such as new products, new services or even completely new business models, digitalization is also accompanied by obstacles that especially affect SMEs with their lower financial resources as compared to large corporations. According to BMWi (2016), these barriers mainly concern data security, the qualification of specialists and skilled workers, lacking standards and high investment costs (Franken & Cutmore-Beinlich, 2018).

All business functions will be more or less affected by the impact of an increasing digitalization in the future. But why exactly should Human Resource Management deal intensively with the topic of digital transformation? The Centre for European Economic Research (ZEW) comes to the conclusion that the number of workplaces in Germany with job profiles showing a high probability of automization is 12 % (Frey & Osborne, 2013). The Institute for Employment Research has shown this trend in 2016. The proportion of employees subject to social security contribution, working in jobs with high substitutability, rose from 15 % in 2013 to 25 % in 2016. Helping professions are even more affected with a share of potential job loss increasing up to 58 %. Specialist jobs show a share of 54 %. Despite differing figures, the entire spectrum of helping and expert professions is affected (Dengler & Matthes, 2018).

Jung (2014) differentiates in this context between routine- and non-routine work as well as manual and intellectual work. An unchanged demand is to be expected for manual non-routine work, such as hairdresser or geriatric nurse. The demand for manual and intellectual tasks, performed by low- and medium-skilled workers, would decrease. This affects, for example, general industrial workers or administrative staff. Non-routine tasks, requiring a high qualification level, will increase in the future. Additional, further jobs are to be expected, for example, for the development and monitoring of machines and processes.

Furthermore, it is foreseeable that traditional working relationships, i.e., insurable employment in full-time with compulsory presence will become less important. On the contrary, the number of project workers, who will collaborate across national borders and time zones within multicultural teams, will increase (Rürup & Jung, 2017).

Human Resource Management needs to be prepared for these development trends. For instance, competence and job profiles need to be re-defined in order to meet new requirements of the digitalization. Especially human resource development will significantly gain in relevance (Rürup & Jung, 2016). Leadership and business organization need to be aligned accordingly to ensure the efficiency and effectiveness of digital transformation.

As with any other cultural change, a digital transformation can only be successful if the workforce joins, i.e., when more people within an organization think, act and communicate in a new direction. This needs preparation. Preparing employees for the digital transformation was one of the two key topics for Human Resource Management in 2017 (Eilers et al., 2017). This requires that the Human Resource Managers themselves are digitally competent. It is precisely at this point it becomes clear that HR is becoming crux of the matter for a successful digital transformation in organizations. If HR selects the "wrong" employees and/or trains the "right" employees incorrectly, there cannot be a workforce capable of co-designing and participating in the big transformation of corporate digitalization.

Digitalization – an international comparison

Different interpretations of the term *digitalization* already indicate that dealing with the present challenges of the digital age might be different if countries are compared with each other. Germany, e.g., shows a very broad understanding of the term *digitalization*, since it completely subsumes all changes induced by digitalization. Andreas Kluth emphasizes this abundance by expressing: "*[…] There's a virtue in having a word that stands for everything, for a universal set of changes spawned by digitization of information*" (Kluth, 2018). The US in contrast are making use of several terms that may be related to the challenges of the digital age: *Tech, Innovation, Digitization* and *Digitalization*. It seems to be striking that the focus here is more on *Tech(nology)* and *Innovation*, i.e., digitalization provides new business opportunities. The task of a company is then to create innovations through the use of new technologies to improve its economic situation. Germany, on the other hand, seems to be more concerned with corporate cultural change driven by digitalization. The country is master of incremental innovations. Improving the existing, making it more efficient and effective, is one of the country's core competences. In the US, on the contrary, thinking and acting appear to be more radical, enabling more disruptive innovations (Jackson, Richter & Schildhauer, 2017; Capgemini, 2017).

Another difference occurs in the frame of Corporate Social Responsibility (CSR) and Sustainability. Germany is intensively faced with these topics, both driven by intrinsic motivation and attitude as well as by global, EU-wide, national and regional funding programs. It can be supposed that the discussion on ethical barriers despite technological feasibility will be more intensive here.

This little example already shows that different countries can learn from each other, whether to increase the speed in digital transformation and improve business opportunities, or in order to pay more attention to ethical issues in the context of ever-increasing technological feasibilities.

Another context, in which differences in dealing with present challenges of the digital age can be explained, is cultural theory. If one considers Hofstede's cultural dimensions, a comparison between Germany and the US shows that there are differences related to uncertainty avoidance. Germany's score for the uncertainty avoidance index (UAI) is 65 whereas the US score is 46 (Hofstede Insights, n.d.). Employees in German organizations try to counter the uncertainty of the future through detailed plans, rules and regulations. However, as the future scenario of a digital age has not yet been clearly established, there must be a feeling of uncertainty. As a result, it can be assumed that the discussion about digital transformation is still driven too much by anxiety and its realization losing speed. The same can only be logically assumed for all countries showing a high UAI, such as Turkey with a value of 85 on this dimension (Hofstede Insights, n.d.).

This contrasts with countries showing a low UAI. Here, a higher willingness for trying new technologies or business practices can be expected, since there is a lower emotional need for plans, rules and regulations (Hofstede Insights, n.d.). This, for example, accounts for the US (UAI = 46) or Singapore (UAI = 8). Both are often mentioned as digital pioneers. What they have in common is a mentality that is open to change, driven by speed and geared toward a strong customer- and implementation-orientation (Depiereux & van Alphen, 2018; Widmaier, 2017).

As a conclusion, it can be stated that a (too) high uncertainty avoidance paves the way to digital progress. Values like openness for change, speed and strict customer orientation should come to the fore of digitalization designers.

Target competences for the digital age

In addition to IT-security and legal uncertainty, inadequate employee skills are a key challenge faced by companies in the context of digital transformation (DIHK, 2015). The integration of digital technologies into the corporate performance process leads to a change of required employee competences. In the sense of a systematic competence management, new target competences need to be defined, diagnosed and developed. Especially HR-development is gaining in

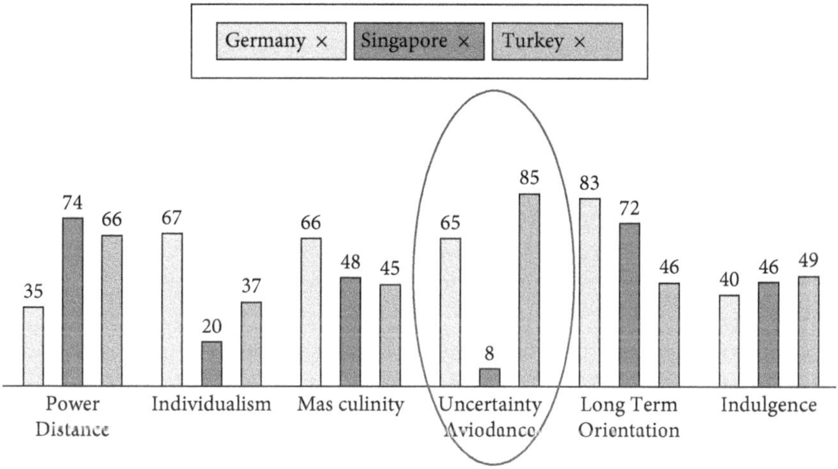

Figure 1: Country Comparison of Uncertainty Avoidance (Hofstede Insights, n.d.).

relevance since qualification is a central success factor for the digital transformation in corporations (Franken & Cutmore-Beinlich, 2018).

But what exactly is a digital competence? In order to clarify this question, a separation of the two terms *digital* and *competence* seems to be useful. The term *competence* aims at capabilities for a self-organized acting in open, complex and often chaotic systems. Competences comprise more than just knowledge or externally approved qualification, since they also include interiorized values, norms and rules (Heyse & Erpenbeck, 2007). They are necessary in a risk society and an economic world, which can be characterized by volatility, uncertainty, complexity and ambiguity (V.U.C.A. economic world; World Economic Forum, 2015). *Digital* means based on digital technology or digital processes, simply said by making use of computer technology. In a narrow sense, this addresses the so-called SMACT-Technologies (Social, Mobile, Analytics, Cloud and Internet-of-Things-Technologies).

A *digital competence* that combines these two insights describes the ability to self-organize in dealing with new technologies. In the broader sense, this understanding should not be limited to a technical-professional requirement, but also relate to personal, activity and decision-making as well as social-communicative competences; i.e., a digital competence should not be limited to handling objects like machines or processes but also be open for dealing with oneself and others. A digital competence, following this broader scope, includes the capability of effectively acting in a new environment that is characterized by digitalization and its strong impact. Although relevant HR-literature differs in its results for the quantity and categorization of digital literacy, there is an overlap concerning those competences with high relevance for the digital age. The following analysis is related to available studies by the World Economic Forum (2018), the McKinsey Global Institute (MGI, 2018), Stifterverband für die Deutsche Wissenschaft e.V. (2018), the Institute for the Future (Fidler, 2016) and the European Political Strategy Centres (EPSC, 2016).

Firstly and more technically speaking, there is a necessity of a basic digital competence. This one targets an effective handling of information- and communication-related technologies. It comprises a sound understanding of how computer systems function, an experienced application of information- and communication-technologies as well as the capability of analyzing and interpreting digital data and being able to create digital content. Secondly, corporations in general and HR in particular are challenged to strengthen innovation skills of their employees. Products, services and whole business models have to be critically reflected and possibly be innovated in order to stay competitive in the future. This requires creativity, critical and analytical thinking, transdisciplinarity and computer-based thinking. Following current significant changes in the way collaboration is organized (in the future), a broadly understood digital competence must also include leadership competence, intercultural competence and social intelligence. Collaboration in the future will increasingly take place project-based, interdisciplinary, multicultural and virtual (Albrecht, 2016). Especially social intelligence should sufficiently be considered if interaction takes place virtually (Deloitte, 2017). Finally, it should be considered that there is a constant need for adaptability. Learning turns to a lifelong task. This requires an inner attitude that aims at continuous development. Such a *Mindset for growth* (Dweck et al., 2014; Accenture, 2017; Kane et al., 2018) is top of a digital competence. In a nutshell, the required profile for a digital competence can be shown as follows:

In this conference contribution, the scientific assumptions have been considered so far. At this point, the business practical point of view on target competences for leaders in the digital age shall be examined. For this purpose, the results of partially structured expert interviews are interpreted. This method complies to the standards of qualitative empirical social research. The respondents were HR Directors, Heads of HR-development and HR consultants. It should be noted that the sample is not representative but has some initial tendencies.

The statements of HR Directors and Heads of HR-development basically confirm the developed competence house (see figure 2), with one exception: To the most widely accepted assumption in the literature, a leader should know how a computer "thinks" the business practical estimation varies. Contrary to scientific

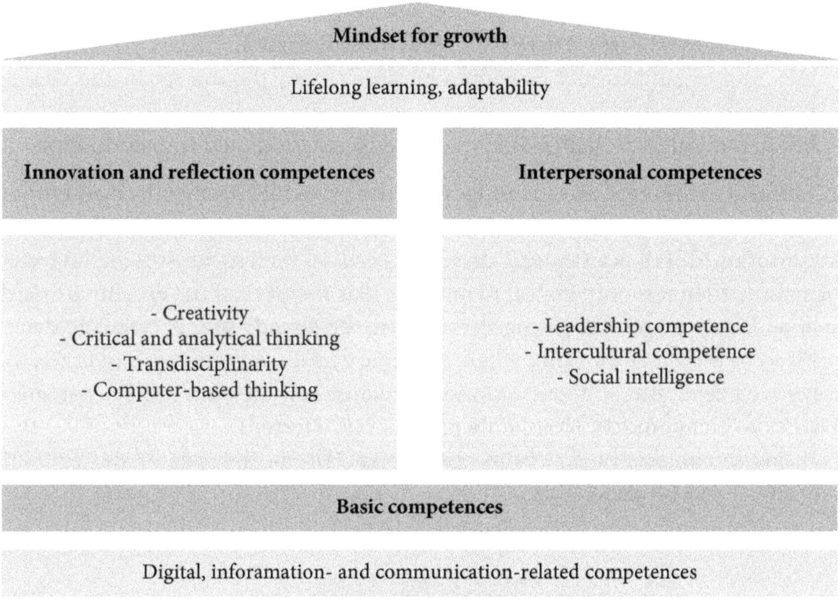

Figure 2: Required Profile of a Digital Competence (own illustration).

results, a clear statement by one of the interviewed HR Directors points out that a computer itself is stupid. What would be way more important is to get a sound understanding of the programmer's ethical attitude. In the sense of this consideration, ethical barriers are required, especially in cases of ethically unacceptable solutions despite technical feasibility.

Another striking estimation is obtained by interviewing HR Consultants. The essence of the statement is that the whole discussion about new competences is not really necessary. In order to ensure effective leadership in the future as well, professional, methodological, and action-related skills would have to be combined more strongly than other (new) competences to be successful. At this point, further empirical research is needed in order to clarify these diverse estimations of the leader's target competence-profile in the future.

New role of HR in the digital age: Business organization

Implications of digitalization also target the organizational positioning of HR. The changing requirements for HR departments can, according to Haufe Akademie (2017), be summed up as follows:

- HR has a creative role.
- HR becomes strategic driver for digital transformation.
- HR- and organizational development are crux of the matter in the change process.
- HR drives cultural change as key success factor for digital transformation.

A central question that directly hinges on is how can HR, against the background of the above-mentioned future requirements, be effectively positioned within an organization? If HR is a strategic driver and crucial for a successful digital transformation, then it is only logical to position it as member of the executive board, such as Finance and Marketing & Sales usually already are. A strategic driver needs to be placed at the point where strategic decisions are taken, and this is the executive board. But still, one question remains: Is it the entire HR department that has to be upgraded, or are only parts of HR affected?

If one separates strategic from operational HR, an upgrade of strategic HR only appears to be reasonable.

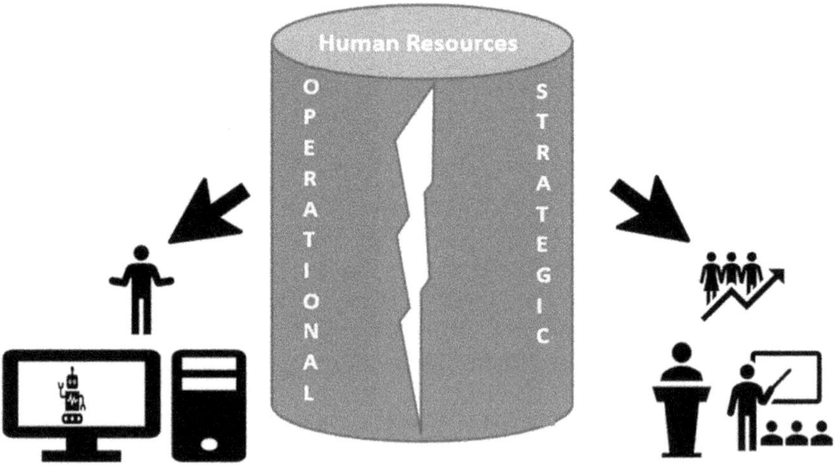

Figure 3: Required Separation Between Strategic and Operational HR (own illustration).

Assuming that the operational HR department is mainly considered with administrative tasks and the strategic HR department with people and culture, two main reasons can be given to justify the above-mentioned proposal of just upgrading strategic HR:

1. Different target competence profile of strategic vs. operational HR-Managers
   The Manager of operational HR needs a high share of professional and methodological competences. These competences relate to dealing with objects, such as processes or legal regulations (Erpenbeck & Ortmann, 2010).
   The Manager of the strategic HR department needs a high proportion of personal and social-communication skills. These competences relate to dealing with oneself and others (Erpenbeck & Ortmann, 2010).
   Both executives in turn need to have a high share of activity and decision-making competences. The compatibility of both profiles in one person seems to be difficult. Assumingly, there will either be an overweighting of objects at the expense of people and culture or an overweighting of human orientation at the expense of structure and task.
2. Different impact of digitalization for strategic vs. operational HRM
   The two HR parts operational vs. strategic will be affected by digitalization in different ways.
   The operational HR processes could almost completely be automized respectively overtaken by Artificial Intelligence (AI) in the future, in order to get rid of waste (according to Lean Production by Taichi Ohno, 1988, waste is Muda and related to non-value adding activities); i.e., in the operational HR department an increasing core removal by Artificial Intelligence (AI) is to be expected in the future.
   Strategic HR, in contrast, will gain in relevance. Since routine tasks can increasingly be substituted by AI, the focus of HR can be put more on value adding activities. HR in the future, as strategic driver, would anyway need a better and profound understanding of the entire corporate value chain (Olesch, 2016).

Integrating HR into the executive board is currently subject to scientific discourse and organizational-related discussions in business practice (Olesch, 2016): "*Human Resources is the biggest challenge for the CEO and corporations in the future*" (4C Group AG, n.d.).

Just as the finance department has made it in the past decades, the HR has to make the leap and become strategic partner for the CEO and the business. Human Capital Management must be equated to Financial- and Capital-Management. Corporate success will more and more depend on top quality human resources and a high-performance corporate culture as well as efficient structure and processes. Business decisions should, therefore, not be taken without the Chief Human Resources Officer (CHRO). This calls for a new positioning of HR as member of the executive board (4C Group AG, n.d.). The future guideline for HR is: Not (only) running the business, but changing the business (Reif, 2018).

In a nutshell, the respective new organizational chart would look like the following:

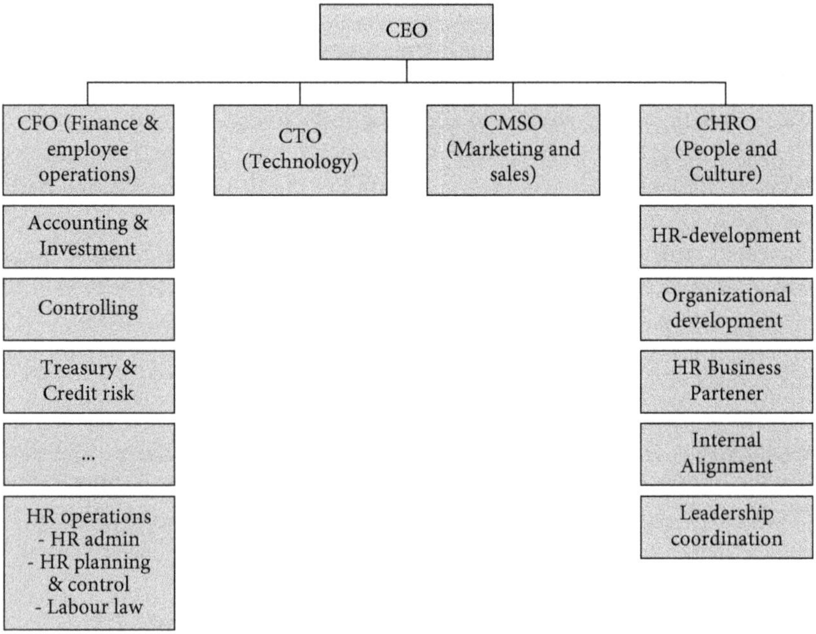

Figure 4: New Organizational Chart for the Digital Age (own illustration).

So far, the assumptions have been presented from a scientific perspective. What is the business practical expectation on the topic? In order to find answers to this question, two workshops were held with representatives of HR-departments, and also interviews were conducted again. Through this approach and as a result, a continuum with two extreme poles can be discovered:

One future scenario for HR is "HR finally really arrives at its role as member of the executive board". The opposite view is that "HR is abolished. There is only Artificial Intelligence (AI) and leaders". The first workshop essentially confirmed the first scenario because the big change process induced by digitalization would be mainly about trust and ethical decisions. In particular against the background of keeping ethics up despite technical feasibilities and efficiency-driven decision recommendations by AI, the role of HR within the executive board was underlined as a critical irritator. There is also a clear warning from the HR business practical point of view that making AI-based decisions, that relate to people, is not (always) a promising idea. Human-oriented decisions should also in the digital future be taken by human beings in order to save the value or even ethical profile of the respective organization. People-centered decisions should also be made by people in the digital future to preserve the value or ethical profile of each organization.

The second workshop also supported the first scenario. Here, however, the participants pointed out that the meaning of the leader's role in the future will increase. Taking a one-dimensional economic point of view, the HR-replacement by AI and leaders seems to be reasonable – at least if one considers that HR usually has the largest share of the overall operating costs.

As a conclusion, there are extremely different scenarios for the future role of HR within an organization from the business practical point of view, reaching from being member of the executive board to being abolished and replaced by AI and leadership. Further empirical research is needed in order to provide a more precise view on the conditions, under which HR will take either the one or the other way in the future. Nevertheless, business examples for integrating HR in the board are available and indicating benefits as follows:

Best-Practice-example Phoenix Contact-Group, Blomberg

Phoenix Contact is a global market leader for electrical engineering. Organized as family business, the enterprise designs the future in a responsible way. HR has already been upgraded since the executive board is represented by the Chief Executive Officer (CEO), the Chief Technology Officer (CTO), the Chief Human Resource Officer (CHRO) and the Chief Financial Officer (CFO). The success of Phoenix Contact speaks for itself: The company is honored as "Innovator of the year 2019", awarded with "Excellence in eSolutions 2019" (Phoenix Contact, 2019), as well as best employer (Germany and Europe) – "Great Place to Work" (Phoenix Contact, 2016). The corporate's CHRO, Prof. Dr. Gunter Olesch, confirms the economic goal improvement. Within four years, the corporation was able to increase its turnover to 1.5 bn EUR (Olesch, n.d.). Regarding the proposed differentiation between strategic and operational HR, it can be assumed that further potential can even be developed in the future.

Conclusion

So far, a lot of questions related to the digitalization's impact for HR remain open. At the present moment, no one is able to finally assess which job will when exactly be replaced by machines and their algorithms. The same accounts for forecasting how long applications of the previously learned will last. There are rather different future scenarios, reaching from apocalyptic to euphoric forecasts of employment. This might lead to uncertainty and anxiety. But exactly these two emotions are bad drivers for an effective design of the digital transformation in organizations. All the more, openness for change, speed and strict customer- and application-orientation can be revealed as success factors.

HR is especially challenged to give strong support to people and culture by increasingly self-organized and coordinated HR-development, agile and empowering leadership as well as by aligning the whole workforce toward a corporate-specific vision for the digital change. The future suitability of exiting target competence profiles, especially for leaders, should be challenged in order to drive the change effectively.

Finally, the comprehensive change process can also lead to a need of newly positioning HR within the business organization. (Especially) Strategic HR should be upgraded and become member of executive board. For deriving general statements on the question, which path business practice will take here, further empirical research is needed. Future research should also analyze the potential benefits stemming from dividing strategic and operational HR by considering both, economic and social Key Performance Indicators (KPIs).

Nevertheless, there is currently a great opportunity for HR to move up to the executive board, if the topic of *People & Culture* is accepted as crucial for success of the digital transformation. Therefore, HR will also need persistence and persuasion. If HR sleeps through this development, the risk of being abolished and replaced by AI is increasing. This also implies that HR needs a new self-conception and more self-confidence. In this context, it should be mentioned that Finance as well as Sales and Marketing have successfully mastered the same step in the past.

Even if readjustments within HR might already be running in business practice, the following recommendations – identified as success factors – for an effective digital transformation shall finally be given:

- **HR has a sound understanding of the enterprise's entire value chain.**
- **HR builds up a strong vision for the digital future and ensures the workforce's reliable alignment.**
- **HR works competence-oriented by integrating proven competences from the past and new digital competences into a systematic competence management model.**
- **HR itself is represented as member of the executive board within the business organization.**

In case that a company is following a sustainable leadership approach, one further aspect should after all be added:

- **HR sensitizes all organizational members for ethical barriers despite technological feasibilities.**

By this, a corporate's way to sustainable competitiveness in the digital age can responsibly be designed by HR and its managers.

References

Accenture (2017). *New Skills Now: Inclusion in the digital economy*. Retrieved July 24, 2019, from https://www.accenture.com/_acnmedia/PDF-63/Accenture-New-Skills-Now-Inclusion-in-the-digital.pdf.

Albrecht, A. (2016). *Virtual leadership as a critical success factor in the new world of work*. In Personal Quarterly 1/2016, 17–22.

Armutat, S. & Grebe, R. (2018). *The EBZ Maturity and Competence Model "Digitization in the Housing Industry"*. Unpublished manuscript.

Bundesministerium für Wirtschaft und Energie (BMWi) (2016). *Monitoring Report Economy DIGITAL*. BMWi, Berlin.

Capgemini (2017). *Digitalization Requires a Radical Change in Organizational Culture*. Retrieved July 23, 2019, from https://www.capgemini.com/2017/06/digitalisation-requires-a-radical-change-in-organisational-culture/.

Deloitte (2017). *Which Key Competences are Needed in the Digital Age? Impact of Automation on Employees, Companies and the Education System*. Retrieved July 20, 2019, from https://www2.deloitte.com/ch/de/pages/innovation/articles/competencies-in-the-digital-age.html.

Dengler, K. & Matthes, B. (2018). Substitution potential of occupations: Few job descriptions keep pace with digitization. *IAB short report 4/2018*. Retrieved August 5, 2019, from http://www.iab.de/194/section.aspx/Publikation/k180213301.

Depiereux, P. & Alphen, C. van (2018). Leadership in the age of digitization – A location Assessment. In Werther, S., Bruckner, L. (Eds.), *Actively Shaping Work 4.0. The Future of Work between Agility, People Analytics and Digitization*, (pp. 29–36). Berlin: Springer Gabler.

Deutscher Industrie- und Handelskammertrag (DIHK) (2015). *Economy 4.0: Great opportunities to do a lot. The IHK corporate barometer on digitization*, DIHK, Berlin Brüssel.

Dweck, C. S., Walton, G. M. & Cohen, G. L. (2014). *Academic Tenacity. Mindsets and Skills that Promote Long-Term Learning*, Bill & Melinda Gates

Foundation. Retrieved July 24, 2019, from https://ed.stanford.edu/sites/default/files/manual/dweck-walton-cohen-2014.pdf.

Eilers, S., Möckel, K., Rump, J. & Schabel, F. (2017). *HR-Report 2017. Focus on Competences for a Digital World 1/2017*, Retrieved July 22, 2019, from https://www.hays.de/documents/10192/118775/Hays-Studie-HR-Report-2017.pdf/.

Erpenbeck, J., Ortmann, S. (2010). *Procedures for determining and developing skills, Leadership skills for top performance. Economic challenges psychological answers*, In Barthel, E., Erpenbeck, J., Heyse V., Ortmann, S. (Eds.), Zawacki Richter, O., *Basic structures of human skills. Tried and tested concepts and instruments*, 77, 188. Münster: Waxmann Verlag GmbH.

European Political Strategy Centre (EPSC) (2016). *EPSC Strategic Notes – The Future of Work. Skills and Resilience for a World of Change*, 10.06.2016. Retrieved July 22, 2019, from https://ec.europa.eu/epsc/sites/epsc/files/strategic_note_issue_13.pdf.

Fidler, D. (2016). *Future Skills Update and Literature Review. Prepared for ACT Foundation and the Joyce Foundation by: Institute for the Future 7/2016.* Retrieved July 24, 2019, from http://www.iftf.org/fileadmin/user_upload/downloads/wfi/ACTF_IFTF_FutureSkills-report.pdf.

Franken, S. & Cutmore-Beinlich, S. A. (2018). Digitization and industry 4.0 – new work, changed workforces, In Armutat, S., Bartholomäus, N., Franken, S., Herzig, V., Helbich, B. (Eds.), *Human Resources Management in Times of Demographics and Digitization. Challenges and Coping Strategies for the Middle Class*, (pp. 57–76). Wiesbaden: Springer Fachmedien.

Frey, C. B. & Osborne, M. A. (2013). *The Future of Employment: How Susceptible Are Jobs to Computerisation?* 17.09.2013. Retrieved August 5, 2019, from https://www.oxfordmartin.ox.ac.uk/downloads/academic/The_Future_of_Employment.pdf.

Hammermann, A. & Stettes, O. (2016). Qualification requirements and qualification. Requirements in the sign of digitization. *IW policy paper* 3/2016. Institut der deutschen Wirtschaft, Köln.

Haufe Akademie (2017). *Strategies for human resource development in the digital revolution. New learning for new working environments, Haufe Akademie E-Books*, 09.06.2017. Retrieved August 7, 2019, from https://www.haufe-akademie.de/blog/themen/e-learning/digitaler-wandel-die-antwort-der-personalentwicklung/.

Heyse, V. & Erpenbeck, J. (2007). *Competence management. Methods, procedures, KODE® and KODE®X in the field test.* Münster: Waxmann.

Hofstede Insights (n.d.). *Compare Countries*, Retrieved July 22, 2019 from https://www.hofstede-insights.com/product/compare-countries/.

Jackson, P., Richter, N., & Schildhauer, T. (2017). Entrepreneurial behaviour and startups: The case of Germany and the USA. In Jackson, P., Richter, N., Schildhauer, T. (Eds.), *Entrepreneurial Innovation and Leadership. Preparing for a Digital Future*, (pp. 1–14). Cham Schweiz: Palgrave Macmillan.

Jung, S. (2014). *Employment adjustment in the business cycle*. Hamburg: Verlag Dr. Kovač.

Kane, G. C., Palmer, D., Phillips, A. N., Kiron, D. & Buckley, N. (2018). Coming of Age Digitally. *MIT Sloan Management Review und Deloitte Insights 6/2018*, Retrieved July 24, 2019, from https://www2.deloitte.com/content/dam/Deloitte/nl/Documents/technology/deloitte-nl-consulting-coming-of-age-digitally.pdf.

Kluth, A. (2018). German 'Digitalisierung' versus American innovation. In *Handelsblatt today*, 23.02.2018, Retrieved July 22, 2019 from: https://www.handelsblatt.com/today/opinion/10-kinds-of-people-german-digitalisierung-versus-american-innovation/23581228.html?ticket=ST-8590973-TOkyJmwCMJj1T5elS6zw-ap5.

McKinsey Global Institute (MGI) (2018). *Skill shift: Automation and the future of workforce*, Retrieved July 22, 2019, from https://www.mckinsey.com/~/media/McKinsey/Featured%20Insights/Future%20of%20Organizations/Skill%20shift%20Automation%20and%20the%20future%20of%20the%20workforce/MGI-Skill-Shift-Automation-and-future-of-the-workforce-May-2018.ashx.

Ohno, T. (1988). Toyota Production System. *Beyond Large-Scale Production*. New York: Productivity Press.

Olesch, G. (2016). *#NextHR: Prof. Olesch, Phoenix Contact, about sustainable HR 05.05.2016*. Retrieved August 5, 2019 from https://www.youtube.com/watch?v=djkXlnn39HA.

Olesch, G. (n.d.). *Phoenix Contact*, Retrieved August 5, 2019 from https://kulturwandel.org/project/phoenix-contact/.

Phoenix Contact (2016). *Phoenix Contact is one of "Europe's Best Employers 2016"* 04.07.2016. Retrieved July 24, 2019, from https://www.phoenixcontact.com/online/portal/de?1dmy&urile=wcm%3apath%3a/dede/web/corporate/press/press_information/1a75acf3-c551-47a2-b3e6-23cec44dd585.

Phoenix Contact (2019). *Phoenix Contact E-Mobility is Innovator of the Year 2019,13.05.2019*. Retrieved July 24, 2019 from https://www.phoenixcontact.com/online/portal/de?1dmy&urile=wcm%3apath%3a/dede/web/corporate/press/press_information/7d38db12-7d1b-492d-84c3-486e972e6033.

Reif, M. K. (2018). *Agile personnel management? Hire a Chief People Officer, 06.12.2018*. Retrieved July 24, 2019, from https://www.reif.org/blog/agiles-personalmanagement-hire-chief-people-officer/.

Rürup, B. & Jung, S. (2016). The state of the global economy and the new challenges for companies. *Audit Committee Quarterly I*/2016, 60–65.

Rürup, B. & Jung, S. (2017). Digitization: opportunities for new growth. In Hildebrandt, A., Landhäußer, W. (Eds.). CSR and digitization. The digital transformation as opportunity and challenge for economy and society. In: Schmidpeter, R. (Eds.), *Management-Reihe Corporate Social Responsibility* (pp. 3–21). Berlin: Springer Gabler.

Stifterverband für die Deutsche Wissenschaft e.V. (Eds.) (2018). *Future Skills: Which skills are missing in Germany?* Retrieved July 23, 2019, from https://www.stifterverband.org/medien/future-skills-welche-kompetenzen-in-deutschland-fehlen.

Widmaier, S. (2017). Digital transformation demands openness and willingness to change from executive. In *PersonalQuarterly 1*/2017, 6–9.

World Economic Forum (2015). *Annual Report 2014-2015, World Economic Forum*. Schwab, K. (Eds.). Cologny/Genf Schweiz.

World Economic Forum (2018). *Insight Report. The Future of Jobs Report 2018, World Economic Forum*. Leopold, T. A. (Eds.). Cologny/Genf Schweiz.

4C Group AG (n.d.). *Human Resources Management (CHRO). It's time for HR!* Retrieved August 5, 2019, from https://www.4cgroup.com/de/chro-humanresourcesmanagement.

Ulrich Tamm

Blockchains: Benefits and Problems for Applications Besides Cryptocurrencies

Abstract: The technical background and the infrastructure of blockchains are analyzed in view of possible applications besides cryptocurrencies. Especially, logistics turned out to be an important field in which the blockchain technology is already implemented or will come into play soon. The aim of this chapter is to yield a closer insight into benefits and problems beyond cryptography with an emphasis on the role of miners. The source of many problems is the fact that processes relevant for cryptocurrencies do not match business processes for further blockchain applications. As an example, a possible fork of a health care blockchain is discussed. On the other hand, a benefit in logistics is that a blockchain for supply chains, additionally, yields mechanisms to locate problems during the transport.

Keywords: Blockchain, mining, double-spend, fork

Introduction

Among the many innovations in the times of digital transformation, cryptocurrencies and their underlying distributed ledger management via a blockchain play a prominent role. In this chapter, cryptographic aspects of this new technology are neglected. Instead, a closer look is taken at the mining process. In blockchains for cryptocurrencies, mining is the solution to avoid the double-spend attack in which someone can try to pay twice using the same coin. In this case, there are two possible decisions about the owner of the coin, which will be discussed until the miners achieve consensus. To this aim, they have to follow a proof-of-work protocol, and also a delay of the acceptance of the payment has to be tolerated.

These two last-mentioned drawbacks are responsible for acceptance problems of cryptocurrencies in practice. The proof-of-work is provided by the solution of a complicated puzzle, for which a lot of computing power is necessary. Since with the rising bitcoin exchange rates mining became more and more attractive and also more difficult, the energy consumption is much criticized nowadays. As a consequence of the delay in the acceptance of a payment, cryptocurrencies are still much slower than, for instance, credit card transactions.

This technical background on blockchains and mining will be briefly provided in the next section. This section will be concluded with a discussion about another drawback, namely, the possibility of a fork and its consequences. A fork occurs when the miners, finally, do not find consensus, in which case the blockchain is split in two separate ones. The result will be two different cryptocurrencies. This happened, for instance, when Bitcoin and Bitcoin Cash separated.

When blockchains are used for business applications and not for payment records, the situation is much different. There is no real incentive for a double-spend attack. In turn, problems, as a fork, may then be much more critical for the business application than for cryptocurrencies. This will be the topic of the third section. With four examples (payments with cryptocurrencies, patient records in health care, delivery documents in logistics, and data of used cars), the consequences, especially of a fork, will be considered. It turns out that several aspects of the data to be stored as value, lifetime, or frequency of transactions of a subject will be of importance in the analysis.

Finally, a closer look is taken at the situation in logistics, for which in the fourth section several already implemented solutions will be compared in view of the mining and forking problem. It will be seen that in order to store transactions of a supply chain several solutions have been implemented. They might be based on Ethereum that is a cryptocurrency, on Hyperledger where mining does not require so much energy, or even on database management organized within the company. Logistics is, further, a nice example for an application where blockchains outperform classical databases in another aspect. Problems during the transport as the damage or even disappearance of a good might be analyzed by backtracking their way in the transport network that is exactly mirrored by an information network in the blockchain.

Technical Background

Blockchain as data structure

A blockchain is often described as a distributed ledger. As a ledger, it is, actually, the backbone for cryptocurrencies allowing to keep track of the transactions. From the computer science point of view, it can be regarded as a database (of transactions). As underlying data structure of this database, Satoshi Nakamoto in his pioneering paper Nakamoto (2008) chose the hash pointer, which consists of two well-known components.

1. A pointer is the address of another data segment – in a blockchain the previous block of transactions. A pointer allows to store a database as a linked list of data segments where the segments do not have to be placed in adjacent storage space but can be anywhere – even on different computers. Thus, it already allows a distributed database.

2. Additionally to the pointer on the previous transaction in each header of a data segment, the hash value of the previous data segment is stored. A hash value is a short checksum that guarantees that a fraud or manipulation will be detected. This manipulation, for instance, the change of a recipient of a cryptocoin will result in a change of the checksum.

Thus, a blockchain can be compared to a book, which has to be read backwards. Each page with blocks of transactions contains a pointer to the previous page. The single transactions are equipped with serial numbers such that it is also possible to follow the single items as cryptocoins subject of this database.

Cryptography comes into play in order to protect the transactions by digital signatures or to encrypt transactions if secrecy is required. The most important tool is the cryptographic hash function which guarantees that it is computationally impossible to find two transactions with the same hash value. This prevents attacks by dishonest users who might try to change the amount of money in a transaction or even to steal a transaction by replacing the name of the recipient into their own name.

It is not purpose of this chapter to discuss the various cryptographic security aspects. For a closer look Narayanan et al. (2016) or Kohn and Tamm (2019) might be consulted. However, it should be stated that, if carefully implemented, the cryptographic infrastructure should be quite solid. In each case, bitcoin works well and passed several stress situations since more than 10 years now. The attacks reported are mostly on the electronic wallets in which the bitcoins are stored and are often due to an improper handling of the cryptographic key.

One security aspect usually considered in cryptography, however, should be mentioned at this point. Several copies of the blockchain are stored in public places such that it is accessible to everybody and, hence, an open book. Everybody can go through the database in which users can choose pseudonyms. This should guarantee anonymity, but this is not really the case. For instance, the pattern analysis of a user's transactions might allow to gain a lot of knowledge or even to identify this user. It is also possible to find out how many cryptocoins are actually assigned to one pseudonym. As a recent example, in a *New York Times* article by Popper (2019), the purpose of bitcoin transactions was analyzed to some detail. The result was that about 60% to 80% of the transactions are speculation and only less than 1% of the transactions are actually used for payments. Big part of the remaining transactions is, probably, used for illegal commerce. This anonymity concern might be a serious drawback for further applications of blockchains in which privacy has to be absolutely guaranteed.

Cryptography can protect against enemies trying to steal money. However, there is a problem which cannot be prevented by cryptographic tools – the so-called double-spend attack. A user might try to use the same cryptocoin for several payments. In order to guarantee the impossibility (better, "almost improbability") of this attack, several control mechanisms have been introduced: the miners, proof-of-work, and delay in the confirmation of transactions.

The miners and the double spend attack

The participants of a blockchain, e.g., the owners of cryptocoins are participants of a peer-to-peer network, i.e., there is no central instance for administration. Thus, the validation of the correctness of a transaction should, in principle, be carried out by a user himself. This validation includes among other tasks to control that the money he receives is really in the hands of the sender, to verify the digital signature, and to check if there was no double-spend. However, not every peer in the network has the time or the abilities for this job. Furthermore, the blockchain after a while will exceed the size of a standard computer memory such that special equipment might be necessary. This validation process is delegated to a special group of peers in the network: the miners.

Besides the validation, another important task of the miners is to generate new cryptocoins. To this task they have to solve a computationally hard puzzle – more exactly, they have to find a hash value of a certain structure. When they have solved this puzzle, the solution can be easily verified by all other miners, and they are rewarded with a certain amount of cryptocoins. Actually, they have generated a new block worth this amount in which their recently validated transactions are included. This approach is called proof-of-work. The difficulty of the puzzle is scaled such that on average each, say 10 minutes as for Bitcoin, a new cryptocoin is generated.

Since computers are getting faster and more miners come into play because of the immense rise of the value of cryptocoins, the difficulty of the puzzle today is such that only very fast and specialized computers can be used for this purpose. This costs a lot of energy for computation and cooling. Because of this, the proof-of-work approach is much criticized. Leading computer experts are working on an alternative, proof-of-stake. The idea is that in the proof-of-work approach a miner would create a fraction of cryptocoins proportionate to his amount of computer power. If, for instance, a miner has 15 per cent of the computer power he would mine about 15 per cent of the new cryptocoins. Why then not using a less energy consuming mining procedure by allowing to generate new coins proportional to the stake, i.e., the amount of cryptocoins a miner holds. Thus, a miner holding 20 per cent of the cryptocoins should mine 20 per cent of the new cryptocoins. There is a strong impetus on the development of such proof-of-stake procedures. A big problem to be overcome is the rich-get-richer effect, which means that miners with fewer bitcoins will finally disappear – cf. Bagaria et al. (2018). Especially, Ethereum promised the replacement of proof-of-work by proof-of-stake. However, the introduction already promised for much earlier is delayed and now announced for 2020 (cf. Ethereum 2.0 News (2019)).

Another problem is the possible presence of dishonest miners. Especially, they control if a user is trying a double-spend. However, what if this user is a miner himself? To prevent a double-spend attack, in each case, a delay for the acceptance of a transaction has to be tolerated. After such a double-spend, the community of miners will split into two parts: one group which accepts recipient A and another group accepting recipient B. Such a splitting of the miners is called a fork. In order to correct (and, hence, avoid) such a fork, a special rule had been introduced: transactions are not immediately included in the blockchain, the pending transactions form chains of different length, and the miners have to append their next validated transaction to the longest chain they see.

A dishonest miner, however, might not follow this rule and, instead, create a new chain. If he has enough computational power, he might succeed to make this the longest chain and the honest miners will follow him and his double-spend. To avoid this attack, a transaction is confirmed only after a certain number, say 5 as in Nielsen (2013), of blocks have been added subsequently to the block in which the respective transaction is included.

This delay is responsible for the relative slow speed of transactions. Even credit card transactions are much faster than transactions with Bitcoin or Ethereum. There is intensive research now by leading computer scientists to overcome this bottleneck in blockchain technology as Ji and Micali (2017) or Li et al. (2018).

Another point is that a single miner or a coalition of miners should not be too powerful. Otherwise the 51 per cent attack would be possible. If one controls more than half of the computational power, than one will mostly be able to build the longest chains.

Forks may arise in different ways, when miners disagree. The most well-known forks are due to discussions about changes in the protocol the miners have to follow. For instance, the split of Bitcoin Cash from Bitcoin was result of a fork – cf. All about Bitcoin Cash hard fork (2019). The miners could not agree about the block size. A so-called hard fork is already announced by Ethereum: when a proof-of-stake protocol will be introduced, the miners can decide if they will use this or the old proof-of-work protocol.

As seen in this section, the miners play a central role in the blockchain technology. Besides the above-mentioned tasks validation of transactions and generation of new cryptocoins, they have to maintain the database and also to discuss about changes in the protocol. Further, it has to be controlled that single miners or coalitions of miners do not become too powerful. Even with far less than 50 per cent of the computational power, different attacks than double-spend are thinkable.

It should also be mentioned that mining is quite expensive now and the invested money should, of course, return to the miners. When the bitcoin exchange rate dropped below 4000 Euro, it was reported that mining was not profitable any more, actually, in between the profitability limit is about 7300 USD – see, for instance, Bitcoin Miner sind weitestgehend Profitabel (2019). In the moment, the bitcoin miners are rewarded for the generation of a new block with 12.5 bitcoins (this will halve to 6.25 bitcoins in May 2020) – the exact figures and more information is seen on Bitcoinhalf (2019), cf. also Dilmi (2019). They will also benefit from the validation of the transactions that results in transaction fees for the users of a blockchain. Hence, mining can be regarded as a profession today.

This becomes obvious when taking into account that spots for the mining pool of Facebook Libra are on sale as described in Libra Whitepaper (2019). Actually, one might always ask: who are the miners? In Bitcoin or Ethereum, for instance, everybody can download the protocol and start mining. Without the necessary equipment, this will not be very successful such that there is some selection by wealth, too, of course. A different approach is taken in the open source developers platform Hyperledger, where the selection is based on trust. Many business-oriented blockchains do not use mining based on proof-of-work at all; for instance, they might be based on Hyperledger or even other concepts to find consensus about the decisions.

Applications Other Than Cryptocurrencies

Ethereum and smart contracts

Most blockchains are cryptocurrencies and thus have a monetary purpose. Money is created by the generation of a new block, and the successful miner may use this money for future payments. Among the more popular blockchains Bitcoin Cash, Bitcoin Gold and, in a wider sense, Litecoin are results of forks from Bitcoin. Ripple had originally been introduced for money transfer between different countries in order to reduce the exchange fees. IOTA is a cryptocurrency for inter-machine payments in the internet of things (in fact, this is not even based on a blockchain). A special role is played by Ethereum. On one hand, firstly, effort is taken to replace proof-of-work by proof-of-stake. Secondly, a special feature is implemented here, which is of big interest for applications beyond cryptocurrencies. This feature is a so-called smart contract. The contract is such that a transaction will be carried out only if several conditions are fulfilled. This can be realized by a small programming code using simple IF ... THEN commands which might be coded into the script of a block. In fact, any text (not only payment information) can be written into a block – this makes the blockchain technology so flexible and interesting for business applications.

Since the transfer of money adds a monetary value to a transaction in the blockchain of a cryptocurrency, this gives incentive to dishonest users to attacks as discussed above: stealing, fraud, and double-spend. For other applications of blockchains, this incentive might not be present such that these attacks have to be reconsidered. Especially, a lot of measures were taken in order to prevent a double-spend: miners, which are not too powerful, a rather long delay until the confirmation of a transaction. One question for further applications might be if these measures are really necessary.

On the other hand, scenarios which are not so much dangerous for cryptocurrencies might turn out as very unpleasant for business applications. Particularly, a fork is sometimes even forced for cryptocurrencies. The client who does not accept one of the branches can easily decide for the other branch. For instance, one can immediately sell all his bitcoins and invest the money in bitcoin cash. Actually, the exact mechanism is based on tokens that are often described as shares of cryptocoins. The exact mechanism will not be discussed here.

Comparison of several applications

In the following, several applications are considered whose single transactions do not have a significant value. This might even include micropayments.

Health Care: One of the most promising applications of blockchains is health care. For a survey of benefits, see Blockchains in Health Care and the Life Sciences (2019). Especially, there it is stated that "*the adoption of the blockchain technology could save the health industry up to $100 - $150 billion per year by 2025*". They go as far as praising "*Blockchain and healthcare is a match made in heaven*" and "*Given that blockchain is a public ledger that's secure and immutable, it's exactly what healthcare needs*".

Advantages are listed in The "Global Blockhain in Health Care" Report (2019): secure management of electronic health records, patient consent management, drug traceability, data security in clinical trials, and incentivization through micropayments. This last feature is a nice application of smart contracts, which might be used to reward patients "*for following a certain treatment plan or sharing their data for clinical research*".

There was already a strong initiative for a standardization of blockchains in health care, which is absolutely necessary as stated in Healthcare Blockchain Relies on Industry Standardization (2019). However, progress seems to slow down in this respect.

From the above statements, it can be concluded that Ethereum might be the proper choice for a blockchain in health care. There are, however, a lot of requirements concerning the privacy of the data. Since patient data are very sensible, they should of course be encrypted. Further, it should be guaranteed that other parties (employers of a patient, competing enterprise in pharma industry) do not gain information by browsing through the blockchain. Cryptology, usually, provides solutions – but many special scenarios have to be considered.

Another serious drawback is the possibility of a fork. If a fork would occur, then the data would be distributed among the branches of this fork. Since most data will be used for a long time in the future, this is not an acceptable situation here. Some problems are reflected in the following.

1. The access rights to the data are, usually, arranged via tokens. Tokens are often described as shares of coins for cryptocurrencies. For health care blockchains, there might arise the impression that patient data are traded as shares in case of a fork. This would yield a very bad impression in public discussions.
2. In each case, the ownership of the data might be an important question. Many parties involved – patients, medical doctors, hospitals, pharmacists, pharma industry, health insurances, etc. – should at least be informed about the changes. Some of them, surely, want to be involved in the decision process.
3. On the other hand, it will be almost impossible to transfer the data to a new database because of the complicated pointer structures and privacy restrictions. Furthermore, the number of tokens is, usually, limited, which might yield a serious restriction here.
4. Standardization is, usually, a very conservative and slow process. A fork in the blockchain would force a change and a decision about the branch to be followed. There might be some time pressure since the date of the fork will be fixed.
5. For business applications with an impact such as a whole national health care system, a fork might be compared to a split of a big enterprise. This is a

complicated process with a lot of consulting and lawyers' advice. Additionally, here the date of a fork will be fixed and cannot be delayed.

6. This is mainly due to the governance of a blockchain as Bitcoin or Ethereum. The discussion about protocol changes is among the miners. Probably, no law can stop the fork in case the miners finally disagree about the future protocol.
7. There may be many further legal questions involved. For instance, it is not clear which branch to follow. With the Bitcoin Cash fork, the canonical successor was Bitcoin – the blockchain not changing the protocol. In a case of a split of Ethereum into proof-of-work and proof-of-stake, for instance, the canonical successor might be the update and not the old protocol. In times of discussion about climate change most business applications would switch to the less energy consuming proof-of-stake protocol.

Logistics: A further much promising application of blockchains is the record of transactions in a supply chain. Several solutions here exist already, and a closer look at them will be taken in the next section. Here we just want to briefly analyze the data in the delivery documents in respect of benefits and problems when they are stored in a blockchain. Actually, supply chains in the pharma industry should also be a part of health care blockchains.

Such delivery documents should be quite immune toward double-spend attacks. There is not really an incentive for double-spend and, if this really would occur, the document is assigned to a good which is delivered. If this, additionally, would accompany a second good, the information would not be very useful at the receiving end. In this situation, one might really ask if all the control mechanisms described for cryptocurrencies – even the miners – are necessary at all. In fact, in the next section, solutions will be presented without an involved mining system based on proof-of-work.

As seen above, the transactions here are accompanying the good to be transported. Furthermore, they are following the same network, i.e., information will be entered at nodes as ports, where the goods arrive and depart (and, perhaps, during the transport). This feature will be of some importance in the next section, where it will be discussed that problems arising during the transport as contamination or stealing of goods might be investigated using the blockchain.

A big advantage of a more or less centrally controlled blockchain without miners is that a fork is not possible. Even though this is always an unpleasant scenario, here, however, the consequences will not be as drastic as in health care. The purpose of a delivery document is, usually, settled when the good successfully arrives at its destination. After that, further transactions with this document will not be carried out. It might be used later on, e.g., for the tax office or for the investigation of problems during the transport. This is, however, a passive role for which storage over an appropriate period should be sufficient.

Storing Data of Used Cars: Very recently, several platforms have been launched in order to store data of used cars, for instance, described in the web pages Blockchain-based Used Car Data Marketplace to Launch in Singapore (2019) or Daimler to Use Blockchain Platform for Valuing Used Cars (2019). This is a very nice example for demonstrating some benefits of a blockchain. The data can be entered from different places and at any time and will in short time be included into the database of used cars. It would be difficult to implement such a collection of data with classical databases as Excel. The benefit for traders and clients is evidently an improvement in transparency. Past sales of these cars, repairs, etc. can be obtained from the database, and it will be difficult to hide negative information. Further, it will be possible to compare the price of similar cars. The cryptographic protection against fraud prevents from changes, for instance, of the mileage.

There are many more blockchain applications in the automobile industry under development or already implemented – some of them are mentioned in Daimler to Use Blockchain Platform for Valuing Used Cars (2019). We choose this one because the type of data to be stored is again different from the previous examples. Again, a double-spend does not make much sense here – payment is explicitly excluded and the data accompany a real object and cannot be easily matched to another car. The data will be updated during the lifetime of a car, which might be quite long. However, the frequency of updates is, probably, not very high.

Blockchains in Logistics

In the previous section, we considered delivery documents in logistics as an example of data with quite a short life time. Of course, there are many more demands in supply chains that should be taken into account also in the blockchain. For a small survey see Özbay (2018), where also several blockchain solutions and use cases of existing implementations or such under development are presented. Here we select a few of them in order to demonstrate that all variants discussed in the previous sections are relevant in practice.

Ethereum: VeChain is a platform introduced by the Chinese blockhain enterprise BitSe and was developed, especially, for applications within a supply chain. The underlying blochchain is Ethereum. Hence, this is a solution including proof-of-work mining that might soon be replaced by proof-of-stake. A prominent partner is DB Schenker (VeChain und DB Schenker: Blockchain in der Logistik, 2018).

IBM: In 2017, Maersk and IBM started a test for shipments of goods of a French enterprise from Rotterdam to Newark. The blockchain solution here is developed using Hyperledger (Cargo via Blockchain, 2017). Thus mining is done by a community of trusted miners. Actually, IBM has implemented further logistics applications, for instance, on food supply chains. This we shall discuss under a different aspect later on.

Guardtime: Another leading expert, besides IBM, for blockchain solutions is the Estonian enterprise Guardtime. Several of their partners in supply chains are listed on their website Guardtime (2019). Actually, the hash pointer (underlying data structure of a blockchain) was not a new concept when Satoshi Nakamoto introduced Bitcoin, and Guardtime had already worked with it before. Thus, they have a long-standing experience and also certified cryptography implementations. SAP is cooperating with Guardtime in blockchain solutions. Interesting for us is the mining process. From a discussion after their lecture at the Workshop "Blockchain and Smart Contracts" Tartu (2018), it can be concluded that maintenance of the database is organized by Guardtime itself.

Corda: A blockchain operating without a consensus algorithm based on mining is Corda, see, for instance, their webpage Corda (2019) or Was ist Corda (2019), which has cooperation on Daimler for several applications, for instance, described on Daimler Carries out First Transaction on Marco Polo Blockchain Trade Network (2019).

So, there already exist a lot of blockchain solutions based on different mining and consensus concepts (Ethereum, Hyperledger, Guardtime). The problem may arise that these solutions will not be guaranteed to be compatible among each other.

An own section is devoted to logistics for another reason. When the transactions are recorded in a blockchain, it is easily possible to trace back in case of problems that may arise during the transport. Here is a clear advantage compared to classical databases, since mechanisms of backtracking are essential for the maintenance of the blockchain. As an example, in a food supply chain some food may be contaminated during the transport. In order to find the nodes in the network where this problem originated, a surprising connection to information theory and signal processing was helpful in the analysis. The spreading process could be compared to the spreading of rumors via gossiping in an information network, Varshney et al. (2017).

Similarly, a way to find out where goods not arriving properly might have been damaged or even stolen had been suggested by Bayrak-Meydanoglu and Tamm (2010). The idea (already sketched in Tamm, 2010) was that the information in the database is assigned to a good to be transported. Since information about this good is, usually, obtained in places where the goods arrive and/or depart or during the transport, transactions concerning this good allow to locate a node or an edge in the underlying transport network. Hence, in the blockchain, an information network is represented with the same nodes and edges as the underlying transport network. For such information networks, there is already a vast amount of literature, and algorithms might exist to help analyzing problems in supply chains via blockchains. For instance, network coding introduced by Ahlswede, Cai, Li, and Yeung (2000) and described in Scientific American by Effros, Koetter, and Medard (2007) allows to locate the origin of problems in an information network and might even help to code or encrypt information. In case of locating the nodes where goods might have been stolen, this could yield an interesting mathematical problem. Since, usually, further criminal investigations will have to be carried out, a quantification and subsequent decision rule for the evidence of a theft at a special location must be specified.

Discussion and Conclusion

Blockchains were analyzed in view of a possible double-spend attack. This is a very serious problem for cryptocurrencies that, unfortunately, cannot be controlled by use of cryptographic methods. In order to avoid and, if necessary, correct double-spends, a much sophisticated system of mining bitcoins had been set up. This led to new problems which only quite recently became evident in the last two or three years due to the exponential increase in cryptocurrency transactions: an unacceptably high consumption of energy and a long delay in the acceptance of cryptocurrency transactions which are, by now, much slower than credit card transactions.

For most business applications, however, the double-spend attack does not appear to be of much significance. There is no real incentive for such an attack, and furthermore, the transactions are often directly connected to a real life subject that cannot be split. Even worse, a fork of a blockchain due to a split of the community of miners might involve many difficulties of technical, organizational, or legal nature for business applications, whereas for cryptocurrencies a fork is quite well controllable. This demonstrates that a tool designed for one purpose is not so easily applicable for another purpose – even in the digital world. Besides, the control mechanism is not a technical one that might be implementable in hardware or software but more of sociological structure: how could a group of deciders receive consensus under several restrictions? How much power should be given to this group (of miners)? In cryptocurrencies, they are responsible for the generation of new digital money and also for the development of the protocol. In business applications, they should rather maintain the database and achieve consensus in case of more possible decisions. In an internet blockchain forum, Can You Create a Blockchain Without Miners (2019), it was discussed if miners are necessary at all for business applications. In each case, the proof-of-work, in general, is not necessary there and might be replaced by proof-of-stake, trusted miners as in Hyperledger or even other concepts. However, the choice between several possible decisions may not only arise in case of double-spend but also, for instance, in smart contracts as it was stated in the above-mentioned forum discussion.

A closer look at already implemented solutions in logistics demonstrates that, in fact, all these mining concepts have been selected for practical applications. The future will tell which approach will finally succeed or if these applications might exist in parallel. There might be compatibility issues that could be problematic for standardization and also for the change of blockchains during the transport. Further, most blockchain solutions have only very recently been implemented or are still in a test phase. They will have to demonstrate resistance against possible attacks.

Finally, it should be mentioned that a hard fork of the Ethereum blockchain is scheduled for the very near future, namely, for December 7, 2019 – see Ethereum 2.0 Istanbul Update (2019). The name of the new branch will be: Istanbul.

References

Ahlswede, R., Cai, N., Li, S.-Y. R. & Yeung, R. W. (2000). Network information flow. *IEEE Transactions on Information Theory*, 1204–1216.

All about Bitcoin Cash Hard Fork. Retrieved September 20, 2019 from https://www.investopedia.com/news/all-about-bitcoin-cash-hard-fork/.

Bagaria, V., Kaman, S., Tse, D., Fanti, J. & Visvanath, P. (2018). Deconstructing the block chain to approach physical limits, https://arxiv.org/abs/1810.08092.

Bayrak-Meydanoglu, S. & Tamm, U. (2010). An information theoretic approach to RFID security problems in supply chains. *Proceedings VIII International Logistics and Supply Chain Congress*, Istanbul.

Bitcoin Miner sind weitestgehend profitabel. Retrieved October 25, 2019 from coincierge.de/2019/forschung-bitcoin-miner-sind-weitestgehend-profitabel-ist-das-bullisch/.

Bitcoinhalf. Retrieved September 20, 2019, www.bitcoinhalf.com.

Blockchain-Based Used Car Data Marketplace to Launch in Singapore (July 05, 2019). Retrieved September 20, 2019, from cointelegraph.com/news/blockchain-based-used-car-data-marketplace-to-launch-in-singapore.

Blockchain in Healthcare and the Life Sciences. Retrieved September 20, 2019, from consensys.net/enterprise-ethereum/use-cases/healthcare-and-the life-sciences.

Cargo via Blockchain: Gigant Maersk testet die Technologie unter realen Bedingungen. BTC-ECHO, (March 5, 2017). Retrieved on September 20 from www.btc-echo.de/cargo-via-blockchain-maersk-machts-vor/.

Can You Create a Blockchain Without Miners. Retrieved September 20, 2019, from www.quora.com/Can you-create-a-blockchain-without-miners

Combat Cyber Risk in Military Supply Chains with Blockchain. Retrieved September 20, 2019, from blogs.sap.com/2017/05/20/combat-cyber-risk-in-military-supply-chains-with-blockchain/.

Corda. Retrieved September 20, 2019 from www.corda.net.

Daimler Carries out First Transaction on Marco Polo Blockchain Trade Network (September 25, 2019). Retrieved September 30, 2019, from /www.coindesk.com/daimler-carries-out-first-transaction-on-marco-polo-blockchain-trade-network

Daimler to Use Blockchain Platform for Valuing Used Cars (September 04, 2019). Retrieved September 20, 2019, from https://www.businessinsider.com/daimler-to-use-blockchain-platform-for-valuing-used-cars-2019-9.

Dilmi, A. (2019). *Blockchain-Technologie am Beispiel Bitcoin*. Bachelor Thesis, FH Bielefeld.

Effros, M., Koetter, R. & Medard, M. (2007). Breaking network logjams. *Scientific American*, 78–85.

Ethereum 2.0 Istanbul Update. Retrieved on November 20, 2019, from cryptomonday.de/ethereum-2-0-istanbul-update-offiziell-am-7-dezember/.

Ethereum 2.0 News: Launch für Ethereum 2.0 für den 3. Januar 2020 geplant. Retrieved on September 20, 2019, from cryptomonday.de/ethereum-2-0-news-launch-von-ethereum-2-0-fuer-den-3-januar-2020-geplant.

Guardtime. Retrieved September 20, 2019, from guardtime.com.

Healthcare Blockchain Relies on Industry Standardization. Retrieved September 20, 2019 from hitinfrastructure.com/news/healthcare-blockchain-relies-on-industry-standardization.

Hyperledger. https://www.hyperledger.org

Ji, C. & Micali, S. (2017). Algorand. https://arxiv.org/abs/1607.01341.

Kohn, W. & Tamm, U. (2019). *Mathematik für Wirtschaftsinformatiker*. Berlin, Heidelberg: Springer.

Li, C., Li, P., Zhou, D., Long, F. & Yao, A. (2018). Scaling Nakamoto consensus to thousands of transactions per second, https://arxiv.org/abs/1805.03870.

Libra Whitepaper. Retrieved on September 20, 2019, from libra.org/de-DE/white-paper.

Nakamoto, S. (2008). *Bitcoin: A Peer-to-Peer Electronic Cash System*. Retrieved September 3, 2019, from https://bitcoin.org/bitcoin.pdf (Bitcoin Foundation).

Narayanan, A., Bonneau, J., Felten, E., Miller, A. & Goldfeder, S. (2016). *Bitcoin and Cryptocurrencies Technologies*. New Jersey: Princeton University Press.

Nielsen, M. (2013). *How the bitcoin protocol actually works*. Retrieved September 20, 2019, from http://www.michaelnielsen.org/ddi/how-the-bitcoin-protocol-actually-works.

Özbay, F. (2018). *Blockchain Solutions in der Logistik*. Bachelor Thesis, FH Bielefeld.

Popper, N. (2019). How does Bitcoin fit into today's economy? *The New York Times*, April 30, 2019, p. 7.

Tamm, U. (2010). Network Coding: A New Field between Information Theory and Operations Research. In A. Erkollar (ed.), *Enterprise and Business Management*. Marburg: Tectum, 37–49.

The Global "Blockchain in Healthcare" Report: the 2019 ultimate guide for every executive (May 26, 2019). Retrieved September 20, 2019, www.healthcareweekly.com/blockchain-in-healthcare-guide.

Varshney, L. R., Tay, W. P., & Ji, F. (2017). An algorithmic framework for estimating rumor sources with different start times. *IEEE Transactions on Signal Processing, 65*(10), 2517–2530.

VeChain und DB Schenker: Blockchain in der Logistik, BTC-ECHO (June 13, 2018). Retrieved on September 20, 2019 from /www.btc-echo.de/vechain-und-db-schenker-blockchain-in-der-logistik/.

Was ist Corda? Retrieved September 20, 2019 from www.btc-echo.de/tutorial/was-ist-corda/.

Workshop Blockchain and Smart Contracts, University Tartu, Estonia (April 2018). Booklet of Abstracts prepared at FH Bielefeld, 2018 (R. Lenz, editor).

Felix Zeidler

Impact of Digital Transformation on the Role of Controlling

Abstract: The impact of current technological progress on the role of Controller and Controlling is actively debated amongst academic scholars and business practitioners. Advocates of a strong future role of Controlling argue that big data, data analytics technology and automation potential will benefit Controllers. Those with a negative view argue that Controlling is an endangered corporate function. Using automated text analysis by applying natural language processing techniques, this chapter analyzes if overall sentiment toward the future of Controlling has changed and if this change is driven by digitalization. I show that there is qualitative indication that digitalization is (quite literally) associated with more risks than chances. Main contribution is to show that natural language processing can be used in research to generate structured research data from text.

Keywords: Digital transformation, digitalization, Controller, Controlling, management accounting, natural language processing, machine learning

Introduction

Digitalization[1] as a topic in business has undergone a remarkable process. For many years, it was almost exclusively associated with either transactional processes of back office tasks or startups in Silicon Valley. It did not seem to have any direct impact on established business models, let alone means to conduct business itself. However, it is now common agreement that recent technological progress requires companies to think very differently also of the way they conduct business (see e.g. Denning, 2018). Companies are increasingly required to question traditional business models and strategies. To this end, corporate function and departments need to rethink their value propositions and way of working as well.

The discussion on the impact of digitalization in finance departments has only recently picked up sharply (see e.g. Krause & Pellens, 2017). In particular, a discussion on the impact on Controlling/management accounting[2] is now ongoing

1 This chapter applies the German usage of the term "digitalization" meaning changes driven by technological progress. Note that the English language uses the term more literally and refers to the conversion of text, pictures or sound into a digital form.

2 The differences of both terms are briefly discussed in Section 2.

amongst practitioners and academics – especially in Germany (see e.g. Weber & Schäffer, 2017; Horváth, 2017). Given the uncertainty associated with digitalization it is not surprising, however, that there is a very ambivalent view on what the future role of Controlling will be.

For decades, Controlling has been regarded as a crucial management support function, using data and analytics to objectify and rationalize complex decision-making, coordinating budgets and plans to ensure departments move toward one goal and developing steering models to enable managers to measure and control the right levers. Given this crucial role of Controlling, it is not surprising that transforming business will lead to changes in the role of Controllers and responsibilities and setup of Controlling departments. Looking at the current discussion, however, it is difficult to extract one clear future path of the role of Controlling. On the one hand, practitioners and academics argue that Controlling has a vital role in business and hence will use technological advances to manifest this role even further. On the other hand, there are voices who paint a much darker picture claiming that many of the traditional controlling tasks will become obsolete in the (very near term) future.

Advocates of a strong future role argue that Controlling, inter alia, will strongly benefit from increasing data availability and data analytics technology as well as from automation of traditionally time-consuming activities such as reporting tasks. Those with a negative view, while recognizing the above arguments, claim that new skills are required to apply analytics in a world with significantly more and different data, which is why people with other backgrounds (e.g. computer scientists) will take over traditional tasks for Controllers. In addition, changes in the way of organizing work within big corporations (e.g. trend toward agility) will have a profound negative impact on the number of Controllers required in corporations. In summary, there are overarching contrary arguments as to what the impact of digitalization on Controllers will be.

This chapter attempts to contribute to this recent discussion in two ways. First, it will address the question if overall sentiment toward the future of Controlling has changed and if this change can be attributed to digitalization. The sentiment analysis is based on existing literature and uses automated text analysis to extract key terms associated with Controlling. The second contribution is in applying techniques from natural language processing (NLP) to extract this relevant text information. In doing so, this chapter is an initial attempt to use unstructured text as source of research data by applying current machine learning methods. This is new as the rare literature on the interface of machine learning and business/economics mostly emphasizes on model building for and prediction and classification of structured (or tabular) data.

This chapter is structured as follows: First, I shortly summarize the role of Controllers and Controlling and describe common hypotheses with respect to possible future development paths. To the end, I then present our analyses.

Related Literature

Role of Controller and Controlling

In a German context, the term "Controlling" refers to either the corporate department and/or a management support process. While an international equivalent to "Controlling" exists, it differs in (i) name and (ii) responsibilities. The term "management accounting" is accepted as the international equivalent (see e.g. Sheridan, 1995; Willson et al., 2003). There are, however, very distinct differences in what management accounting encompasses compared to Controlling. A very narrow view claims that management accounting can be reduced to cost accounting (i.e. "Kostenrechnung" in Germany). The most distinct difference is that management accountants in an international context are also responsible for external accounting tasks, which in Germany is commonly the responsibility of the distinct financial accounting department. For the remainder of this chapter, I will use the term "Controlling and Controller" and focus on the ongoing German discussion on the future roles. Due to a strong and growing overlap between international management accounting and German Controlling, most of the aspects discussed are transferable to international management accounting.

When approaching the question on the impact of digitalization and business transformation on Controlling and Controllers, it is helpful to summarize what both of these terms exactly mean. While it is widely accepted that "*Controlling is a key success factor for companies in German-speaking countries*" (ICV & IGC, 2012, p. 2), there is disagreement about what Controlling essentially is. A large part of research in Controlling (in Germany) actually focusses on the question what Controlling is and contradicting views among academics (see e.g. Weber & Schäffer, 2016) exist. In addition, there is not one approach to Controlling in business, and it is probably not wrong to state that every company has a largely different view on what Controlling means and what Controllers do. Hence, it is necessary to provide a concise summary on the essence of Controlling and the responsibilities of Controllers, which most practitioners and academics would agree on.

In this chapter, I mostly share the view of the International Controller Association (ICV) – which is largely based on Albrecht Deyhle's work – according to which Controlling is a management activity, which ensures that decision-making processes are objective-driven. As such, Controlling requires several distinct activities and practices such as planning, analytics, monitoring and control. Controlling applies to both individual management decision as well as to the management of the corporation as a whole. Given the importance of Controlling, managers commonly require support in carrying out this management activity. This support task is largely conducted by Controllers who support their managers in several ways. On the one hand, they support by taking over some specific tasks such as coordination of planning/budgeting activities or proposing and performing reporting tasks. On the other hand, they also function as an "economic conscience" for managers. By giving objective and independent advice, they intend to prevent managers from making irrational decisions based on divisional or personal interest. Looking at these responsibilities, it is apparent that roles and responsibilities of Controllers to a large degree are dependent on the manager itself given skills, experience and preferences of managers will differ (ICV & IGC, 2012).

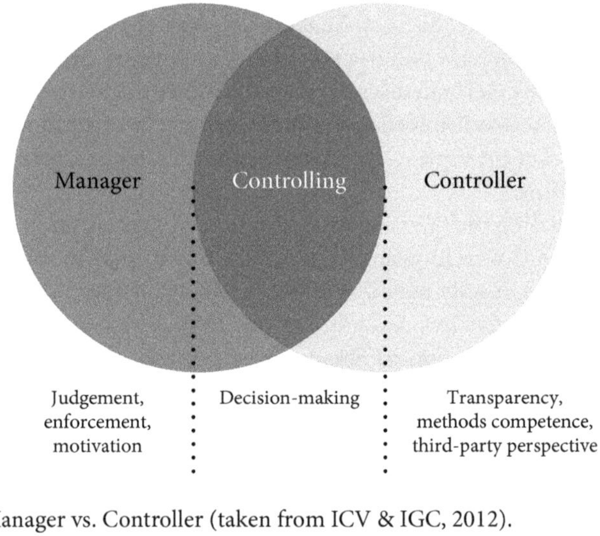

Figure 1: Manager vs. Controller (taken from ICV & IGC, 2012).

Management support by Controllers can, therefore, be summarized by three activities: unburden (helping managers with tasks), complement (being economic conscience) and constrain (assuring goal congruence) activities (Weber & Schäffer, 2016). These activities then lead to the following areas of management support:

1. Economic transparency: define, provide and communicate figures and metrics (e.g. Reporting)
2. Rational corporate management: moderate and design controlling process (e.g. coordinate Planning/Budget cycle)
3. Management control systems: coordinate and manage design and interaction of different management control systems (e.g. ensure availability of appropriate steering model that is aligned throughout company)
4. Project consulting: support managers on projects, not only routine tasks (e.g. determine economic value of an investment project)

Given the broad spectrum of tasks, it follows that it is complex and difficult to assess if Controllers will benefit from developments driven and caused by digitalization. Holding current developments against the aforementioned, four areas of management support the future of Controlling and Controllers could go both ways.

While it is feasible to assume that Controlling as a management activity itself will remain important – after all, who would argue that taking decisions in an objective-driven manner and ensuring rational corporate management is to question in a technological-driven environment. There is uncertainty, however, who actually will conduct the associated tasks in the future.

On the one hand, it appears there is strong evidence and currently little debate that routine tasks such as reporting – to date still a major task for Controllers – will be largely automated and the remainder conducted by managers themselves ("self-controlling"). Given modern BI (business intelligence) solutions, reporting tasks become less and less time consuming and enable managers to put together "their" set of relevant figures in a tailor-made fashion. Controllers will still be required to ensure that the right metrics are used, definitions are aligned, metrics fit the steering model, etc. However, in total, significantly less Controllers will be required (Weber & Schäffer, 2017).

On the other hand, there are many areas where the impact on Controlling and Controllers is less clear. On the area of economic transparency, for example, digitalization has been a blessing in a sense that more data is available. This provides corporations with more granular and direct access to data of customers, processes, machines, etc. Management can use this data to create information and knowledge and base decisions on data-driven facts where previously they applied gut feeling. However, Controllers may lack the skill required to make use of this data and may be replaced by other professionals (e.g. data scientists)

It is thus not surprising that a fierce debate has evolved as to whether or not the Controller is an endangered species.

Machine learning in economics and management accounting

Recent Machine Learning literature is widely regarded to be relevant for research and practice in business and economics. However, adoption of these methods has been slow and lacking behind other fields (e.g. biology).

Literature on machine learning with specific focus on management accounting/controlling is rare. While many papers acknowledge that "big data" will change management accounting and will require new methods and approaches (see e.g. Warren et al., 2015), the vast majority does not explicitly explain or examine how machine learning may or may not support "big data", let alone which new algorithms or approaches are suitable for research or practice.

Furthermore, in economics, research on applications of machine learning algorithms has evolved only very recently. In one of the first papers, Mullainathan & Spiess (2017) give an overview of machine learning techniques and explain (i) how machine learning works (compared to traditional statistics) and (ii) how these new techniques can be helpful for economic research. Athey and Imbens (2019) build on this and give an in-depth overview on differences between machine learning and traditional econometrics that is heavily using traditional statistics. They proceed by emphasizing methods from machine learning that are particularly useful for empirical research in economics. Both papers focus on using machine learning for prediction tasks for regression and classification. Lopez de Prado (2019) also takes a stand for application of machine learning algorithms in economics, however, focuses specifically on financial machine learning. He argues that machine learning algorithms are often misconceived as black boxes and have, therefore, not been widely used in finance. However, given the increased availability of data, he considers machine learning algorithms and techniques to be better suited for finance than traditional model-based approaches.

All of the existing literature on the interface of machine learning and economics/business focusses on methods and approaches to model-structured (i.e. tabular) data for prediction or classification. Machine learning is used as a tool to gain insights from structured data.[3] This is especially surprising for the field of Controlling research given many articles in the last few years emphasize the potential of "big data" and point out opportunities that stem from the availability of unstructured text data (see e.g. ICV, 2014).

3 For a great overview of state of the art techniques and methods, see e.g. Jurafsky & Martin (2019).

Sentiment Analysis

Data and methodology

The analysis is based on all articles published in the journal "Controlling & Management Review" from the years 2011 to 2019. The journal is known for being relevant for both business as well as academia in the German-speaking Controlling community and is therefore well suited for the analysis.[4] The overall unfiltered data sample contains 1.834 articles (i.e. text files). Given many of the articles relate to content that was not deemed to be relevant for the analysis at hand (e.g. announcements for upcoming conventions or reviews of books), the sample was further reduced to 461 text files containing articles regarding topics relevant to the field of Controlling. I identified relevant topics by the "article type" flag given by the journal itself.[5]

In order to generate sentiment scores over time, two questions need to be addressed from a methodological perspective:

1. How should I measure sentiment?
2. On which elements (i.e. tokens) of the article texts should I apply this measurement?

Determining the semantic orientation or polarity of words is critical for sentiment analysis. Any automated text analysis requires some kind of knowledge about the meaning of the specific words in the text analyzed. In the context of a sentiment analysis, it is important if a specific word has a negative or a positive connotation. For example, for the analysis at hand it is important to understand if the sentence

"*Das Controlling ist gefährdet.*" (Controlling is at risk/endangered.)

has a negative or positive meaning. While there are numerous large data sets available for English, it is much harder to conduct such analysis on German texts given less available word polarity data. I base my analysis on data from Waltinger

4 Note that it is the author's intention to also include the second relevant journal "Controller Magazin" into this analysis. However, given copyright aspects, it was not possible to include the data at the point of writing.

5 The following article types were used for the analysis: "praxis artikel", "schwerpunkt", "praxis magazin", "wissenschaft", "editorial", "magazin", "praxis", "unternehmenssteuerung", "spektrum", "controlling managmenent", "accounting reporting", "controller manager", "originalpaper", "praxis artikel", "praxis magazin", "kosten ergebnisrechnung", "kosten und ergebnisrechnung", "controller und manager".

(2010).[6] The data set contains 10.141 unique German words with numerical polarity scores determining the positive, negative or neutral direction of a specific word. The data set only contains a subset of the overall German vocabulary[7]. This a restriction to this analysis as it increases the probability of not being able to calculate sentiment scores for some words. However, this restriction is somewhat mitigated by the fact that the sentiment of a sentence or an expression is commonly determined by a few key words. For example, the sentiment of the above sentence is largely driven by the word "gefährdet" that using our word polarity data set gives the overall sentence a strong negative score of -0.5.

Next to defining the measure of sentiment, it is important to address the question on which level this measure should be applied. Given it can be calculated on single word level, there are many options. For example, one could calculate sentiment scores of each article by (i) determining word polarity score on each word occurring in the text and available in the word polarity dictionary and then (ii) aggregating these scores for each article by, e.g., calculating the median. This would yield a median polarity (i.e. sentiment) score per published article. However, this approach appears very broad and not well suited for the specific question if the overall sentiment toward Controller and Controlling has changed. It is, therefore, necessary to calculate the sentiment associated with Controller and Controlling and not the sentiment of an entire article given the latter could be largely distorted by "noise created from prose" not actually related to the term "Controller" or "Controlling".

In order to apply polarity scores more precisely, the following procedure is used:

3. Split each article into individual sentences
4. Determine sentences where keyword (e.g. "Controlling") is subject of sentence
5. Extract grammatical objects from identified sentences
6. Calculate polarity scores of (3)
7. Calculate median of (4) for each sentence ("sentence sentiment")

Applying this method yields sentiment scores on sentences containing information on the terms "Controller" and "Controlling" and ensures that word "polarity scores" is only calculated on words that are used to give these keywords

---

6 The data is publicly available via http://www.ulliwaltinger.de/sentiment/GermanPolarityClues-2012.zip.

7 According to *Duden* (German universal dictionary), the German active vocabulary contains around 70.000 words and the overall vocabulary contains approximately 500.000 words.

a semantic meaning. Steps 1 and 3 are achieved using a technique called dependency parsing where the grammatical structure of a sentence and relationships between words within a sentence are analyzed. Figure 2 shows a dependency parse of a short example sentence.

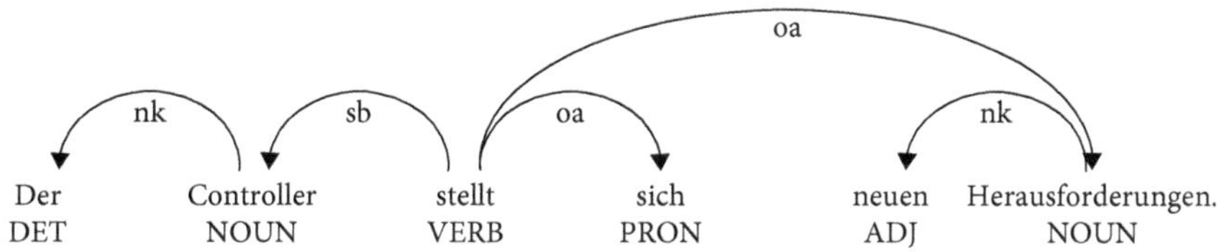

Figure 2: Example of Dependency Parse.

The figure shows the part-of-speech tags indicating if a word is, e.g., a verb or a noun. In addition, it indicates the syntactic dependencies of a sentence. Here it indicates, e.g., that *Controller* is the subject of the sentence. Applying this technique on text data enables us to extract text that fulfills certain grammatical criteria. For example, it is possible to identify the subject or all nouns of a sentence.

I use the natural language processing library Spacy that is using the programming language Python. The library has a German language model based on news and media data[8] embedded. The linguistic annotations are based on statistical predictions using deep learning techniques.

Descriptive analysis

The data set contains 461 articles from the years 2011 to 2019 with an average of 48 articles per year. The least number of articles in the sample are from 2011 (18 articles), whereas the most number of articles are published in 2017 (73 articles). On average, each article consists of five pages and contains 2.028 words. Overall, the sample of all articles contains 2.365 pages and 809.397 words.

Applied research on Controlling focuses on a myriad of topics. Figure 3 shows the percentage of articles containing specific keywords (i. Controller, ii. Controlling, iii. Planung and iv. Digitalisierung). As the entire sentiment analysis is based on sentences containing keywords such as Controller and/or

8 Sources of the language data can be found online on the pages https://figshare.com/articles/Learning_multilingual_named_entity_recognition_from_Wikipedia/5462500 and https://www.ims.uni-stuttgart.de/.

Controlling, it is important to understand if these terms occur in the majority of analyzed articles. The figure shows that this is indeed the case. This is also not surprising given the high focus of applied Controlling research on the role of Controllers and Controlling. The analysis shows further that a major amount of articles contain the term "Planung" (engl. Planning/Budgeting). This is in line with the general understanding that one of the key roles of Controlling is to coordinate and challenge the regular corporate planning cycles. Most Controller in practice will probably agree that aspects of the planning cycles are a major focus of discussion points in Controlling.

What is somewhat surprising is, however, that the term "Digitalisierung" (engl. digitalization) only first occurs in 2015. This shows that the discussion on technological developments and its impact on Controlling is rather new. The increase in occurrences strongly indicates that the discussion is now very prominent in applied research in Controlling given in 2019 the term is used in around 50% of all articles.

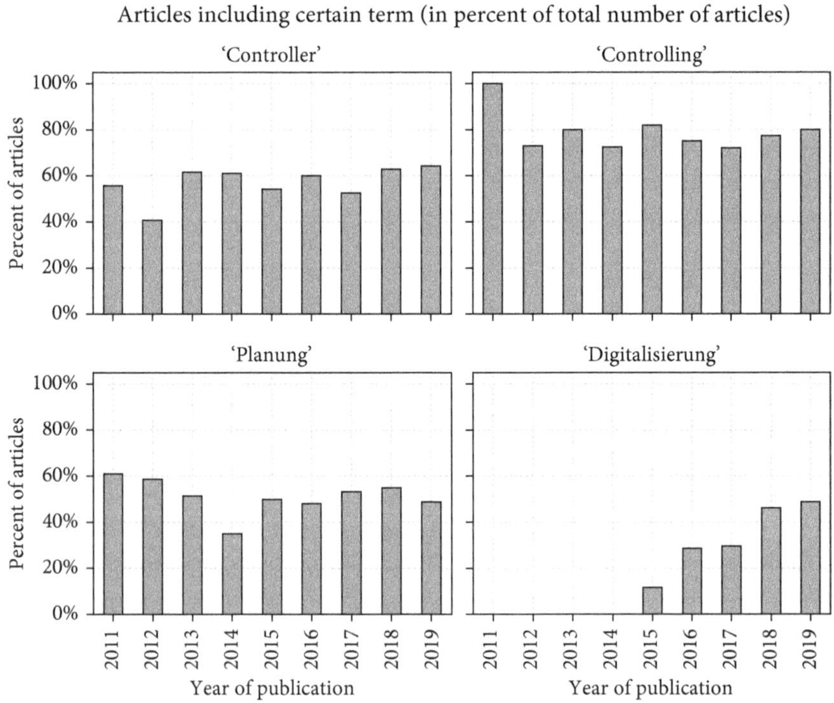

Figure 3: Search Terms.

Sentiment analysis

The sentiment analysis is based on all sentences containing the keywords "Controller" and/or "Controlling". Sentences are only considered for further analysis if the keyword is the subject of the sentence to ensure that the key topic of the sentence is the keyword itself. This yields 2.460 sentences that are further analyzed. Below are two identified sentences for illustrative purposes:

- *"Controller müssen **Geschäftskenntnisse** aufweisen."*
- *"Das Controlling läuft **Gefahr**, den **Anschluss** zu verlieren."*

Based on the identified sentences, I extract all grammatical objects from these sentences. For example, the words extracted from the above two examples are "Geschäftskenntnisse" (business skills), "Gefahr" (danger) and "Anschluss" (here: are behind/lose touch). This yields a set of words for each sentence that classifies for the sentiment analysis.

In a first step, I separate the set of words in those belonging to articles from the years 2011 to 2014 (pre digital) and those belonging to articles from the years 2015 to 2019 (post digital). The reason behind this is that from Figure 3, it is apparent that a discussion about digitalization only started in the year 2015 and has significantly increased since then. While it could be true that articles prior to 2015 discuss digitalization using different terms, it is reasonable to assume that the main discussion on the future of Controlling has started in 2015 using the keyword digitalization as a catchword or slogan. This would be in line with the broader German public debate on digitalization.

If sentiment towards the role of Controllers and Controlling has changed driven by impact of digitalization, it would be hence likely that word polarity of words describing the role of Controllers and Controlling differs between these time spans.

In Figure 4, the findings are summarized by two word clouds. Each word cloud contains the 150 most common terms extracted from the identified sentences. In each cloud, the size of a word indicates the number of occurrences relative to all other words, i.e., the bigger a word in the word cloud, the more often it occurred in a sentence.

The visualization indicates that there appears to be in fact a difference in topics associated with the terms "Controller" and "Controlling". In the time span from 2011 to 2014, terms such as "Entscheidungen" (decisions), "Partner" (partner) and "Rolle" (role) occurred very frequently which is in line with the aforementioned common topics. It has been a vivid debate that Controllers need to change its role toward business partners and as such must help decision-making by

Figure 4: Wordclouds.

management. Turning toward the time span from 2015 to 2019, other terms are dominating. Terms like “Risiken” (risks), “Daten” (data) and “Gefahr” (danger) or “Aufgabenprofil” (task profile) have replaced or outnumbered previously dominating terms and seem to be predominantly discussed. Two of the four terms have a negative connotation (risk and danger), indicating that the discussion in applied research has not only focused somewhat on the specific future role (“Aufgabenprofil”) of Controllers and Controlling but moreover that the outcome of this discussion/development is expected to be rather negative for both. The qualitative analysis indicates that the role of digitalization has changed the tone in applied research, and there is at least indication that the impact of digitalization is rather negative than positive. At least, there are no terms such as “chances” or “opportunities” that are frequently used in context of describing Controller and Controlling.

While the qualitative analysis indicates a rather negative sentiment toward Controller and Controlling, the quantitative analysis does not provide evidence for such conclusion.

Indicated by Figure 5, the average word polarity score per sentence and year does differ over time (blue line). However, there is no clear trend identifiable. While it appears that sentiment score in 2015 is highest and then decreases strongly, this finding is not backed statistically. In particular taking into account that standard deviation of average word polarity score per sentence and calculating the 95% confidence intervals surrounding these averages (grey dashed lines), it becomes apparent that there is no clear development of sentiment score over time.

This begs the question: Why the qualitative and visual findings are not supported by a quantitative analysis?

This is largely driven by the fact that the two predominantly used “negative” terms “Risiko” and “Gefahr” are at least somewhat compensated by many different "positive" terms, i.e., there are not two but many – which is why they do not stick out in the word clouds – counterparts to the dominant negative terms used to describe the role of Controllers and Controlling in light of digitalization.

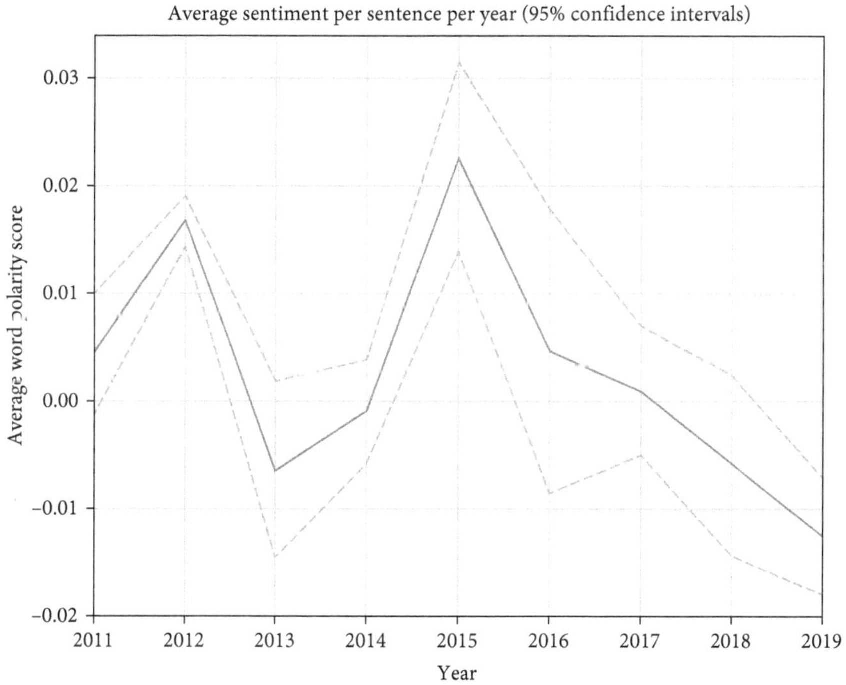

Figure 5: Sentiment Scores Over Time.

Conclusion and Outlook

The study presented in this chapter served two distinct purposes.

First, I wanted to provide new insights on the role of digitalization and its impact on Controlling. Given the different and often contrary views among scholars and business practitioners, it was one purpose to provide new evidence toward one view by analyzing if and how sentiment toward the role of Controllers and Controlling has changed. To this end, I analyzed 461 articles from Journal of Controlling and Management and used natural language processing techniques in combination with existing word polarity scores to aggregate and summarize a predominant view on the future of Controlling. While a naïve and qualitative aggregation of words indicated that digitalization is associated with terms that have a strongly negative connotation (e.g. risk and danger), this conclusion was not supported by quantitative and statistical analysis.

The second purpose of this chapter was to explore if and how techniques from natural language processing can be utilized for research. One common shortcoming for research is lack of data. By making unstructured text available for structured data analysis, machine learning techniques can help to increase the availability of research data. The chapter showed that using techniques from language processing, it is easily possible to selectively extract relevant text from data. Given readily available libraries (here: Spacy for Python), it is possible to parse text data. As such, this is a source of new information and a promising field for new research. Future research – not only in management accounting – should consider text analysis as an additional source of data given the fact that unstructured data can easily be made accessible in a way that it can be integrated in structured data analysis.

However, it should be stated that the extracting logic used in this chapter is only considered to be of exploratory nature. Future research on Controlling and the impact of digitalization should consider more detailed text extraction mechanism (e.g. including adjectives and verbs and clustering techniques) to generate more meaningful aggregations and summarizations of existing literature.

References

Athey, S., Imbens, G. (2019). *Machine Learning Methods Economists Should Know About*. Annual Review of Economics. Vol. 11, pp. 685–725.

Denning, S. (2018). *The Age of Agile. How Smart Companies Are Transforming the Way Work Gets Done*. New York.

Hoffjan, A. (2008). *Vergleich des anglo-amerikanischen Management Accounting und des deutschen Controllings*. Controlling, Vol. 12, December 2008.

Horváth, P. (2017). *Controlling ohne Controller?*, Controlling, Sonderausgabe September 2017, S. 1–3.

ICV (2014). *Big Data – Potenzial für den Controller*. Dream Car der Ideenwerkstatt im ICV 2014.

ICV, IGC, (2012). *The essence of Controlling—the perspective of the Internationaler Controller Verein (ICV) and the Internatinal Group of Controlling (IGC)*. Journal of Management Control, Vol. 23, Issue 4, February 2013, pp. 311–317.

James, G., Witten, D., Hastie, T., Tibshirani, R. (2017). *An Introduction to Statistical Learning*. 8th edition, New York.

Jurafsky, D., Martin, J. (2019). *Speech and Language Processing.* 3rd edition (draft). Stanford University.

Krause, Stefan/ Pellens, Bernhard (Editors) (2017). *Betriebswirtschaftliche Implikationen der digitalen Transformation*, Zfbf 72/2017, S. 267–284.

Lopez de Prado, M. (2019). *Beyond Econometrics: A Roadmap Towards Financial Machine Learning.* Working Paper, Cornell University, 2019.

Mullainathan, S., Spiess, J. (2017). *Machine learning: an applied econometric approach.* Journal of Economic Perspectives, Vol. 31, pp. 87–106.

Schäffer, U., Weber, J. (2017). *Digitalization will radically change controlling as we know it.* Controlling & Management Review, Vol. 1, pp. 2–9.

Schäffer, U., Weber, J. (2019). *Zehn Thesen zur Entwicklung des Controllings.* Controlling & Management Review, Vol. 6, pp. 46–49.

Sheridan, T. (1995). *Management Accounting in Global European Corporations: Anglophone and Continental Viewpoints.* Management Accounting Research, Vol. 6, Issue 3, pp. 287–291.

Waltinger, U. (2010). *Sentiment Analysis Reloaded: A Comparative Study On Sentiment Polarity Identification Combining Machine Learning and Subjectivity Features.* In Proceedings of the 6th International Conference on Web Information Systems and Technologies (WEBIST '10), April 7-10, 2010, Valencia.

Warren, J., Moffitt, K., Byrnes, P. (2015). *How Big Data Will Change Accounting.* Accounting Horizons, Vol. 29, Issue 2, 2015, pp. 397–407.

Weber, J., Schäffer, U. (2016). *Einführung in das Controlling.* 15th ed., Stuttgart.

Willson, J. D., Bragg, S. M., Roehl-Anderson, J. (2003). *Controllership, the work of the managerial accountant.* 7th edition, New York.

Daniel Antonius Hötte, and Arthur Felk

Digital Transformation and the Law – the Impact of Information Technology on the Legal Business

Abstract: Until recently, the traditional way of practicing law has essentially been untouched by external influences. While significant changes in the division of labor, process optimization and diversification of work during the late 20th century shaped the development of modern economies, the market for legal services – despite its significant size and importance – remained astonishingly unaffected by that progress. The reasons, among others, were a low technological impact or even a complete absence thereof, the highly personal character of the services provided, legal language and the method of legal reasoning that could not be dealt with via technical means. With the global effects of digitalization, these structures are fundamentally being shaken. Technologically charged new market entrants now force changes that affect the very nature of the legal business and expose it to profound challenges in an international context and in more and more of its traditional domains.

Keywords: Legal technology, Legal Tech, digitalization, legal business model, Alternative Legal Service Providers (ALSP), Billable Hour, AFA, more for less, efficiency, legal automation, artificial intelligence, User Experience (UX), legal design thinking

Introduction

Digital transformation has been changing the economic environment of companies in many industries for several years now: sometimes with disruptive effects. Until recently, however, practicing law in law firms and in in-house legal departments was largely untouched by this development. Technology merely replaced existing analogue activities. Writing letters was substituted by emails and going to the library became superfluous due to online legal databases.

In other words, legal practice remained at the level of digitization (Cohen, 2017; Gartner, 2019), and the business model based on it did not change substantially. The latter is generally based on billing according to statutory fee regulations – as in most countries legal practice is a regulated market – or billing according to hourly rates (including so-called fee cabs for defined projects or so-called retainer for permanent matters).

Currently, aforesaid status is changing fundamentally. With regard to different levels of the legal value chain, technical solutions are being introduced and changing the way the law is practiced and delivered. These technical solutions are commonly referred to as "*Legal Technology*" or in short "*Legal Tech*" (Wagner, 2018, p. 1). This chapter examines the evolution of Legal Tech as an international phenomenon and its influence on the legal services market.

Digitalization of the Law

Legal Tech and thereby digitalization of the law has gained momentum in recent years. The precise meaning of Legal Tech is examined in chapter 2.1 while the global impact is observed under chapter 2.2.

Legal Technology

Legal Tech is the support of legal services by means of information technology systems and can be divided into three areas with regard to its functionality (Goodenough, 2015; Wenzler, 2018).

The first area (Legal Tech 1.0) covers applications within the organizational-administrative environment of legal practice such as workflow management without interfering with the core of legal work itself. The second area (Legal Tech 2.0) can already be described as Legal Tech in a narrower sense and allows the creation of contracts or comparable documents based on a questionnaire. In addition, such Legal Tech applications allow to obtain legal recommendations for precisely defined situations or to automatically generate documents such as appeals against administrative orders, which then can either be printed out or even sent directly via email. From a technical point of view, these applications are frequently based on so-called expert systems, which operate based on a knowledge base and support the user comparable to an expert providing advice (Cohen, 2018).

Besides this, progress in speech recognition makes it increasingly possible to read and analyze texts. On that basis, Legal Tech applications are trained for specific (legal) tasks, using structured data sets in order to significantly reduce time required for reviewing and preparing documents. Such applications have become a market standard in the field of due diligence, a sub-area for corporate transactions and in the field of so-called internal investigations (Goodenough, 2015). Lawyers working in these areas are supported by well-balanced technical systems doing the "ground work", whereas the more sophisticated legal problems are still to be solved by the lawyers themselves.

The third area (Legal Tech 3.0) reaches even beyond (Remus & Levy, 2016). It aims to create applications that automatically handle even more complex legal issues without limiting the area of law or the kind of question in advance (Balkin, 2015). In other words, such systems would come close to a human lawyer being broadly qualified to solve legal issues. This would require not only the collection and analysis of complex legal information in natural language but also the output of tailor-made legal solutions. Systems of this kind do not seem to be available in the foreseeable future. This chapter exclusively refers to Legal Tech 2.0 whenever mentioning Legal Tech.

In addition to the above-mentioned areas of Legal Tech, there are approaches to make blockchain technology accessible for legal constellations, like transforming the register system. (Wagner, 2018, p. 21). However, as for now, those ideas do not show any impact on the practice of law (The Law Society Of England and Wales, Lawtech Adoption, 2019) and, therefore, will not be discussed here (for more details see Baker & McKenzie, 2017, pp. 18, 20). The same applies to the approach of integrating technical solutions into the legislative process itself in order to make regulations directly machine-readable (Breidenbach & Glatz, 2018).

Legal Tech as an international development

More than in any other discipline, national borders limit the practice of law. This is mainly because of the legislative power, which, with the exception of the European Union, is assigned to the individual states and their legislative bodies. This inevitably leads to different national laws. The differences between those national legal regimes lead to different training of young lawyers and to restrictions of legal advice to the law of the particular country in which the adviser is qualified and licensed.

With Legal Tech, a phenomenon has now arisen that is affecting the legal sector globally. The development of Legal Tech began in the technological centers of Silicon Valley in California and the nearby law schools of the Universities of Stanford and Berkeley and has massively been driven by startups (Vogl, 2019). They often collaborate with universities and form so-called legal incubators. Their number in the US alone currently adds up to 60 incubators (American Bar Association, 2019; Hook, 2019). The pace of Legal Tech development in Europe, especially in the UK and Germany, has also accelerated rapidly in recent years. The number of Legal Tech startups in the UK alone rose from 75 in 2017 to 110 in 2019 (Thomson Reuters, Legaltech, 2019). At present, a German online database for Legal Tech startups counts a total of 190 companies in Germany; however, the numbers also cover providers of Legal Tech 1.0 (Legal Tech in Deutschland, 2019). Moreover, Legal Tech applications and startups countries have emerged in various countries demonstrating the impact of this development around the globe (see country reports in Glatz, 2018, p. 289). International professional networks have been established such as the European Legal Technology Association (ELTA), headquartered in Berlin or the Legal Tech platform Legal Geek based in the UK. The latter has meanwhile developed into the most important European networking platform for Legal Tech startups and is now also active in the US (Thomson Reuters, Legaltech, 2019).

Importantly, investors establish Legal Tech innovation and networking platforms and provide venture capital for those solutions with a convincing value proposition. The aim is to sustainably enrich the legal business market with Legal Tech solutions in order to secure a lead in international competition (Thomson Reuters, Movers and Shakers, 2017). Since the underlying technology of Legal Tech applications can be used in different jurisdictions, this provides the opportunity to expand internationally. In 2018, the total global amount of investment in Legal Tech became higher than ever before. From a moderate total investment of USD 233 million in Legal Tech companies worldwide in 2017, the growth exploded to a total of USD 1.6 billion in 2018 (Dolm, 2019). This trend continues to hold steady in 2019 –by September 2019, the international investment volume in Legal Tech companies had already reached just under USD 1.2 billion (Ambrogi, 2019). Meanwhile, more than 1.240 Legal Tech companies are active in different fields of law including legal education around the world (Stanford CodeX, 2019).

When looking at the legal market itself, it becomes obvious why investments appear to be attractive. According to a recent study, the global legal services market size was valued at USD 794.50 billion in 2018 (Grand View Research, 2018) and is expected to grow to the amount of USD 1011 billion in 2021 (The Global Legal Post, 2019). North America accounts for almost half of the global market. (The Business Research Company, 2019) whereas the size of the western European market is considered to be worth approximately USD 186 billion in 2019. Within that region, the UK (USD 42 billion) and Germany (USD 34,6 billion) are the largest national markets for legal services (Thomson Reuters, Legaltech, 2019). In terms of growth, Asia, specifically China, Hong Kong and Singapore are the fastest growing legal markets (Greentarget, 2018).

In summary, Legal Tech is a cross-border development that is likely to break with the traditional focus on national laws and related legal markets.

Impact on the Legal Business

The spread of constantly new Legal Tech applications brings movement to the legal business. It should be borne in mind that the practice of law is still characterized by the fact that professionals – usually lawyers – provide legal services and are then remunerated either according to the applicable fees or according to billable hours. Even in large international law firms, the characteristics of this approach remain the same, and there is very limited scope for scaling, as marginal costs do not decrease. Instead, increases in revenue can only be achieved by a proportionally higher degree of workforce deployment (Semple, 2017). In addition, legal services are commonly not understood as a process consisting of several (sub-) processes, which may need to be improved, but often as one coherent sequence without clear sections. Because legal services are provided in person, there is no obvious ground for optimization regarding efficiency – apart from a good self – and office organization. In addition, the hourly remuneration model offers little incentive to save time, as this would instantly lead to a lower amount to be invoiced to the clients.

Legal Tech has begun to transform the legal business by acting as a catalyst triggering and accelerating developments that have been taking place in other industries for some time. The main trends are briefly discussed below.

Diversification of legal services

Many Legal Tech applications view the legal working method as a process and analyze the particular levels within the value chain (Deloitte, 2016). Consequently, current offerings target at specific aspects and operate where they see the greatest potential impact for their software solution. This technical and economic understanding results in a partial breakup of the supposedly homogeneous legal working method. Thus, Legal Tech extracts and transforms individual parts of the legal work. Therefore, such providers do not offer comprehensive legal advice, but operate in a clearly defined sub-area of the legal business. For instance, consumers are offered legal assessments and the automated creation of documents for specific legal questions, e.g., regarding compensation for delayed flights (Georgetown Law/Thompson Reuters, ALSP, 2019). However, individual enforcement in court – to the extent needed – is left to affiliated lawyers (Roger Smith, 2018).

In commercial law, various Alternative Legal Service Providers (ALSP) offer technically supported solutions for labor-intensive processes that increasingly cover more complex areas such as document review, ediscovery or compliance issues (Georgetown Law/Thompson Reuters ALSP, 2019). The turnover of the ALSPs is growing significantly, as a recent study shows for the US market (Georgetown Law/Thompson Reuters, ALSP, 2019). This happens also at the expense of traditional legal services providers (Georgetown Law/Thompson

Reuters, ALSP, 2019). In 2018, the annual turnover already amounted to USD 10.7 billion that represents a growth rate of 12.9 percent for the US market compared to the previous year (Georgetown Law/Thompson Reuters, ALSP, 2019).

These new innovative tech-driven service providers are splitting a formerly uniform legal service up by identifying individual sub-processes and then consider them separately. This splitting is also referred to as "*unbundling*" (The Law Society of England and Wales, 2017, p. 22). For sub-processes that are also offered by ALSPs, the question arises as to whether they should be outsourced or whether legal advice should continue to be provided from a single source. These sub-processes are characterized by the fact that legal services that have been formerly carried out by lawyers are automated and can thus be offered faster and more cheaply.

In-house lawyers are particularly targeted by ALSPs, as their products are focused on recurring legal tasks that often have to be handled by legal departments. In-house lawyers are in a position to assess the quality of the products themselves from a legal point of view and to supplement advice on individual cases – if necessary – themselves (Deloitte Legal, 2018). This leads to a new direct customer-client relationship between legal departments and Alternative Service Providers with regard to legal services (Greentarget, 2018). As a result of this development, legal departments are increasingly able to use free capacities through technical support for standard tasks in order to devote more attention to more complex legal tasks (Eversheds Sutherland, 2016).

For traditional law firms, the pressing question is what role they will play in the future and how they react to Alternative Legal Service Providers as new market entrants. Some of the big law firms react to the changes described and found their own subsidiaries, which see themselves as technology providers in the legal services sector. The law firms use these units to establish contact with the start-up scene or cooperate directly with successful up-and-coming market entrants. Examples from the German legal business are the Freshfields Lab, newly founded in 2019 by Freshfields Bruckhaus Deringer, the Clifford Chance Tech GmbH by Clifford Chance LLP or Baker & McKenzie's partnership with the legal tech startup platform ReInvent. The stated objectives of these initiatives are to improve their existing legal services, to optimize legal processes and to develop a new legal portfolio (JUVE, 2019). Other commercial law firms such as Hengeler Mueller or CMS Law complement their traditional legal business with in-house Legal Tech departments, offering direct access to software solutions when required (Thomson Reuters, Legal Insights Europe, 2019). On the UK market, for instance, the internationally active commercial law firms Allen & Overy, Dentons and Slaughter and May established their own Legal Tech incubators or labs (Thomson Reuters, Legaltech, 2019). This enables them to provide hybrid legal services combining a mix of traditional legal services and new software enriched solutions depending on the requirements of the client. A current report on law firms' investment strategies regarding legal technology in the UK reveals that more than half of the UK Top 50 law firms focus on further investing in new innovative technology rather than conducting business as usual (HSBC UK, 2019). At the same time, a large proportion of law firms, especially smaller ones, are hesitant about the current challenges and regard themselves more as "*smart followers*" than as "*early adopters*" (Wenzler, 2018, pp. 45, 46).

Summing up, the exclusive control of law firms over the legal business is fading and a diversified market for legal services is emerging, in which various providers specialize in different sub-processes. The underlying technology acts as an accelerator of this diversification.

Business model

The traditional business model for lawyers focuses on the individual use of human capital. The lawyer's work is regarded as a whole and invoiced according to the services rendered (Georgetown Law/Thompson Reuters, State of the Legal Market, 2019). The basic idea is to ensure a remuneration that is as performance related as possible and tailored to the difficulty of the individual case. Since there are no predefined parameters for the classification of the individual complexity level, time-based remuneration emerged for calculating the costs of legal services (Georgetown Law/Thompson Reuters, State of the Legal Market, 2019). An increasing complexity by and large leads to an increase in time required for addressing a specific legal matter and, therefore, higher costs for the legal services provided. This concept of the so-called billable hour is based on the minute-by-minute recording of all legal work performed. Until now, standard activities have mainly been carried out by young lawyers with one to two years of professional experience, who thus form the bottom of the traditional organizational pyramid structure in big law firms (The Boston Consulting Group/Bucerius Law School, 2016). Although billing on an hourly basis has long been under pressure, the billable hour has remained the most common payment model in most (large) law firms. Even where clients request alternative fee arrangements such as a fixed fee or the like, the billable hour is generally the starting point for calculating the costs of a matter (Aderant, 2018; Aderant, 2017).

The increasing usage of Legal Tech and the increased presence of ALSPs on the market means that wherever former human labor is replaced by a technical solution, hourly billing no longer makes sense. Instead, ALSPs more and more frequently determine the market price for a particular service. In this respect, legal services costs become more calculable for clients, as a fixed fee replaces costs on an hourly basis. This is a significant difference from the previous approach, which regarded legal services as the use of human capital at corresponding (premium) prices, which was always difficult to calculate in advance (Cohen, 2018). As a technical surrogate, Legal Tech is hence accelerating efficiency processes and restructuring the price modelling. Previously common business models, which largely charge young lawyers for research work on an hourly basis, are losing client acceptance and being replaced by information technology and intelligent systems (McKamey, 2017). The pressure is immediately noticeable in areas where ALSPs are increasingly taking over some legal work previously awarded to law firms (Georgetown Law/Thompson Reuters, ALSP, 2019). However, the effect extends beyond automated processes and changes the clients' overall perspective on legal services in a way that the service is seen more as a product and dissociated from the effort behind it.

Based on the above, it can be assumed that the previous business model and in particular the previous payment model with an invoicing of human deployment on an hourly basis will not continue to exist in its current form. A total 73 percent of all law firms recently surveyed agree with this assessment and are convinced that investments in technological innovations will lead to a replacement of the billable hour in favor of alternative pricing structures in the long run. Hence, efficiency due to the use of technology will not only improve the legal service itself but also establish new pricing mechanisms (HSBC UK, 2019).

Efficiency

While in-house legal teams have long had to be measured against efficiency criteria that record the number of legal matters per employee, law firms are more likely to be optimized with regard to revenue per professional. This does not mean that legal matters are processed inefficiently; however, the system of billable hours evidently rewards the use of time and not its saving.

The already discussed effects of Legal Tech – namely the unbundling and the presence of ALSPs in a diversifying market – have led to the effect that clients and law firms alike focus on efficiency in the provision of legal services to an extent never seen before. Clients are increasingly splitting legal services into their individual components (Thomson Reuters, Legatech, 2019). On this basis, it is then to decide which aspects will remain with the in-house law department and what to outsource to law firms, to ALSP or even non-law firm entities (Greentarget, 2018).

The legal business is exposed to the expectation of providing better services at lower prices. This is strikingly described as "*more for less*" (Cohen, 2018, p. 40). This expectation, which is widespread in the manufacturing industry, has so far been met by the legal sector with the fact that no economies of scale can be achieved and, therefore, a significant increase in efficiency cannot be achieved. The use of technology changes this assumption, and it becomes clear that for those sub-processes that can be technically replaced or effectively supported, a rise in efficiency can be achieved. Technical solutions for sub-processes, which can be completed at high speed and produce directly structured results, make the further – traditionally provided – legal services appear slow in the context of a comprehensive consultation. The attempt to stick to the traditional hourly remuneration in this respect can no longer be enforced so easily against clients.

For law firms, as traditional providers of legal services, this means on the one hand that the accelerated operation of technical systems can no longer be compensated simply by expanding the activities of young lawyers (The Boston Consulting Group/Bucerius Law School, 2016). On the other hand, there is increasing pressure to make traditional advice itself more efficient and also to create a link with the Legal Tech applications that are used either by themselves or by ALSPs. The law firm can only position itself convincingly vis-à-vis the client if it is able to orchestrate the various sub-processes and bring them together in the form of a comprehensive legal advice (Georgetown Law/Thompson Reuters, State of the Legal Market, 2019). This also applies with regard to the introduction of technological solutions where the challenge now is to bundle the advantages of different software applications (The Law Society of England and Wales, 2017).

Despite further (cost) pressure, current challenges for law firms also offer the potential to create unique selling points that ultimately may also lead to market advantages through the use of innovative technology. This requires the implementation of a legal project management to handle product, strategy and process innovation within a law firm. However, the insight that all legal services provided by law firms are also processes and every process can be improved which in the end leads to a better delivery of client outcomes has yet to be established. Process optimization in the legal business through the use of methods being established in other areas such as lean manufacturing still offers a great deal of potential.

Customer focus and user experience

The traditional way of delivering legal advice often continues to be stuck in old patterns. Form and language of legal advice pay little attention to the individual needs of clients who in many cases have no legal background or little experience in the legal field in question (The Law Society of England and Wales, Lawtech Adoption, 2019).

In contrast to this, Legal Tech and ALSPs pay particular attention to their user experience (UX) and have a strong customer focus. Legal Tech applications are capable to adapt legal context not only through customized language but also graphically with the use of charts, icons or graphics in order to increase client's perception and acceptance depending on their individual circumstances. It goes without saying that Legal Tech applications are often accessible via smartphones and deliver immediate support.

In other areas outside the law, clients are used to being presented with services in an appealing way, to being provided with updates and to having direct access to understandable work results via interfaces. It turns out that, in spite of "*more for less*" considerations, UX is becoming more and more important from the client's point of view. Legal Tech applications, which are particularly dedicated to UX and offer not only faster and cheaper solutions, but also those that are easy to understand and implement, are more successful in the market (Wenzler, 2018). Again, it helps to transfer methods, that have already been tried and tested elsewhere, to the legal sector, for example, the comparatively recent approach Legal Design Thinking (Harvard Law, Center on the Legal Profession, 2019). Where user experience is concerned, Legal Tech appears to be a driver of innovation and change that forces traditional law firms to rethink their way of providing services.

Outlook

Legal Tech has entered the legal market, and there is every indication that it will continue to influence the development of the legal services market in the coming years.

It proves difficult to accurately predict the scale of the changes. In this respect, the above-mentioned trends can only serve as a basis for projections into the near future. The largest variable appears to be the dynamics of technological advancements and the potential for direct applications to legal services. It will be crucial which legal matters can be addressed using artificial intelligence so that Legal Tech can further enter domains previously reserved for humans. This will require further progress in understanding natural (legal) language and its use in the interaction with lawyers and/or clients. There are, however, already promising approaches such as so-called legal chatbots capable of answering general legal questions (The Law Society of England and Wales, Lawtech Adoption, 2019).

Irrespective of the speed of technological progress, it seems unlikely that the legal business could return to the homogeneity that it had 10 years ago. Instead, ALSPs have gained a market share and are currently expanding it – partly at the expense of traditional players. The latter have to decide whether to maintain their business model and limit it to legal advice not automated so far with the risk that this could become a niche market in the future or face the challenges of a technology-driven market and consider offering a finely tuned, broader range of legal services. The challenge for law firms is to remain the primary point of contact for legal services, and this seems to be only possible in the long term with the appropriate integration of technical solutions. If not, there may only remain a market for individual legal advice that is tending to shrink, such as enforcement in court or in negotiations.

Legal Tech has a global effect on the provision of legal services. Sophisticated legal markets currently seem to have a head start, but there is good reason to believe that technical support for legal services will also find its way into other markets. The effects of this development can be particularly great where legal advice was previously reserved exclusively for those with a large budget to spend on legal advice, since Legal Tech can then provide affordable access to justice for a larger group of people.

References

Aderant (2017). *The 2017 Aderant Business of Law and Legal Technology Survey*. Retrieved October 29, 2019, from http://mkt.aderant.com/acton/attachment/29032/f-0103/1/-/-/-/-/Aderant%20Business%20of%20Law%20Survey%202017.pdf.

Aderant (2018). *The 2018 Aderant Business of Law and Legal Technology Survey*. Retrieved October 29, 2019, from https://www.aderant.com/wp-content/uploads/2018/05/2018-Business-of-Law-Survey-Global.pdf.

Ambrogi, Robert J. (2019). At $1.2 billlion, 2019 is a record year for legal tech investments – and it's only September. *LawSites*. Retrieved October 29, 2019, from https://www.lawsitesblog.com/2019/09/at-1-1-billion-2019-is-a-record-year-for-legal-tech-investments-and-its-only-september.html.

American Bar Association (2019). *Legal Incubators. Lawyer Incubator Directory*. Retrieved October 29, 2019, from https://www.americanbar.org/groups/delivery_legal_services/initiatives_awards/program_main/program_directory/.

Baker McKenzie & R 3 (2017). *Blockchains and Laws. Are they compatible?* Retrieved October 29, 2019, from https://www.bakermckenzie.com/en/-/media/files/expertise/fig/br_fig_blockchainsandlaws_jul17.pdf.

Balkin, Jack M. (2015). The Path of Robotics Law, *California Law Review Circuit Vol. 6, June* 2015.

Breidenbach, Stephan & Glatz, Florian (2018). *Rechtshandbuch Legal Tech.* München: C.H. Beck.

Cohen, Mark A. (2017). Legal Delivery is Becoming Digitized. What Does That Mean? *Forbes Media.* Retrieved October 28, 2019, from https://www.forbes.com/sites/markcohen1/2017/05/21/legal-delivery-is-becoming-digitized-what-does-that-mean/#6770d7764e62.

Cohen, Mark A. (2018). The Legal Industry in Transition – How Did We Get Here and How Has Technology Changed the Marketplace? In M. Hartung, M.-H. Bues, G. Hartleib (Ed.), *Legal Tech. How Technology is Changing the World*, pp. 39–43. Baden-Baden: Nomos.

Deloitte (2016). *Developing legal talent. Stepping into the future law firm*, pp. 3–5. London: the Creative Studio.

Deloitte (2018). *In-house Legal Service Delivery*, pp. 1–17. London: DTTL.

Dolm, Nick (2019). 713% Growth: Legal Tech Set An Investment Record In 2018, *Forbes Media*. Retrieved October 28, 2019, from https://www.forbes.com/sites/valentinpivovarov/2019/01/15/legaltechinvestment2018/#3ad374ba7c2b.

Eversheds Sutherland (2016). Raising the bar – Digital technology and the enhancement of legal services. *The Looking Glass Report 2016*, pp. 24–27.

Gartner (2019). Glossary, Information Technology: Digitization. Retrieved October 29, 2019, from https://www.gartner.com/en/information-technology/glossary/digitization.

Georgetown Law, Center on Ethics and the Legal Profession & Thompson Reuters (2019). *Alternative Legal Service Providers 2019.* Fast Growth, Expanding Use and Increasing Opportunity. Retrieved October 29, 2019, from https://legal.thomsonreuters.com/content/dam/ewp-m/documents/legal/en/pdf/reports/alsp-report-final.pdf.

Georgetown Law, Center on Ethics and the Legal Profession & Thompson Reuters (2019). *Report on the State of the Legal Market 2019.* Retrieved October 29, 2019, from http://ask.legalsolutions.thomsonreuters.info/LEI_2019-State_of_Legal_Mkt.

Glatz, Florian (2018). Blockchain und Smart Contract – Eine neue Basistechnologie im Recht? In M. Hartung, M.-H. Bues, G. Hartleib (Ed.), *Legal Tech. Die Digitalisierung des Rechtsmarkts*, pp. 287–293. Baden-Baden: Nomos.

Goodenough, Oliver R. (2015). Legal Technology 3.0, *Huffpost.* Retrieved October 29, 2019, from https://www.huffpost.com/entry/legal-technology-30_b_6603658.

GrandView Research (2018). *Legal Services Market Size, Share & Trends Analysis Report By Service (Taxation, Real Estate, Litigation, Bankruptcy, Labor/Employment, Corporate), By Firm Size, By Provider, By Region, and Segment Forecasts, 2019 – 2025*. Retrieved October 28, 2019, from https://www.grandviewresearch.com/industry-analysis/global-legal-services-market.

Greentarget (2018). *Legal Industry Outlook 2018*. Retrieved October 29, 2019, from https://greentarget.com/wp-content/uploads/2018/01/2018-Legal-Industry-Outlook_Final.pdf.

Harvard Law, Center on the Legal Profession (2019). Designs on the Law. The arrival of design thinking in the legal profession, *THE PRACTICE, ADAPTIVE INNOVATION, Volume 5 Issue* 2, January/February 2019. Retrieved October 29, 2019, from https://thepractice.law.harvard.edu/article/designs-on-the-law/.

Hook, Alison (2019). *The Use and Regulation of Technology in the Legal Sector beyond England and Wales. Research Paper for the Legal Services Board*. Retrieved October 29, 2019, from https://www.legalservicesboard.org.uk/wp-content/uploads/2019/07/International-AH-Report-VfP-4-Jul-2019.pdf.

HSBC UK (2019). *Peer Group Analysis. Investment Trends in Legal Technology*. Retrieved October 29, 2019, from https://www.business.hsbc.uk/-/media/library/business-uk/pdfs/financing-investments-in-legal-tech-2018.pdf.

JUVE (2019). Legal-Tech-Umfrage: Kanzleien setzen auf Effizienzgewinn, *JUVE*, 31.07.2019. Retrieved October 29, 2019, from https://www.juve.de/nachrichten/namenundnachrichten/2019/07/legal-tech-umfrage-kanzleien-setzen-auf-effizienzgewinn?view=print.

Legal Tech in Deutschland (2019). *Umfassende Datenbank mit Unternehmen und Anwendungen, die Technologieeinsatz mit juristischem Bezug innerhalb Deutschlands anbieten*. Retrieved October 29, 2019, from https://www.legal-tech-in-deutschland.de.

McKamey, Mark (2017). Legal Technology: Artificial Intelligence and the Future of Law Practice, *Appeal Vol. 22*, pp. 45–58.

Remus, Frank & Levy, Frank S. (2016). Can robots be lawyers? Computers, Lawyers, and the practice of law. Retrieved October 29, 2019, from https://ssrn.com/abstract=2701092.

Semple, Noel (2017). *Canadian Bar Association Legal Futures Initiative*. Accessibility, quality, and profitability for personal plight law firms. CHAPTER 5 – vertical devision of labour, pp. 85–100.

Smith, Roger (2018). *The Legal Education Foundation – Digital Delivery of Legal Services*. Retrieved October 29, 2019, from https://www.

thelegaleducationfoundation.org/wp-content/uploads/2019/03/Digital-Technology-Winter-2018.pdf.

Stanford Law School, CodeX (2019). *Discover Legal Technology*. Retrieved October 29, 2019, from http://techindex.law.stanford.edu/.

The Boston Consulting Group & Bucerius Law School (2016). *How Legal Technology Will Change the Business of Law*. Retrieved October 29, 2019, from https://www.bucerius-education.de/fileadmin/content/pdf/studies_publications/Legal_Tech_Report_2016.pdf.

The Business Research Company (2019). *Legal Services Market By Types (B2B Legal Services, B2C Legal Services, Criminal Law Practices and Hybrid Commercial Legal Services), By Size, By Practice, By Key Players and By End Users – Global Forecast To 2021*. Retrieved October 28, 2019, from https://www.thebusinessresearchcompany.com/report/legal-services-market.

The Global Legal Post (2019). *Tech change driving forecasted $ 1011 billion global legal services market*. Retrieved October 29, 2019, from http://www.globallegalpost.com/big-stories/tech-change-driving-forecasted-$1011-billion-global-legal-services-market-90340488/.

The Law Society of England and Wales (2017). *Capturing technological innovation in Legal Services*. Part 1: Technological Innovation In Practice, pp. 22–46. Retrieved October 29, 2019 from https://www.lawsociety.org.uk/support-services/research-trends/capturing-technological-innovation-report/.

The Law Society of England and Wales (2019). *Lawtech Adoption Research*. The lawtech landscape, Drivers for lawtech adoption, Barrierts to lawtech adoption, Lawtech adoption trends, pp. 11–30. Retrieved October 29, 2019 from https://www.lawsociety.org.uk/support-services/research-trends/lawtech-adoption-report/.

The Law Society of New South Wales (2017). *The Flip Report*. The Future of Law and Innovation in the Profession. Chapter 1 – Drivers of change: clients' needs and expectations, pp. 14–30. Retrieved October 29, 2019 from https://www.lawsociety.com.au/sites/default/files/2018-03/1272952.pdf.

Thomson Reuters (2017). Movers and Shakers: *UK Lawtech Start-Ups 2017*, pp. 7–17. Retrieved October 29, 2019 from http://info.legalsolutions.thomsonreuters.co.uk/legalgeek?utm_campaign=AS39490/001&utm_source=5170103A&utm_medium=BlogLegalSolutions.

Thomson Reuters (2019). *Legal Insights Europe. Embedding innovative legal tech in law firms*. Retrieved October 29, 2019, from https://blogs.thomsonreuters.com/legal-uk/2019/01/25/embedding-innovative-legal-tech-in-law-firms/.

Thomson Reuters (2019). *Legaltech Startup Report 2019*. A maturing market, pp. 3–17. Retrieved October 29, 2019 from https://legalsolutions.thomsonreuters.co.uk/content/dam/openweb/documents/pdf/uki-legal-solutions/report/tr-legaltech-startup-report-2019.pdf.

Vogl, Roland (2019). *Talking Tech with CodeX: Roland Vogl Discusses the Technological Transformation of Legal Practice*. Retrieved October 29, 2019, from https://law.stanford.edu/2019/03/19/talking-tech-with-codex-roland-vogl-discusses-the-technological-transformation-of-legal-practice/.

Wagner, Jens (2018). *Legal Tech und Legal Robots*. München, Wiesbaden: Springer.

Wenzler, Hariolf (2018). Big Law & Legal Tech. In M. Hartung, M.-H. Bues, G. Hartleib (Ed.), *Legal Tech. How Technology is Changing the World*, pp. 44–48. Baden-Baden: Nomos.

Ela Sibel Bayrak Meydanoğlu, Margareta Teodorescu, Sevgin Batuk, and Selin Karaca

Enhancing Digital Reputation: New Tools for Monitoring Corporate Reputation in the Digital Age

Abstract: Since digital platforms have become a business tool instead of merely being a digital communication one, digital corporate reputation has undeniably become one of the most valuable assets of companies. Brands can take advantage of their online presence by increasing their popularity and enhancing their reputation digitally. Yet, there is a reverse side of the coin, too. The digital world can be an amazing instrument for bringing businesses to the next level or, just as well, to their very end. As any information – be it true or false – can be spread digitally at an unprecedented speed, the need for companies to put into place tools that allow monitoring and assessing digital content across various websites has dramatically increased. In this chapter, we propose a short review of the corporate reputation concept and its advantages, objectives, methods and process in the digital context. We also analyze some of the most newly developed and frequently used tools for monitoring digital reputation and examine how they managed to help organizations increase their digital and marketing awareness and capabilities as well.

Keywords: Corporate reputation management, digital reputation, monitoring and profiling tools

Introduction

Irrespective of the degree of digitalization in the business world, it is indisputable that reputation is one of the most valuable assets of a company. Yet, it was only after the digital revolution that this concept started to be used extensively not only in marketing, but also across other fields of economics and business administration as well.

Today, in the digital world, information travels fast. Its exponential replication and amplification by means of social media is of paramount importance for companies. For example, the first tweet ever was sent on March 21, 2006 by Jack Dorsey, the creator of Twitter. For the first billion tweets, it took more than three years, until the end of May 2009. Today, it takes less than two days for one billion tweets to be sent. According to Worldometers' RTS algorithm, around 6,000 tweets are tweeted on Twitter every second, on average (Internet Live Stats, n.d.). This corresponds to over 350,000 tweets sent per minute, 500 million tweets per day and around 200 billion tweets per year. And Twitter is, among other digital platforms like Facebook, LinkedIn or Myspace, just one example.

As long as companies have an online presence, they have to worry even more about their reputation. As an increasing number of consumers rely on online research in order to make their buying decision, brand's and company's reputation can make or break the business. Not only is it essential that companies understand and apply online reputation management, but ignoring this can cause companies a serious loss of customers and money, or harm their reputation.

Besides some studies in the relevant literature which distinguish between online and offline corporate reputation management (e.g. Jones, Temperley, & Lima, 2009), some studies exist that define these two concepts as an integrated process (e.g. Meier & Portmann, 2013). Since this study focuses on digital reputation management, a separate approach was adopted. In this chapter, we have a twofold goal. Firstly, we provide a short review of some of the most relevant theoretical aspects of the corporate reputation concept and its advantages, objectives, methods and process in the digital age. Secondly, we conduct an analysis of some of the best and newly developed tools companies use in order to monitor and manage their digital reputation. Selected examples from the business community will shed an additional light on how these tools can be integrated into companies' strategies and help them improve their online presence. Even if the literature provides several studies analyzing digital corporate reputation and its monitoring tools, case studies or business-life examples of how these tools can be used for improving organizations' digital reputation are almost inexistent. The aim of this chapter is to close this gap by providing an analysis of several case studies selected from the real business world.

This study highlights firstly several definitions of the corporate reputation term, defines its role for companies and describes its major advantages. Following, the chapter presents the corporate reputation concept in the digital context, its objectives and selected methods for protecting and strengthening reputation on digital platforms. The sub-processes making up the digital corporate reputation management process are described in the next section. The last part of the study provides a detailed analysis of how digital reputation can be monitored and of the tools companies may use in order to successfully monitor their online activity. The study ends with the conclusion section.

Table 1: Definitions for "Corporate Reputation"

Author(s)	Definition
Tucker & Melewar (p. 378), 2005	*"Corporate reputation is the perception of an organization based on its stakeholders' interpretation of that organization's past, present and future activities and the way in which these are communicated."*
De Castro, López & Sáez (p. 362), 2006	*"Collective representation of actions and outcomes of the past and present of the organization, that describe its capability to obtain valuable outcomes for different stakeholders."*
Barnett, Jermier & Lafferty (p. 34), 2006	*"Observers' collective judgments of a corporation based on assessments of the financial, social, and environmental impacts attributed to the corporation over time."*
Beal & Strauss (p. 13), 2009	*"It is pure perception that may or may not be based on fact. It is the esteem that an entity has in the eyes of its stakeholders."*
Kadıbeşegil (p. 59), 2018	*"Corporate reputation is the contribution of the trust created by a company in the total market value of the company. It is the carrier of the company's untouchable values. It refers to being an admired, appreciated company by the society."*
Cornelissen (p. 180), 2014	*"Subject's collective representation of past images of an organization (induced through either communication or past experiences) that is established over time."*

Corporate Reputation and Its Role for Companies

Reputation means "*the opinion that people in general have about someone or something, or how much respect or admiration someone or something receives, based on past behaviour or character.*" (Cambridge Dictionary). Several studies regarding corporate reputation and its management define this term very differently. Table 1 presents some of these definitions.

Having good reputation brings operational, strategic and financial advantages to a company:

- Good reputation enables gaining quality employees and keep them in the company (Taylor, 2001; Doorley & Garcia, 2007), increases the sense of belonging among existing employees and their efficiency as well (Ross, 2008).
- Reputation is an important selection criterion in the purchasing process (Taylor, 2001). Good reputation can boost revenue by triggering sales

(Fombrun & Gardberg, 2000) and gives companies the advantage of pricing their products and services (Ross, 2008).

- Reputation shows what consumers think about a company or the quality of its products or services and affects financial performance. Good reputation can open doors to new markets, facilitates capital access and attracts investors, increases brand loyalty, makes it easier to adopt and hold new products/services in the market (Akmehmet, 2006), and increases the credibility of companies and their ability to overcome crises without or with less damage (Ross, 2008).
- Reputable companies have a high credit among stakeholders and get their support (Ross, 2008).
- Reputation differentiates companies from its competitors (Ross, 2008).

Creating a good corporate reputation takes long time and great effort. However, in the digitalized world, it takes just a few seconds to damage it. Dove's ad posted on Facebook on October 4, 2017 is a good example that illustrates how quickly social media can impair well-known, reputable big companies. In the Dove's ad, a black woman is turning into a white one after using the Dove brand cleaner (see Figure 1).

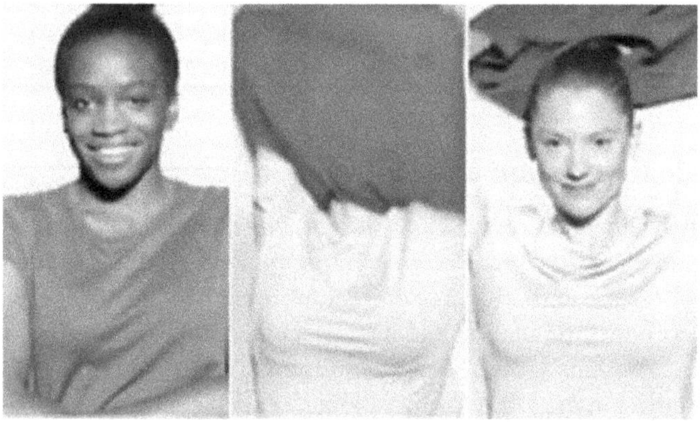

Figure 1: The Image from Dove's Advertisement (Slawson, 2017).

This ad led to a debate on racism on social media platforms around the world after a makeup artist (an influencer) put screen grabs of the ad clip together and shared them on Facebook. The post got shared by many people in a short time. From October 6 to 13, the ad was discussed in more than 30,000 posts and 45.55

% of these had a negative sentiment. More than 12,000 times Dove was mentioned with a variant of the word "racist" or "racism" (Glavinić, 2017). Dove removed the post, did not publish any other related content and apologized for the offense (Slawson, 2017). The crisis caused by Dove's ad was discussed frequently from October 11 to 7, then it diminished. Although no explanations regarding its negative impact could be found on digital platforms, the story lasted long enough for a lot of people to get exposed to a negative image of Dove, and it was expected that it had an impact on Dove's short-term sales results (Glavinić, 2017). In her study, Bogomoletc (2019) reviewed 200 from 3931 comments on the crisis statement of Dove on Facebook from October 7, 2017 and found that 70.5% were negative. After examining the negative comments, five common themes were found: racism, boycott, negative feelings, team, and apology. Although Dove received a lot of criticism from social media, it continued to draw attention to strong advertising efforts focused on women's diversity and self-esteem and did not suffer from the consequences on consumer loyalty.

Corporate Reputation Management in the Digital Age

Digital corporate reputation, its objectives and methods for ensuring digital corporate reputation

As the Dove example shows, managing corporate reputation on online platforms is not an easy process. However, this process is essential for organizations. Digital reputation is defined as *"the process of organizing, structuring, managing by consciously controlling and measuring news and shares in the digital world in order to create positive perceptions about an organization."* (Çiftçioğlu, 2016, p. 48).

Retaining and reinforcing reputation on digital platforms cannot be considered independent from the overall reputation management of an organization. Therefore, the following objectives for traditional reputation management described by Schultz and Werner (2005, p. 4) are also valid for digital reputation management:

- *"Maintaining a favorable reputation in the workplace and marketplace,*
- *enhancing and building the organization's good name and reputation,*
- *establishing acceptable practices, policies, procedures, systems and standards that will avoid damage to the organization's reputation,*
- *establishing guidelines for dealing with situations where the company's reputation has been tarnished,*
- *preparing and equipping the management team to take full responsibility for managing the company's reputation."*

Today, shares made in different online platforms may affect an organization significantly, and negative shares can damage its reputation. There are some methods to protect and strengthen reputation on digital platforms (Er, 2008):

- **Technical Precautions:** These precautions (e.g. protection of databases and websites, creation of a technical infrastructure to provide uninterrupted service) prevent possible damages to reputation occurred as a result of hacker attacks, disruption of electronic services and leakage of private information.
- **Reflecting corporate identity on digital platforms:** Corporate activities on digital platforms should be carried out in accordance with the organization's mission and vision, which should be easily accessible on the website. All corporate design elements (e.g. logo, slogan) and corporate communication should also be available on digital platforms.
- **Addressing all stakeholder groups (staff, customers, investors, media, suppliers, international community and non-governmental organizations):** This can be done by having multilingual website for international stakeholders, opening a special page for investors relations, sharing audio/videos messages of executives and listening to customer problems via special chat rooms.
- **Improving the power of self-expression:** Organizations should increase their visibility on digital platforms, for example, through successful search engine optimization or advertisements leading to the organizations' websites. They should ensure consistency between what they are saying and what they are doing. For instance, if an organization defines itself as being environmental-friendly, but its activities do not comply with this behavior, then this will likely be criticized on digital platforms. Organizations should ensure transparency on digital platforms (e.g. via publishing reports on social responsibility activities or financial information on the website), provide reliable/real information and original content, and make realistic promises.

Digital corporate reputation management process

Reputation management is a repetitive process in which the following subprocesses are applied one after the other:

- **Due Diligence Process:** This process is carried out in order to determine the current reputation perception of the organization's target audience on digital platforms. For this, it is necessary to determine which digital platforms (e.g. social media, blogs, websites, complaint sites and search engines) the target audience uses and to identify the relevant news content and shares. Companies may search for answers to questions such as "who will follow us?", "why they follow us?", "what tools they use to follow us?", "what do they talk about us?" The tools with which the target audience interacts and communicates as well as their usage time are also identified. These tools have to be monitored and, based on this, profiling has to be carried out (Çiftçioğlu, 2016). Next section considers several monitoring and profiling tools closer.

- **Positioning Process:** This *"(…) is a process in which the data obtained during the due diligence process is analyzed, evaluated, the current reputation perception and the reputation perception value targeted by organizations on digital platforms are determined, and an action plan has to be put forward to reach the targeted reputation value."* (Çiftçioğlu, 2016, p. 121). This process consists of two sub-processes:

  1) Setting online reputation targets.
  2) Creating and managing online reputation action plans.

In the digital world, reputation targets can be determined according to either a defensive approach such as introducing the organization and protecting the reputation, or an aggressive approach such as opening the company to new markets, acquiring more customers, increasing customer loyalty and gaining superiority over competitors. After setting the goals, a digital action plan has to be determined. For this, the organization has to identify risks in the virtual world, possible situations that may create a crisis, and relevant promotional content and activities (e.g. designing and structuring websites, content creation and social networking strategies) on digital platforms (Çiftçioğlu, 2016).

- **Evaluation Process:** This *"(…) is a continuous repetitive managerial process that measures the extent to which the online positioning actions, policies and strategies were achieved."* (Çiftçioğlu, 2016, p. 163). Within this process, the effectiveness and efficiency of the actions taken by an organization to build and maintain online reputation as well as the success of its defined targets are measured. The online reputation management performances of other companies in the sector are compared with that of the organization, too. The evaluation process aims at measuring indicators such as "corporate visibility", "credibility", "reality", "transparency", "trust", "social trust" and "positive stakeholder relations", which are mentioned as indicators of reputation in the literature on reputation management.

Different methods can be used to measure reputation indicators. One of these is personality analysis, which means that links and words on the web page of an institution are examined and, based on this, its identity is being analyzed. The result is then compared with the aimed reputation identity. It is also possible to evaluate reputation perception of an organization by conducting a content analysis of its media tools. The organization's past and current shares as well as the digital data are compared in order to evaluate the development of the reputation profiling of the organization in the digital world. In addition, social media metrics (e.g. rating of company shares, frequency of mentioning company name or products, number of followers) and rating systems in which customer ratings are followed are frequently used tools for evaluating organizations' trust and reputation (Çiftçioğlu, 2016).

Monitoring Digital Reputation

> *"Monitoring is defined as the process of identifying and gathering all opinions, information and news related to an organization that are shared on digital platforms that do or do not threaten the reputation of the organization."* (Çiftçioğlu, 2016).

The raw data obtained at the end of the monitoring process is analyzed within the process of company-related profiling. Through profiling, it is possible to determine changes in consumers' perception related to reputation by comparing the data of different periods. Profiling is also important to evaluate the impact of campaigns and activities carried out to improve and strengthen the perception of organizations' digital reputation (Çiftçioğlu, 2016, p. 109). *"Eluting shares and news on digital platforms that may be related to institutional reputation and analyzing them considering the context in the relevant period forms the center of the profiling process"* (Çiftçioğlu 2016, p. 109).

Depending on their size and the role reputation management plays for them, organizations can use different monitoring and profiling tools. They can execute the monitoring and profiling by themselves or get support from companies such as Reputation Changer or PriceWaterhouseCoopers that are active in the digital reputation management field (Çiftçioğlu, 2016; Er, 2008). Other than the usual online monitoring tools such as RSS feeds, Google Alert or Yahoo Alert, some special ones have been newly developed as a result of the increasing importance of digital reputation. Some of these tools are presented below, together with relevant case studies or business-life examples that highlight how organizations can use them for improving their digital reputation.

1. Awario:

Social listening is a way of proactively monitoring all comments, complaints, positive or negative emotions about a brand on the internet, especially in social media and among online communities. One of the social listening tools that helps companies to manage their reputation is Awario. The capability of performing emotion and competitor analysis is one of the most important characteristics of this tool.

Emotion analysis is a new type of text analysis that aims at determining individuals' subjective opinions (Collomb, Costea, Joyeux, Hasan, & Brunie, 2014). Its main purpose is to identify people's mood, behavior and ideas from textual documents (Eliaçık & Erdoğan, 2015, p. 782). Several digital platforms help companies to reach emotions of audience by comparing the fluctuations in positive and, respectively, negative emotions. During particular events, the emotions and contents can be reviewed by setting up specific keywords such as, for example, company name (Breakenridge, 2012, p. 110).

As Awario's vice president Masha Maksimava stated, dealing with negative feedback quickly and preventing the potential reputation crisis is an important issue in the digital environment (Bown, 2019). Awario's platform monitors brand-related conversations in real-time on key social networks and the web, provides emotion analysis to help identify conversations that require immediate action, and creates emotion graphs that show positive and negative comments (Awario, 2018). Emotion graphs play an important role especially for social media professionals working with brands. By using these graphs, they can detect and react to reputation crises in due time (Stoica, 2018).

Furthermore, Awario supports also competitor analysis. By creating monitoring alerts, companies can get feedback about customers' emotions and satisfaction regarding a specific brand or company. As Awario enables comparing the brand words related to a company with those related to its competitors (Awario, 2018), negative alerts/comments about competitors can be used in order to learn from their reputational failures and to gain new customers (Bredava, 2018).

In her study, Bredava (2018) analyzes Hilton, one of the most famous hotel chains in the world, and examines how Hilton uses Awario for social listening and for monitoring and providing feedback to its customers on social media. Figure 2 shows that the number of positive comments from social media users is higher than that of negative ones, Twitter being the most popular platform for posting both of them.

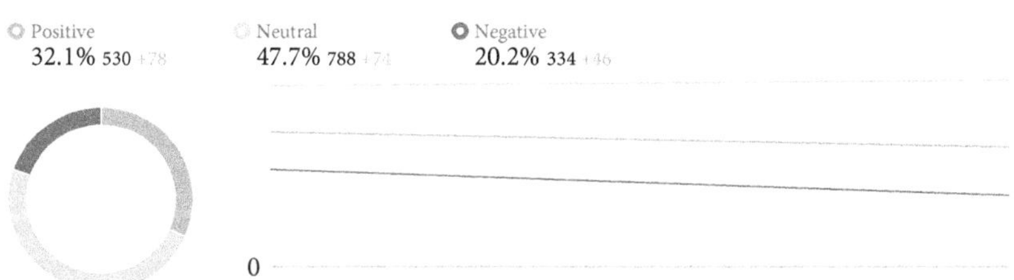

Figure 2: Sentiment Analysis of Hilton Hotels (Bredava, 2018).

2. Brandwatch

Brandwatch is another social listening tool. It uses millions of online resources and provides instant data and real-time results. Brandwatch helps companies to monitor data and make comparisons with competitors. It also allows for accessing the demographic information about the target audience and saving time with automatic reporting as well (Kızılırmak, 2015).

Toys "R" Us, the world's leading retail toy company, uses Brandwatch Analytics for tracking, measuring and optimizing its Instagram accounts. According to a social media program launched in 2016, Toys "R" Us allowed their more than 860 stores to have their own Instagram accounts. The aim of this program was to increase the number of store visits and empower each store to manage their online content. Two important questions arose in this process. The first was how to determine the growth rate and activity of each post, and the second how to decide which content performed best. That meant solving a twofold problem. The company had to find both a way to visualize the content of all its 860 Instagram accounts and a tool that allows for handling and analyzing the whole online content (Brandwatch, n.d.).

After setting up Instagram accounts in Brandwatch, all accounts could be viewed in one place and their content analyzed in real time. By using this tool, Toys "R" Us succeeded to identify common findings across all regions and products. Finding key factors by assessing this information helped the company to considerably improve its consumer experience by simultaneously managing its more than 860 Instagram accounts (Brandwatch, n.d.).

3. Reputology

Another social listening tool that helps organizations track their online reviews is Reputology. It monitors common platforms such as Google and Facebook, as well as industry-specific review websites, and provides emotion analysis, reviews monitoring, performance measuring and quick response (Reputology, n.d.). This tool suits best to companies that have multiple locations, as it allows for evaluating their overall reputation (Awario, 2018).

Caruso Affiliated, one of the largest, privately owned real estate development companies in the United States, sought out Reputology to assist in ensuring that reviews and guest feedback were addressed in a timely manner. With thousands of people visiting Caruso Affiliated's properties on a weekly basis, the company regularly deals with both positive and negative online reviews. By using Reputology, the team at Caruso Affiliated now has an enhanced, streamlined and organized way of handling online reviews. Reputology provides the team with daily reports outlining positive and negative comments, and, additionally, with regular reports, the team can assess its online reputation management strategy on a monthly basis.

4. ReviewTrackers

ReviewTrackers is a software that analyzes customer feedback (Seotech, 2017) and helps brands achieve customer success using data and technology (Darroch, 2016). This tool monitors online business reviews on over 100 websites and keeps companies informed by setting up e-mail alerts. Comprehensive, customized reports can be generated that address companies' needs. Furthermore, it collects customer feedback and shows what customers are talking about the most.

Ziebart, an automotive aftermarket service provider, was aware that customer feedback could be valuable in reaching a better understanding of how to provide a better customer service level. Before using ReviewTrackers, Ziebart's marketing team was unable to respond to reviews in a reasonable amount of time due to the large number of reviews on different digital channels. By leveraging data and technology, the tool provided the company with comprehensive review monitoring, timely feedback and warnings, and helped measuring and optimizing its customer experience. Using ReviewTrackers, Ziebart has become more efficient in tracking online reviews and increased its responsiveness to customer feedback. This has led to improve brand reputation and higher ratings (ReviewTrackers, n.d.).

5. Grade.us

Grade.us is a tool that allows customers to make ratings on websites (Gradeus, 2018; Gradeus, n.d.) and enables monitoring online reviews and ratings. A survey about online reviews conducted by ReviewTrackers (2018) for the period October 2017–March 2018 found that 63.6 % of customers search on Google before visiting a new business. Negative reviews drive customers away, and they often do not trust companies that get ratings under four stars. Thus, the role of online reviews and ratings for companies remains uncontroversial.

BizMktg, a digital marketing agency, served one of its most important customers, North Creek Dental Care, by using Grade.us. When North Creek opened a new clinic, BizMktg understood the importance of online reviews for the dentistry team and began to search for solutions for managing its digital reputation. It found out that Grade.us could help North Creek with monitoring and increasing the number of positive reviews by upgrading review ratings. BizMktg designed an evaluation framework using the Grade.us platform (Figure 3) and

North Creek Dental Care delivered this customized Grade.us evaluation form to all patients via e-mail. Since then, reviews and ratings have increased periodically, and the total volume of evaluation forms has soared both on review sites and on the web. North Creek Dental Care succeeded to get 4.83 stars out of 5 in search engine results and increased considerably its number of new customers (Sussman, 2018).

Figure 3: Rating Platform for North Creek Dental Care (Sussman, 2018).

Conclusion

This study provides a short overview about some of the most important theoretical aspects related to the corporate reputation management in the digital world. After defining the corporate reputation term and its role for companies, we describe some of the major advantages of building a good corporate reputation. We exemplify this by using the example of Dove's ad posted on Facebook in October 2017, which illustrates the rapid impact social media can have on organizations' reputation. The chapter presents thereafter the objectives of digital corporate reputation and the methods for ensuring it as well. Following this, a thorough analysis of the corporate reputation management process in the digital world is provided. The study ends by analyzing some of the most important, newly developed tools companies use for monitoring and managing their digital reputation. We use selected cases from the business community in order to examine and exemplify how these tools can help organizations increase their digital and marketing awareness and improve their online presence as well. In doing so, we choose relevant, large-sized organizations from different sectors, having different business goals and online target audience.

Even if information – positive or negative – spread rapidly across digital platforms, the virtual environment should not be considered as a threat to reputation. There are anti-corporate users on digital platforms, but there are also users who voluntarily build fan sites for the organization as well. Such users contribute to strengthen corporate reputation, as the fans and defenders of an institution usually act to defend its reputation against any attacks and threats (Beal & Strauss, 2009).

To reduce reputational risks on digital platforms, large-sized companies or companies operating on international platforms may get support from professional monitoring companies. However, it should be kept in mind that for accurate and reliable digital reputation analysis it is necessary to work with companies that have sufficient knowledge, experience and software expertise (Çiftçioğlu, 2016).

References

Akmehmet, D. (2006). *Kurumsal İtibar Yönetimi ve Bir Uygulama* (Unpublished master's thesis). Marmara University, Istanbul.

Awario. (2018, November 27). *8 Best Online Reputation Management Tools for Your Brand*. Retrieved July 16, 2019, from https://searchengineland.com/8-best-online-reputation-management-tools-for-your-brand-308621.

Barnett, M. L., Jermier, J. M., & Lafferty, B. A. (2006). Corporate Reputation: The Definitional Landscape. *Corporate Reputation Review*, *9*(1), 26–38.

Beal, A., & Strauss, J. (2009). *Radically transparent: Monitoring and managing reputations online*. Indianapolis, Indiana: John Wiley & Sons.

Bogomoletc, E. (2019). Dialogic communication in faux pas paracrises. What do users want to discuss on brands' official Facebook pages? *Journal of Promotional Communications*, *7*(1), 3–19.

Bown, J. (2019, July 10). Sosyal medyada şirketinizin itibarının sıfırlanmaması için nelere dikkat etmeniz lazım? *BBC*. Retrieved July 16, 2019, from https://www.bbc.com/turkce/haberler-dunya-48929435.

Brandwatch. (n.d.). *Toys"R"Us Customer Story*. Retrieved July 24, 2019, from https://www.brandwatch.com/case-studies/toysrus-customer-story.

Breakenridge, D. (2012). *Social media and public relations: Eight new practices for the PR professional*. New Jersey: Pearson Education.

Bredava, A. (2018, November 15). *Social Listening Study: Reputation Analysis of 8 Major Brands* [Web log post]. Retrieved July 16, 2019, from https://awario.com/blog/social-listening-study-2018/.

Çiftçioğlu, A. (2016). *Online İtibar Yönetimi* (1st ed.). Bursa: Dora Yayınları.

Collomb, A., Costea, C., Joyeux, D., Hasan, O., & Brunie, L. (2014). A study and comparison of sentiment analysis methods for reputation evaluation. *Rapport de recherche RR-LIRIS-2014-002*. University of Lyon, INSA-Lyon.

Cornelissen, J. (2014). *Corporate Communication: A Guide to Theory and Practice* (4th ed.). London: Sage Publications.

Darroch, D. (2016, July 28). *Interview with Chris Campbell, CEO at Reviewtrackers* [Web log post]. Retrieved July 25, 2019, from http://www.symmetry50.com/blog/2016/7/28/chris-campbell-reviewtrackers.

De Castro, G. M., López, J. E. N., & Sáez, P. L. (2006). Business and Social Reputation: Exploring the Concept and Main Dimensions of Corporate Reputation. *Journal of Business Ethics*, *63*(4), 361–370.

Doorley, J. & Garcia, H. G. (2007). *Reputation Management: The Key to Successful Public Relations and Corporate Communication*. USA: Routledge.

Eliaçık, A. B., & Erdoğan, N. (2015). Mikro Bloglardaki Finans Toplulukları için Kullanıcı Ağırlıklandırılmış Duygu Analizi Yöntemi. In *UYMS*. 782–793. Istanbul: Istanbul Teknik Üniversitesi.

Er, G. (2008). *Sanal Ortamda İtibar Yönetimi: Kurumsal İtibar Yönetimi ve İnternet'te İtibarı İzlemenin, Korumanın ve Güçlendirmenin Yolları* (1st ed.). İstanbul: Cinius Yayınları.

Fombrun, C. J., & Gardberg, N. (2000). Who's Tops in Corporate Reputation?. *Corporate Reputation Review*, *3*(1), 13–17.

Glavinić, I. (2017, October 27). *How Dove's Reputation Crisis Unraveled On Social Media* [Web log post]. Retrieved August 5, 2019, from https://www.mediatoolkit.com/blog/dove-reputation-crisis/.

Gradeus. (2018, December 5). *Grade.us: The Review Management Platform for Marketers, Agency, and Local SEO Specialists* [Video File]. Retrieved July 28, 2019, from https://www.youtube.com/watch?time_continue=4&v=_VUhxg3iGGs.

Gradeus. (n.d.). *Automate Your Effort to Acquire, Monitor and Amplify Customer Reviews*. Retrieved July 28, 2019, from https://www.grade.us/home/how-it-works.

Internet Live Stats. (n.d.). *Twitter Usage Statistics*. Retrieved September 11, 2019, from https://www.internetlivestats.com/twitter-statistics/.

Jones, B., Temperley, J., & Lima, A. (2009). Corporate Reputation in the Era of Web 2.0: The Case of Primark. *Journal of Marketing Management*, *25*(9-10), 927–939.

Kadıbeşegil, S. (2018). *İtibar Yönetimi* (9th ed.). Istanbul: Mediacat Yayınları.

Kızılırmak, D. (2015, March 27). *En İyi Sosyal Medya Takip Araçları.* Retrieved July 24, 2019, from https://www.dijitalajanslar.com/sosyal-medya-takip-araclari/.

Meier, A. & Portmann, E. (2013). *Fuzzy Management Methods: The FORA Framework A Fuzzy Grassroots Ontology for Online Reputation Management.* Berlin Heidelberg: Springer-Verlag.

Reputation. (n.d.). In *Cambridge Dictionary*. Retrieved August 5, 2019, from https://dictionary.cambridge.org/dictionary/english/reputation?q=reputation.

Reputology. (n.d.). *Manage Reviews from One Place.* Retrieved July 21, 2019, from https://www.reputology.com/.

Reputology. (n.d.). *Success Stories.* Retrieved July 21, 2019, from https://www.reputology.com/case-study-form?study=caruso.

Review Trackers. (2018). *2018 ReviewTrackers Online Reviews Survey.* Retrieved July 28, 2019, from https://www.reviewtrackers.com/reports/online-reviews-survey/.

Review Trackers. (n.d.). *Ziebart is Tuned Into the Voice of the Customer.* Retrieved July 28, 2019, from https://www.reviewtrackers.com/wp-content/uploads/Review-Trackers-Case-Studies_Ziebart.pdf.

Ross, L. G. (2008). *Corporate Reputation: 12 Steps to Safeguarding and Recovering Reputation.* New Jersey, USA: John Wiley & Sons.

Schultz, H. B. & Werner, A. (2005). Reputation management. *Human Resources Management, 13*, 1–15.

Seotech. (2017, July 14). *11 Başlıkta Online İtibar Yönetiminin Püf Noktaları*. Retrieved July 25, 2019, from https://seotech.com.tr/11-baslikta-online-itibar-yonetiminin-puf-noktalari/.

Slawson, N. (2017, October 8). Dove apologises for ad showing black woman turning into white one. *The Guardian*. Retrieved July 11, 2019, from https://www.theguardian.com/world/2017/oct/08/dove-apologises-for-ad-showing-black-woman-turning-into-white-one.

Stoica, V. (2018, April 11). *Awario Review: Why it's an Essential Social Media Monitoring Tool* [Web log post]. Retrieved July 16, 2019 from https://www.vasilestoica.pw/awario-review/amp/.

Sussman, G. (2018, June 28). *A Grade.us Case Study – BizMktg – Helping Businesses Win Online* [Web log post]. Retrieved July 23, 2019, from https://blog.grade.us/grade-us-case-study-bizmktg/?gaconnectorId=5429c98e-b3af-c92a-83c7-45e7dea6cc5f.

Taylor, S. (2001). *Defending Your Reputation. A Practical Guide to Crisis Communications*. London: Thorogood.

Tucker, L. & Melewar, T. C. (2005). Corporate Reputation and Crisis Management: The Threat and Manageability of Anti-corporatism. *Corporate Reputation Review*, *7*(4), 377–387.

Tolga Tuzcuoğlu

Digital Transformation and the Changing Role of Controlling in Business Enterprises

Abstract: Recently digital transformation is reshaping the business world and resulting in fundamental changes in companies with respect to business models, organizational structures and internal processes. Considering the general consequences on business practices, the aim of this chapter is to examine the impact of digital transformation on controlling (management accounting) from a variety of perspectives. Focusing on this objective, the chapter analyzes the changing role of controllers (management accountants), organizational restructuring trends in finance and controlling, as well as the recent instruments and concepts applied in controlling processes and practices. Digital transformation inherently possesses both chances and risks for controlling. The extent to which digital transformation trends and their impacts are recognized timely and action plans are formulated in advance in a proactive way determines the level of opportunity seizure and success for controlling.

Keywords: Controlling, management accounting, digital transformation

Introduction

This chapter examines the changing role of controlling in business enterprises in the era of digital transformation. Focusing on the latest trends, applications and business practices, the chapter discusses the implications of digital transformation from the perspectives of controlling organization, operations, and the competences of controlling associates.

Whereas digitization can be basically regarded as the conversion of analog data into digital implying the emergence of the use of computers in organizations, digital transformation can be considered as the next step of digitization impacting the whole business practices of organizations (Sugahara, Daidj & Ushio, 2017). In a broader sense, it can be described with the integration of various technological innovations that improve the way how the business is done (Scardovi, 2017).

Throughout their life cycle, business firms may witness upward and downward periods. Indeed, in the digital transformation era, companies are confronted with elevated volatility, uncertainty, complexity and ambiguity. In such an environment, the life cycle of companies is subject to more frequent downturns and even consecutive negative phases. Considering their traditional role as processing information in order for company management to make strategic decisions, controllers currently play a pivotal role more than ever. In the light of the current business circumstances as well as digital transformation trends, there is and will be more to expect from controllers. In other words, the role that controlling plays for the organization has been evolving parallel to the current business trends and digital transformation requirements.

Foundations

Controlling: Concept and Role Change

Controlling can be defined as a process in which all kind of business relevant information is processed and reported for company management at diverse positions in an effort to support and facilitate the attainment of organizational goals. Information processing is mainly carried out in a formal accounting system. Due to the technological advancements, accounting systems have evolved in such a way that all business functions are brought together through enterprise resource planning (ERP) systems and managers are able to access data, create reports and carry out analyses by themselves (Horngren, Sundem, Burgstahler, & Schatzberg, 2013). Similarly, developments in information technologies (IT) in the previous two decades transformed the role of controllers from information gatherers into in-house management advisors (Drury, 2018, p. 11). In this context, controllers are now more involved in assuring data availability, interpretation and enhancing visualization for decision-makers.

Starting from the late 1960s, the role that controllers play for business enterprises experienced a significant structural change. According to Li (2018), controllers mainly dealt with cost calculations especially in production facilities in the 1960s. In the subsequent decade, job descriptions started including profitability analyses and support for decision-making processes. With the emergence of globalization trends in the 1980s and 1990s, the focus of controllers turned to novel areas such as value creation processes, stakeholder analyses, benchmarking and balanced scorecards leading to a shift from operational to strategic considerations. As for the strategic approach, the Chartered Institute of Management Accountants in the UK (CIMA, 2000) relates strategic management accounting to the utilization of external data and non-financial internal information in addition to internally generated company data.

In the same way, Plag (2012) points out that as the role of controllers evolved from information providers to internal consultants, change management became a focal point for controlling. In this context, the author summarizes four key reasons:

1. Controllers counsel and support the management regarding the implementation of central restructuring, reorganization, change or transition projects and quality management initiatives such as lean management, value stream design, six sigma, etc.

2. Controllers undertake benchmarking activities, the results of which are likely to introduce new models or approaches that have not been implemented before.
3. Changes in the controlling tools such as dashboard reporting, predictive analytics or a revision of performance indicators that are followed up on by company management are likely to affect organizational units and initiate change.
4. The role and mindset change in controlling including new competence requirements can be broadly regarded as a change driver in the organization.

Küng (2012) explains that supporting the decision-making processes of company top management requires particular soft skills in addition to analytical and conceptual thinking. Such soft skills mainly pertain to communication, influence and negotiation. Regardless of being reactive or proactive, defining, communicating and implementing measures to attain strategic goals can be thought of as a contract or agreement with the relevant parties within the organization. Therefore, conclusion of such agreements, in which controlling is one of the parties necessitates especially competences regarding negotiation, conflict management and compromise. On the other hand, controllers as business partners are regarded as proactive idea generators and drivers for securing the long-term profitable growth of the organization, relieving the management's decision-making burden without any hierarchical boundaries (Langmann, 2019).

Based on the aforementioned views, the role change in controlling in the historical context can be briefly summarized in Figure 1.

As Figure 1 suggests, controlling evolved from the sole execution of financial calculations to financial planning, decision support and in-house consulting, where this transformation is further expected to be in the direction of change initiation in the organization. Parallel to the changes in executed tasks, the focus of controlling shifted from a sole operational standpoint to a future oriented strategic perspective. In the same way, the acquirement of qualitative skills in addition to that of technical gained priority.

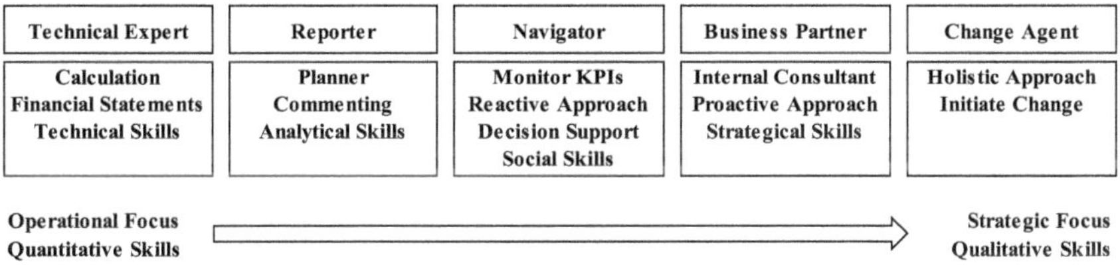

Figure 1: Controlling Role Change (own illustration).

Digital transformation: The impact on controlling

The impact of digital transformation on controlling is a multifaceted phenomenon posing numerous challenges. To illustrate, Schäffer and Weber (2016) argue that the digitalization challenges to be faced by controllers are mainly eightfold which are summarized below:

1. *Data Management* encompasses the task of controllers to ensure data quality and integrity as well as positioning of their role with respect to data science among statisticians, mathematicians and computer engineers.
2. *Self-Controlling* pertains to enabling company managers and associates to generate their own report and conduct their own analyses in which controllers are expected to set up the scene for a self-service environment which can be achieved by standardization.
3. *Agile Control* poses the challenge to cope with short-term and long-term uncertainties due to changing business models in which automated forecasting through predictive analytics is likely to support the decision-making processes, indeed their review at comparatively shorter intervals.
4. *Efficiency* is associated with the gains emanating from the standardization, automation and centralization of controlling activities creating room for controllers to add value to the organization.
5. *Business Partnering* requires the active participation of controllers in the digital transformation processes especially the evaluation of novel and digital business models in relation to resource allocation and profitable growth.
6. *Analytics* is the competence development in the fields of statistics, information technologies and data science enabling controllers to comprehend complex big data structures.
7. *New Skills* are to be continuously sought and acquired by controllers not limited to merely technical competences such as statistics and data science but to include interpersonal skills regarding communication, conflict management and resilience as well as developing a broad understanding of business in general.
8. *Controlling Mindset* is the required perception change for controllers including the switch of their traditional focus on profitability, growth and efficiency rather to the risks and chances associated with the digital business models and uncertainties.

Broadly speaking, the impact of digitalization on controlling can be mainly examined from organizational and process-related perspectives. Centralization trends and the establishment of shared service centers (SCCs) can be regarded as the organizational consequences of digital transformation. On the other hand, as summarized by Langmann (2019), the central concepts of digital transformation in relation to finance and controlling processes can be mainly classified under four dimensions, which are big data analysis, business analytics, robotic process automation (RPA) and machine learning, respectively.

Centralization and shared service centers

There is a growing trend among especially multinational companies to set up worldwide SSCs of their own in certain regions that offer administrative and operational services such as with respect to accounting, payroll, warehouse management, indirect purchasing, foreign trade and human resources processes. Whereas the improvements in the communication and IT fields have enabled the establishment of global service centers, cultural, time zone and language differences can be thought of as the challenges of this approach (Dressler, 2012, p. 107).

Quoting from the study on future trends in controlling conducted by Schäffer and Weber (2015), Becker, Ulrich and Fibitz (2016) report that the level of standardization in controlling processes are relatively high and expected to increase in the future. In addition, the authors explain that the establishment of SCCs is one of the primary results of standardization and centralization. Pointing out the work of Schmitz, Lawrenz and Drerup (2016), the authors refer to *reporting factories* as a special version of SSCs, in which standardized reports are distributed, thanks to the advancements in data management tools (Becker et al., 2016, p. 11).

The notion of shared services can be traced back to two decades that is currently a hot topic for business enterprises that are seeking alternative ways to secure their competitiveness through primarily focusing on their core competences. In other words, assigning support functions to shared SSCs that are bundled in low cost countries create additional financial benefits (Fries & Noldus, 2016). Clustering standard business activities together in a centralized way in particular locations, SSCs offer cost advantages through labor cost arbitrage over decentralized alternatives which are present in all company locations especially for business enterprises of medium and large size (Dornbusch, 2016).

Fach and Lawrenz (2016) illuminate that SSCs incorporate transactional and highly repetitive tasks with relatively low customer interaction and need for decision-making which are mainly financial accounting relevant tasks such as invoice-to-pay (creditor postings), bill-to-cash (customer invoicing), etc. The authors argue that the SSC concept can be applied to controlling activities through *Centers of Excellence* (CoEs).

Pointing out the work of Fach (2014), the authors quote a threefold development path for CoEs:

1. *Reporting Centers*, coined alternatively as reporting factories, generate automated standardized reports from a central platform possibly without commenting in which line managers are the primary customers.
2. *Decision Support Centers* offer ad-hoc analyses including forecasting activities for controlling business partners and group controlling.
3. *Decision and Planning Centers* present extensive analyses for the top management and drive the planning processes for the organization as a whole.

Big data

According to the World Economic Outlook report of the International Monetary Fund (IMF, 2019), the global economy entered into a slowdown phase starting from the second half of 2018 onwards and dropped from almost 4.0% (2017) to 3.2% (2018, second half). Projections show that the growth rate is expected to be 3.6% in 2020, which is below the 2017 level. Especially in periods that are characterized with financial downturns and macroeconomic imbalances, controllers are not in such a position to support the decision-making processes with an inward-looking approach and utilize information merely from own company financials. In addition to changing macroeconomic circumstances, the mindset change in business practices triggered by the digital transformation trends requires now the close monitoring, analysis and conclusion of external information.

The use of external data has some advantages over internal data. Whereas the information in company financials reflect the past and are historical, market data may be available on a daily basis hence with less information lag incorporating fair values as well. On the other hand, external data have less availability compared to internally generated information.

At this point, two approaches that can be suggested are:

1. The time lag in the analysis of internal data is to be eliminated.
2. Methods aimed at incorporating and concluding external data are to be introduced.

Flowing into the organization's data warehouse similar to internally generated ERP data, external information in the form of voluminous unstructured "big data" are integrated in reporting, financial forecasts as well as used for detecting market trends through data science techniques such as sentiment analysis (Langmann, 2019). In this sense, big data can be defined by referring to such characteristics as variety, velocity and volume, which is indeed subject to advanced analytics techniques and technologies so as to derive cause-and-effect relationships (Corea, 2019). The effects of digital transformation will be felt comparatively in a more intensive way in multinational companies and large enterprises operating in the fields of, e.g., banking, insurance, telecommunications, utilities which are characterized with voluminous customer data and daily transactions (Langmann, 2019).

While controlling has been traditionally dealing with internally generated structured data accessible from the company ERP systems, digital transformation trends as well as the business partnership roles require controllers to consider external data from diverse sources. In other words, the integration of big data analytics in the controlling processes is likely to result in accelerated decision-making, improved management reporting and analyses, high-accuracy and real time forecasting, expansion of existing businesses and creation of novel business models (Weichel & Herrmann, 2016).

On the other hand, Gadatsch (2016) explains that controllers are primarily familiar with structured information derived from the company ERP systems that are the basis for reporting, analysis and forecasting processes to support the company management and strategic decision-making. In addition, the author considers big data not only relevant for IT experts but also for controllers, who may process real time external data such as from machines, sensors, social media, etc. hence creating additional value for corporate decision-making.

Similarly, Gentsch and Kulpa (2016) argue that controlling is one of the big data relevant organization units in a business enterprise owing to the fact that it deals with information to support company management and strategic decision-making to secure profitability and competitiveness. In this context, information to be used in this process is not limited to internally generated data but also from external resources, which implies big data in the brand-new digital business world.

Business analytics

Business analytics encompasses the use of statistical analysis methods such as regression analyses, decision trees, neural networks, etc. to support the decision-making processes in the enterprises (Langmann, 2019).

Predictive analytics implies the application of statistical tools and techniques in an effort to forecast future trends, conditions or values with particular probabilities of realization, the outcomes of which are incorporated in future oriented reporting as well as decision support by enterprises. Segmentation, association, classification, regression analysis and prognosis are the five process steps in predictive analytics methods in which data are grouped based on similarities, frequencies and patterns. Within this scope, causalities are determined, unclassified elements are categorized, relationships are explained and finally future values are derived, respectively (Iffert, 2016). Hence, the outcomes of predictive analytics can be used to detect signals for the upcoming events, which may imply an early warning system (Gentsch & Kulpa, 2016).

Another application area of business analytics includes data visualization, which enables individuals to understand and comprehend information. It is also an accompanying subject of big data in that traditional data illustration methods such as tables, pie charts, column graphs or figures with simple lines may be inadequate to visualize large volume of data as well as associations and causalities therein; moreover treemapping, heatmaps and sankey charts can be the examples for new visualization methods (Losbichler, Eisl & Plank, 2016). Microsoft Power BI, Tableu, QlikView, Oracle BI are some examples from business intelligence software used for visualizing information.

The acquirement of data visualization competences is vital for controllers arising from the fact that controllers are no longer suppliers of information but rather in-house consultants deriving conclusions from data analysis for strategic decision-making. The numbers presented by controllers are to tell a story, and business intelligence software can be regarded as storytelling instruments in the controllers' toolbox.

Robotic process automation

Robotic process automation (RPA) refers to software carrying out predefined tasks either on the user interface side or on the servers just as humans working in front of computers; in addition, once the process to be executed is defined with decision trees, the robot software follows these instructions and executes standard and repetitive operational tasks (Van der Aalst, Bichler, & Heinzl, 2018).

Automation of processes through RPA in the fields of accounting, finance and controlling are many. Robot software applications are employed in invoice-to-pay processes where RPA checks the invoices, notifies the relevant associate in case of discrepancies, post the invoices, releases the payment and conducts reconciliation with the creditor (Langmann, 2019). In addition, RPA is employed in standardized month-end closing processes, repetitive report generations and processing customer orders.

Machine learning

Machine learning, often used interchangeably with artificial intelligence (AI), is the application of mathematical data analysis methods with the aim of determining significant associations and employing them in future cases (Finlay, 2018). On the other hand, artificial intelligence can be thought of as a software with self-learning capacity implying self-generation of codes or algorithms that are not instructed or programmed by humans (Corea, 2019). Hence, artificial intelligence can be thought of as a broader concept, encompassing machine learning that pertains to the imitation of human decision-making skills by computers (Finlay, 2018).

In practice, machine learning techniques are employed to reduce uncertainty in which they are integrated in prediction models or in predictive analytics (Finlay, 2018). One of the application areas of machine learning in controlling is the cash flow projections, where the payment patterns of customers are processed based on particular variables such as historical payment behaviors, social media networks, the residence of the customer, etc. Through advanced data processing, machine learning techniques assess the weight of each possible determinant on the payment behavior while improving the prediction power each time the application is run (Langmann, 2019).

Findings

Up to now, we have reviewed the impact of digital transformation on controlling with respect to the changing roles of controllers as well as the changes in organizational structures, processes and the novel tools introduced in the transition phase. Broadly speaking, this impact can be summarized with three main dimensions, which are people, processes and products, respectively. Table 1 presented below is a concise summary of the implication of each dimension with practical examples.

As it may be inferred from Table 1, the "people" dimension implies how the job descriptions and the expected competences of controllers are affected by digital transformation. Likewise, the "process" dimension pertains to the reorganization of the controlling function within the company as well as the altering scope of controlling operations. The "product" dimension encompasses the newly introduced controlling tools and methods in the transformation process.

The classification of various impacts under the aforementioned main pillars facilitates the analysis of chances and risks associated with digital transformation in controlling. Firstly, the decision support role of controllers as internal

Table 1: Implications of Digital Transformation on Controlling

Dimension	Implication	Observation
People	Job Descriptions	Shift of controller roles from business reporters to change agents and data scientists
	Competences	Requirement of novel technical skills especially in the field of data science as well as soft skills such as communication and conflict management Intensive focus on strategic objectives rather than operations
Process	Organizational Structures	Establishment of shared service and competence centers
	Operations	Standardization and automation of controlling activities
Product	Instruments and Output	Integration of external data with company specific internal data
		Application of big data analytics and advanced statistical tools

counsellors will still be of central importance in the new digital business world as it has been the case traditionally. Nevertheless, the provided support to decision-makers is changing its form in that controllers are to integrate voluminous external market data together with firm specific data into analyses. Such an integration requires the application of new techniques such as big data analytics, advanced statistical predictive methods, artificial intelligence and machine learning. As for a key challenge, such an alteration foremost entails the acquirement of particular technical knowledge and competences which have ordinarily not been in the scope of controllers. Likewise, processing, integrating and analyzing external data is yet another challenge to be met in the near future.
Standardization and automation of operational tasks of controllers present an invaluable opportunity by creating room and capacity for strategic processes. Shifting the focal point from report generation to future-oriented analyses is likely to reinforce the role of controllers as in-house consultants. In other words, as the capacity spent on strategical tasks increases compared to that of operational, the value that is created for the company increases. In the same way, such a shift is by nature expected to cause controlling to get more involved in the assessment of current and future business models, therefore, initiating change in the organization.

The question that arises at this point is where to position controllers in the digital transformation process in the organization. Equipped with statistics and

IT knowledge, controlling can be thought of as an extension of the IT department. Adding the depth of knowledge and breadth of experience in business and management, the positioning can be expanded with regard to a business IT or strategic business development department. The emergence of new roles is likely to position controllers as data scientists and system architects working as back-end as well as front-end consultants and change agents primarily interacting with the decision-makers within the organization. Hence, the positioning of controlling in the organization in the new era is yet another challenge.

Discussion and Conclusions

Controlling is confronted with a number of compelling challenges associated with the consequences of digital transformation in today's world. Digital transformation mainly brings about considerable changes on the roles and skills sets of controllers as well as on the organizational structures, tools, methods and operations of controlling.

High level of standardization and automation emanating from digital transformation leads to both organizational as well as role changes in controlling. The shift of focal point from operational to strategic tasks due to the automation of certain daily routines such as report generation enables controllers to concentrate more on the added-value-areas for the organization by evaluating current and possible future business models. In order to act in this direction, big data and business analytics, RPA, artificial intelligence and machine learning will be the common methods and instruments in the standard toolbox of controllers. In other words, controllers are required to acquire technical skills in the field of statistics, data science and business analytics to cope with the changes with respect to digital transformation.

Standardization, automation and new competence acquirement may not be realized from today to tomorrow especially in international companies operating worldwide in different locations and should be regarded as a long-term strategic objective. The attainment of this objective requires an investment which is twofold; firstly in physical capital implying IT infrastructure and secondly in human capital pertaining to the acquirement of required future competences.

Accordingly, business enterprises are foremost recommended to treat digital transformation as a project, prepare a roadmap for guidance in this journey and define the milestones to be reached. Benchmarking with other companies already on this track as well as working with independent consulting firms are further points that can be considered. In any case, it is vital that companies take the initiative voluntarily to start this journey now before being compelled to do so due to the external circumstances that are highly probable to arise in the near future.

References

Becker, W., Ulrich, P., & Fibitz, A. (2016). Kontextfaktoren der Controlling-Organization. In U. Schäffer, & J. Weber (Eds.), *Controlling & Management Review Sonderheft 3*-2016, 8–14. doi: 10.1007/978-3-658-15682-4_1.

CIMA (2000). *Management Accounting Official Terminology*. London: CIMA.

Corea, F. (2019). *An Introduction to Data: Everything You Need to Know About AI, Big Data and Data Science*. doi: 10.1007/978-3-030-04468-8.

Dornbusch, D. (2016). Creating Value in Shared Services. In U. Schäffer, & J. Weber (Eds.), *Controlling & Management Review Sonderheft 3-2016*, 54–58. doi: 10.1007/978-3-658-15682-4_1.

Dressler, S. (2012). Der Controller als Berater für Sourcing-Entscheidungen. In U. Krings (Ed.), *Controlling als In-house-Consulting*, 93–117. doi:10.1007/978-3-8349-3757-5_4.

Drury, C. (2018). *Management and Cost Accounting* (10th ed.). Hampshire: Cengage Learning.

Fach, P. (2014). Wie viel Shared Services verträgt Controlling. In A. Gadatsch, A. Krupp, & A. Wiesehahn (Eds.), *Controlling in Forschung und Praxis: Tagungsband zur 8. Sankt Augustiner Controlling- Fachtagung*, 35, 110–114, Sankt Augustin 14.03.2014.

Fach, P., & Lawrenz, A. (2016). Shared Services Trends 2020. In U. Schäffer, & J. Weber (Eds.), *Controlling & Management Review Sonderheft 3*-2016, 60–66. doi: 10.1007/978-3-658-15682-4_1.

Finlay, S. (2018). *Artificial Intelligence and Machine Learning for Business: A No-Nonsense Guide to Data Driven Technologies* (3rd ed.). UK: Relativistic.

Fries, A., & Noldus, S. (2016). Shared Services Trends 2020. In U. Schäffer, & J. Weber (Eds.), *Controlling & Management Review Sonderheft 3*-2016, 46–52. doi: 10.1007/978-3-658-15682-4_1.

Gadatsch, A. (2016). Die Möglichkeiten von Big Data voll ausschöpfen. In U. Schäffer, & J. Weber (Eds.), *Controlling & Management Review Sonderheft 1*-2016, 61–66. doi: 10.1007/978-3-658-13444-0_1.

Gentsch, P., & Kulpa, A. (2016). Mit externen Big Data neue Möglichkeiten erschließen. In U. Schäffer, & J. Weber (Eds.), *Controlling & Management Review Sonderheft 1*-2016, 32–39. doi: 10.1007/978-3-658-13444-0_1.

Horngren, C. T., Sundem, G. L., Burgstahler, D., & Schatzberg, J. (2013). *Introduction to Management Accounting* (16th ed.). Boston: Pearson.

Iffert, L. (2016). Predictive Analytics richtig einsetzen. In U. Schäffer, & J. Weber (Eds.), *Controlling & Management Review Sonderheft 1*-2016, 16–23. doi: 10.1007/978-3-658-13444-0_1.

IMF (2019). *World Economic Outlook: Growth Slowdown, Precarious Recovery* (April 2019). Retrieved from https://www.imf.org/en/Publications/WEO/Issues/2019/03/28/world-economic-outlook-april-2019.

Küng, G. (2012). Strategisches Verhandeln für Controller: Die relevanten Wins im Win-Win-Prozess. In U. Krings (Ed.), *Controlling als In-house-Consulting*, 23–42. doi:10.1007/978-3-8349-3757-5_4.

Langmann, C. (2019). *Digitalisierung im Controlling.* doi: 10.1007/978-3-658-25017-1.

Li, W. S. (2018). *Strategic Management Accounting: A Practical Guidebook with Case Studies*. Singapore: Springer Nature.

Losbichler, H., Eisl, C., & Plank, T. (2016). Neue Visualisierungsformen auf dem Prüfstand. In U. Schäffer, & J. Weber (Eds.), *Controlling & Management Review Sonderheft 1*-2016, 46–53. doi: 10.1007/978-3-658-13444-0_1.

Plag, M. (2012). Der Controller als Change Manager. In U. Krings (Ed.), *Controlling als In-house-Consulting*, 43–62. doi:10.1007/978-3-8349-3757-5_4.

Scardovi, C. (2017). *Digital Transformation in Financial Services.* doi: 10.1007/978-3-319-66945-8.

Schäffer, U., & Weber, J. (2015). Controlling im Wandel – Die Veränderung eines Berufsbilds im Spiegel der zweiten WHU-Zukunftsstudie. In *Controlling: Zeitschrift für erfolgsorientierte Unternehmenssteuerung*, 27(3), 185–191.

Schäffer, U., & Weber, J. (2016). Digitalization will radically change controlling as we know it. *WHU Controlling & Management Review*, 60(6), 34–40. doi: 10.1007/s12176-016-0093-9.

Schmitz, M., Lawrenz, A., & Drerup, B. (2016). Reporting Factory in Controllerbereichen. In W. Becker, & P. Ulrich (Eds.), *Handbuch Controlling*, 427–458. Wiesbaden: Springer Fachmedien.

Sugahara, S., Daidj, N., & Ushio, S. (2017). *Value Creation in Management Accounting and Strategic Management: An Integrated Approach.* doi: 10.1002/9781119419921.

Van der Aalst, W. M. P., Bichler, M., & Heinzl, A. (2018). Robotic Process Automation. *Business & Information Systems Engineering*, 60(4), 269–272. doi: 10.1007/s1259.

Weichel, P., & Herrmann, J. (2016). Wie Controller von Big Data profitieren können. In U. Schäffer, & J. Weber (Eds.), *Controlling & Management Review Sonderheft 1*-2016, 8–15. doi: 10.1007/978-3-658-13444-0_1.

Lale Akarun, Necati Aras, Fatma Başak Aydemir, Ümit Bilge,
Cemre Selcen, Aslı Sencer (corresponding author), Tuna Tuğcu,
Sertaç Yerlikaya, and Sedanur Yıldız

A Survey on Digital Maturity Models for SMEs

Abstract: Under the effects of advances in information and communication technologies and rapidly changing markets, digital transformation (DX) has become the key focus for supply chains in changing the way they function to proactively adapt to their environments. At this point, assessing the current digital state of the supply chains accurately and comprehensively with reliable digital maturity models emerges as a crucial issue for the success of DX. Furthermore, noting that the DX performance of the complete supply chain is bounded by the performance of the weakest players, this assessment should find its way in all parties of the supply chain ranging from big manufacturers to the small and medium sized enterprises (SMEs) as suppliers. In this study, we review the digital maturity models in the literature with a special focus on SMEs. We compare these models with different perspectives by first highlighting the special characteristics of SMEs, then analyzing the development process considering that the maturity model is a design artifact.

Keywords: Digital transformation, Digital maturity model, Industry 4.0, Small and medium sized enterprise

Introduction

In the last decade, immense breakthroughs have occurred in information and communication technologies: Connectivity of not only digital devices but all equipment, goods and people to the internet, has enabled continuous monitoring and assessment of all resources. The small connected sensors, and their communication networks, known as Internet of Things (IoT), and Industrial IoT (IIoT) have enabled the collection of valuable data, creating the paradigm of "Big Data" (Zezulka et al., 2018). Cloud computing offers a scalable and economical solution for big data analytics. The analysis of this data using machine learning has revolutionized all fields, and artificial intelligence has become a household term. Flexible robots that can learn and work alongside humans is now a reality. On the other hand, humans of the future will be "augmented humans", equipped with wearable devices and decision analysis tools using data analytics. Computing power from the cloud to edge devices has improved, enabling scalable and unbounded computing resources. Software as a Service (SaaS), Platform as a Service (PaaS), and Infrastructure as a Service (IaaS) paradigms have enabled different outsourcing models for information technologies (Kavis, 2014). These giant advances enable significant improvements from economical production to end-to-end management of supply chain. New information technologies are also environment-friendly and allow sustainable production since they can reduce energy consumption, carbon emission, packaging material, transportation and storage costs as well as waste of raw materials (Gabriel & Pessl, 2016). However, investigating, planning, utilizing, and deploying such emerging technologies require a change of mindset and skills, a potential problem especially for SMEs.

These advances have revolutionized not only production, but all aspects of business; making transformation inevitable. This transformation is known as Digital Transformation (DX). These giant advances have allowed the supply chain to be integrated in different forms, i.e., vertically among the hierarchical levels of the manufacturing system or horizontally between the functional units of an enterprise, or end-to-end among the supply chain parties. This digital integration provides fast interactions and collaborations between the parties that further enable the supply chain to implement dynamic business models in which a new level of value is created for the customer. Examples are numerous depending on the part of the supply chain that digitally integrates and collaborates. An end-to-end integration between the suppliers and the manufacturer provides the supply chain with the ability to instantly alter the order specifications, order quantities, delivery locations as well as the payment schemes. The level of agility and the customer value is further improved as the scope of digital integration is increased to include the distributors, retailers, and customers.

Indeed, the value creation by new business models is not only pushed by the advances in ICT, but also pulled by the frequently changing customer requirements. From the customer behavior perspective, advances in ICT have created a new customer who demands high flexibility with low cost and rapid response in all services. Hence, it is inevitable for the supply chains to consider these two forces while digitally transforming their processes.

DX is about transforming processes digitally by integrating different parties in the supply chain and generating smart systems based on data analysis and decision-making methodologies. Apparently, the level of value created in the supply chain by DX depends on the level of integration provided by ICT and the level of intelligence of the decision-making environment. A successful DX supports the supply chains for being proactive rather than reactive; hence, it provides agility to the supply chains in adapting to their rapidly changing environments.

In many studies, the processes of DX of an enterprise are enumerated as the following stages: creating DX awareness, analyzing the current digital state, generating digital targets, and developing road maps and implementing them (Wang, Wang & Anderl, 2016). Apparently, the success of DX in an enterprise is dependent on the success of all of these stages. At this point, assessing the current digital state of the supply chains accurately and comprehensively with reliable digital maturity models emerges as a key factor for the success of DX.

In this study, we consider the digital maturity models in the literature with a special focus on small and medium sized enterprises (SMEs). Our aim is to compare these models with respect to several aspects by highlighting the special characteristics of SMEs and generate further research directions.

Our motivations are manifold in this academic research. First of all, to pursue the aforementioned goals of DX in supply chains, the assessment of digital maturity should find its way to all parties of the supply chain ranging from big players to the SMEs, which may take many responsibilities apart from the role of suppliers. Noting that the DX performance of overall supply chain is bounded by the performance of the weakest players, the DX of SMEs deserve no less interest than the bigger parties in the supply chain. Quite the contrary: the DX of the supply chain performed under the ignorance of the digital maturity levels of the SMEs is subject to significant failures in value creation. Nevertheless, in spite of their smaller sizes, SMEs have gained significant responsibilities in new product development, shipment, maintenance, and repair services in the last decade. Wang et al. (2016) support this assertion by highlighting the critical role of SMEs in decreasing the batch sizes to one as a requirement of high flexibility requested by the new customer. So, the digital assessment of SMEs emerges as a significant research area in evaluating the level of digitalization of supply chains.

Secondly, as the backbone of the manufacturing industry, SMEs have realized their significant impact on the supply chain performance. However, SMEs face different challenges and barriers as compared to larger companies, and few of them can successfully digitalize their processes (Mittal, Khan, Romero & Wuest, 2018). This issue is highlighted in the EU Horizon 2020 Project, SME 4.0 (2019) in which the SMEs that can successfully manage their DX are referred to as SME4.0. So, the research in this area is expected to find considerable interest among SMEs.

Thirdly, although there are numerous studies in the literature for generating digital maturity models for multi-national enterprises (MNEs), only a few of them focus on supporting SMEs' evolutionary path and paradigm shift toward smart manufacturing. Indeed, SMEs are considerably different from MNEs in many aspects, such as financial resources, technical resource availability, product specialization, organizational culture, employee participation, alliances with universities and research institutions, and collaboration. Considering these different characteristics, specialized digital maturity models are needed for SMEs (Mittal et al., 2018; Wang et al., 2016).

Finally, we realize that over a hundred maturity models have been developed in the last decade to support IT management. In great majority of these studies, the authors do not explicitly mention how they develop their maturity model or explain how they validate it. Furthermore, the documentations of evaluation approaches are usually poor. Becker, Knacksted and Pöppelbuß (2009) consider a digital maturity model as a design science artifact and generate their well-known eight-step procedural framework for the design of maturity models. Since following these steps is a scientific assurance of the maturity model as a design science artifact, we further extend our study to discover the scientific level of existing digital maturity models for SMEs.

Method

We start by exploring the digital assessment methodologies that are specialized for SMEs. We base our search on the most recent and comprehensive review paper by Mittal et al. (2018) where 15 studies relevant to SMEs are identified and compared in accordance to their relevance to the SME specific requirements, as summarized below. Their findings indicate that none of these studies incorporate all aspects of SMEs. Indeed, only five of them partially consider these concerns. In our study, we consider the frameworks where some concerns of SME characteristics are included (Wang et al., 2016; Ganzarain & Errasti, 2016; Jung, Kulvatunyou, Choi & Brundage, 2016; Lee, Jun, Chang & Park, 2017; Lichtblau et al., 2015).

Our first set of evaluation criteria includes i) aim of research, ii) dimensions of the framework, iii) SME characteristics considered, iv) type of integration considered (horizontal/vertical/end-to-end), v) application sector, vi) existence of a self-assessment tool, vii) existence of a road map in addition to the assessment framework. The attributes summarized in Table 1 are selected to overcome the aforementioned drawbacks and provide a correct guidance in developing a digital index specialized for SMEs. Secondly, we consider the study by Becker et al. (2009), where a procedural model is proposed for the development of maturity models as a design artifact, and to remedy the widespread shortcomings when these steps are ignored. Based on the eight requirements for the development of maturity models indicated above, we compare our selected frameworks. We finalize our study by identifying guidelines for generating a comprehensive and valid digital assessment model for SMEs.

Table 1: Comparison of digital maturity models.

Model	Aim	The Evaluation Framework and the DX Process	SME Characteristics	Type of Integration	Industry	Self Assessment Tool	Roadmap
GPMI4.0 Wang et al. (2016) Wang et al. (2017) Wang et al. (2018a) Wang et al. (2018b)	To generate a self-assessment framework for SMEs by the use of Generic Procedure Model I4.0 (GPMI4.0) and to give SMEs a guidance on how to address Industrie 4.0, i.e., identify enterprise-specific technology solutions, optimize existing processes, advance existing business models, exploit new business models.	- General DX framework that includes stages for Preparation, Analysis, Idea generation, Valuation and Implementation. - Assessment by Toolboxes for Products, Production, Intralogistics, Assembly, Engineering, IT security and Business model. Each toolbox represents an assessment criterion that includes six sub-criteria referred to as application levels. - Evaluation in 5 classes generated in accordance to the technological and sequential development stages that vary between zero level and I4.0 vision.	Product, Production, Intralogistics, Assembly, Engineering toolboxes should consider the concerns for technical and financial resource availabilities, as well as the standards considerations and alliances for R&D. High product specialization at SMEs should be noted. IT security toolbox should consider technical and financial resource availabilities, as well as lack of standards considerations and alliances for R&D. Business model toolbox should include employee participation, organizational concerns and collaboration culture. Financial constraints and technical resource availabilities are partially considered since a step-by-step improvement in digitalization is suggested.	Vertical Horizontal End-to-end	Manuf.	Yes	The Valuation stage of DX includes the roadmap that is supported by the targets generated in Idea Generation. Explanations are given on its procedure, methods and results.
Collaborative Diversification Model Ganzarain and Errasti (2016)	To develop a Collaborative Diversification Model for SMEs where new opportunities for collaborative business can be created by exploiting the strengths of companies within Industry 4.0.	- General DX framework that includes stages for Envision 4.0 Vision, Enable 4.0 Roadmap, Enact 4.0 Projects. - Main perspectives are Market, Product, Process, and Value network. - Scoring with maturity levels for: 1: Initial, 2: Managed, 3: Defined, 4: Transformed, 5: Detailed BPM	Market and Value network criteria should include concerns for collaboration, employee participation and organizational culture. Product and Process criteria should consider technical and financial resource availabilities, as well as lack of standards considerations and alliances for R&D. High product specialization at SMEs should be noted.	Horizantal End-to-end	Advanced manuf., Energy, Advanced electronics, Digital business	No	Enable 4.0 Roadmap stage of DX includes the roadmap, but no details are given on how it follows the assessment.
SMSRL Model Jung et al. (2016) Jung et al. (2017)	To help large and small manufacturers determine their current Smart Manufacturing System Readiness Level (SMSRL) and develop a customized improvement plan.	- General DX framework that include stages for Profiling the current state, Assessing the current state with respect to a reference model and Developing an improvement plan. - Main dimensions of the profiling stage are C1: Organizational Maturity, C2: IT Maturity, C3: Performance Management Maturity, C4: Information Connectivity. - Assessment methodology is based on CMMI, i.e., activity maturity scoring, incidence matrix-based similartiy measure. The scores in each dimension are used to generate a single SMSRL index.	C1: Organizational maturity, C2: IT maturity, C3: Performance maturity, C4: Information connectivity maturity should consider the concerns for technical and financial resource availabilities, as well as the standards considerations and alliances for R&D. High product specialization at SMEs should be noted. The reference model is a way of including standardization, but the measures are difficult to be evaluated by SMEs.	Vertical Horizontal	Manuf.	No	Developing an improvement plan stage of DX includes the roadmap. The details of the roadmap are planned for future studies.
ANP Model Lee et al. (2017)	To evaluate and rank the SMEs that are clustered with respect to the importance of their value chain. Analytic Network Process (ANP) methodology is used to create a network structure that incorporates correlations among evaluation criteria.	- No general DX framework is provided. - Assessment is made with 10 sub-criteria that are grouped under 4 main criteria: Leadership (Leadership & Strategy), Process (product development, production planning, process control, quality control, facility management, logistics management), System automation (information management, facility automation), Performance (performance assessment). Each sub-criterion includes 3-6 assessment items. - Clustered SMEs are evaluated and ranked by Analytic Network Process. Scores are reflected under 5 levels for Checking, Monitoring, Control, Optimization, and Autonomy.	Leadership criterion should include concerns for collaboration, employee participation and organizational culture. Process, System automation and Performance criteria should consider technical and financial resource availabilities, as well as lack of standards considerations and alliances for R&D. High product specialization at SMEs should be noted.	Vertical Horizontal	Manuf.	No	Not specified.
IMPULS Lichtblau et al. (2015)	To develop an online self-assessment tool, IMPULS based on Industry 4.0 Readiness Framework so that companies in all sizes can assess their own levels of digitalization and compare their performance.	- No general DX framework is provided. - Main dimensions are Strategy and organization, Smart factory, Smart operations, Smart products, Data-driven services, and Employees and companies. - Scoring is made in 6 levels including 0-level to classify in three classes as Newcomers, Learners, and Leaders.	Strategy and organization, and Employees and Companies criteria should include concerns for collaboration, employee participation and organizational culture. Smart factory, Smart operations, Smart products, Data-driven services criteria should consider technical and financial resource availabilities, as well as lack of standards considerations and alliances for R&D. High product specialization at SMEs should be noted. IMPULS is applicable to all small enterprises with 0-19 employees and less than €1 Million sales, but no concerns of SME characteristics are stated.	Vertical Horizontal	Manuf.	Yes	Not specified, but action items are identified for improvement.

Special characteristics of SMEs

Before going into our findings, we further dwell in the differentiating characteristics of SMEs that will be used to generate perspectives in comparing digital maturity models specialized for SMEs. Mittal et al. (2018) identify 17 features that differentiate SMEs from MNEs based on the following studies in the literature: (Kennedy & Hyland, 2003; Terziovski, 2010; Wuest & Thoben, 2012; Kumar, Khurshid & Waddell, 2014; Vasudevan & Chawan, 2014; Dyerson, Spinelli & Harindranath, 2016; Müller, Dotzauer & Voigt, 2017). These features are classified under eight clusters as financial resources, technical resource availability, product specialization, standards consideration, organizational culture, employee participation, alliances with universities and research institutions, and collaboration (Tables 2 and 3 in Mittal et al., 2018).

It appears that SMEs are already doing significantly better than MNEs when it comes to producing specialized products. Noting that all SMEs outperform MNEs in this context, it is advised not to include this criterion in digital maturity models for SMEs (Mittal et al., 2018).

However, SMEs are not able to keep their favorable position against MNEs for the rest of the clusters, and they require improvement in all. SMEs are absolutely in a disadvantageous position in financial resources and technical resource availability such as use of advanced manufacturing technologies and software including data analytics. Standards considerations are low in SMEs. Next, SMEs have less complex organizational structures making them more preferred in DX. However, this is not enough to place SMEs in a favorable position in organizational culture cluster since they lack the required formality. Furthermore, flexibility of leadership and decision-making environments in SMEs are restricted to the leader with a weak focus on knowledge transfer within the organization. In terms of employee participation, SMEs have human resources in multiple domains making it difficult for them to generate specialized domains such as the automation technology in an MNE. Furthermore, SME employees are also more likely to lack the exposure to mentors, workshops, and supervised industrial training. Therefore, although SMEs might gain deep experiences by focusing on a specific area, there is still a lack of employee participation. It is not easy for SMEs to generate cross-disciplinary networking opportunities. As a result, they are not able to update themselves with the ongoing, cutting-edge research and establish alliances with universities and research institutes. Finally, SMEs are in an unfavorable position in terms of collaboration. The knowledge and wisdom of SMEs are often focused in a specific domain, so they outsource many essential activities. They use a small number of suppliers/vendors and consequently have an extreme dependence on them. So, the collaborative network of SMEs is not that strong.

All in all, SMEs need to develop their own, unique smart manufacturing or Industry 4.0 (I4.0) vision and roadmap. Our study provides insights that help toward developing a realistic digital maturity model for SMEs that reflects their industrial realities more accurately.

Findings

We present our findings first by explaining each framework in Table 1.

Generic Procedure Model to Introduce Industrie 4.0 in Small and Medium-sized Enterprises (Wang et al., 2016)

Wang et al. (2016) provide the most holistic view of DX processes that include the stages for i) preparation, ii) analysis, iii) idea generation, iv) valuation, and v) implementation. Digital assessment is considered as the integral part of the analysis and idea generation stages in DX.

With the aim of giving SMEs a guidance on how to address I4.0 by identifying technology-based solutions, optimizing existing processes, and exploiting new business models, toolboxes are generated to assess I4.0 competencies from different perspectives. The first version of the Generic Procedure Model to Introduce I4.0 (GPMI4.0) toolbox includes four perspectives: products, production, intralogistics, and assembly (Wang et al., 2016). Later, it is enhanced to include three new perspectives: IT security, new business models, and engineering in I4.0 (Wang, Fakhry & Anderl, 2017; Wang, Tran & Anderl, 2018a; Wang, Faath, Goerne & Anderl, 2018b).

An assessment with respect to an I4.0 perspective is made on a table where the rows include the application levels of I4.0, ranging from the basic, up to the most advanced levels for that perspective. Each application level is assessed in columns, in accordance to its development stage where I4.0 vision is the maximum. The toolboxes help to generate an overview of I4.0 competencies by allocating the development stage of each application level.

The idea generation stage provides a set of fields of actions toward I4.0 targets by using the actual positioning of the company in its sector, the capabilities of its suppliers, and the expectations of its customers. Next, the costs of these actions are evaluated in the valuation phase to provide a road map in the form of clear action plans. Finally, the roadmap actions are implemented for successful results.

The *product* toolbox is used to explore which hardware is used, how they communicate, the functionalities of data storage and information exchange, types of monitoring by using the data, product-related IT services, and business models generated around the product. The *production toolbox* considers the application levels of digitalization in production processes. It gives an overview of the integration of the production system with the functional units in the enterprise as well as the parties in the supply chain. *Intralogistics* toolbox is concerned with the flow of information, material, parts and goods within the facility with the aim of optimizing the internal production and distribution processes. The *assembly toolbox* considers the assembly processes that are not covered in the production toolbox with a special focus on the flexibility of the architecture, level of IoT integration of the assembly system, information storage of assembly processes in the form of products, resources, etc. *IT security toolbox* aims to assign protection measures to threats and vulnerabilities of a system for I4.0. (Wang et al., 2017). *Engineering toolbox* is used to assess the engineering competence of the enterprise regarding I4.0. Its aim is to measure how inputs are optimized during the new product development phase so that a higher level of digitalization is obtained in the production field (Wang et al., 2018b). The *business model toolbox* is focused on the development of the new business models with aspects from product development to production improvement (Wang et al., 2018a). In addition to the assessment of factors effecting the efficiency of lot size one production or shortening delivery times, sale models and revenue models are considered to understand if the business model is accurate for the status obtained in the other toolboxes.

Three stage maturity model in SMEs toward industry 4.0. (Ganzarain & Errasti, 2016)

The aim of this three-stage maturity model is to develop new value propositions for new business opportunities for SMEs working in collaboration with different companies and exploiting the strengths of each of the companies within I4.0. The framework seeks to identify collaborative opportunities among companies in the fields of digital business, advanced manufacturing, energy, and advanced electronics. Three stages of DX are developed based on strategic guidance toward I4.0 by Schumacher, Erol and Sihn (2016). These are identified as; i) envision as vision, ii) enable as roadmap, and iii) enact as projects. Here, the roadmap stage includes identifying the requirements to achieve the I4.0 strategy defined in the previous stage and analyze the technologic capabilities with the perspectives of market, product, process, and value network.

The assessment is made through a five-level maturity scale, i.e., 1-Initial: lack of I4.0 vision; 2-Managed: existence of a structured I4.0 vision, customer segmentation and expectations, and non-prioritized projects; 3-Defined: existence of a comprehensive I4.0 strategy with capability specification, definition of value propositions and evaluated project proposals; 4-Transform: existence of a clear vision turned into actual projects with defined resources and capabilities; 5-Detailed Business Model: readiness for the future challenges of I4.0 with managed projects, covered risk factors, and adapted new business models.

An overview of a smart manufacturing system readiness assessment (Jung et al., 2016)

Smart Manufacturing System Readiness Level (SMSRL) is focused on first, helping manufacturers determine their current level in smart manufacturing and second, developing a customized improvement plan. The proposed assessment is held in the following three stages: i) profiling the current state, ii) assessing the current state, and iii) developing an improvement plan.

In the profiling current state stage, the scope is determined; then, information is collected and consolidated with the stakeholders for the activities within the scope. The profiling is made with respect to these dimensions: C1: Organizational Maturity, C2: IT Maturity, C3: Performance Management Maturity, and C4: Information Connectivity. Assessment of the current state is made in comparison with the reference activity model proposed by Jung, Choi, Kulvatunyou, Cho, and Morris, (2017). Computational methods such as counting measures based on the capability maturity model integration (CMMI), as well as incidence scoring schemes or matrix-based similarity measures are used to generate a single SMSRL index.

Finally, the dimensions of the simulated SMSRL results can be clustered by k-means analysis to develop an improvement plan.

A smartness assessment framework for smart factories using analytic network process (Lee et al., 2017)

A smartness assessment framework is developed based on analytic network process (ANP) evaluation and clustering of SMEs with respect to the importance of their value chain. ANP is used to create a network structure that can incorporate correlations among criteria that are influential for evaluating the performance assessment of a smart factory. It is shown that in practice the information on SME clusters and the interdependencies among criteria are the essential characteristics to be considered in developing an assessment framework.

The level of management activities analyzed through three phases are as follows: strategic planning, management control, and operational control. The operational requirements must be addressed in order to make the management activities smarter. Therefore, an evaluation framework is generated where operational requirements can be analyzed with 10 different sub-criteria that are placed under four main criteria. *Leadership* includes the leadership and strategy sub-criterion. *Process* includes the sub-criteria for product development, production planning, process control, quality control, facility management, and logistics management. *System automation* includes the sub-criteria for information management and facility automation. *Performance* includes performance assessment sub-criterion. Each sub-criterion includes 3–6 assessment items. A hierarchical cluster analysis is made to classify SMEs in terms of the importance of sub-criteria for process sub-criterion that reflects a classification in terms of their value chain. Next, the weights of each sub-criterion are determined for each SME cluster in accordance with an ANP evaluation. Hence, an evaluation framework is generated for three clusters of SMEs, respectively.

Scoring the maturity level of a smart factory is reflected under five levels, i.e., (1) Checking: no monitoring; (2) Monitoring: external monitoring with gathered data; (3) Control: monitored data can be used in meaningful analysis; (4) Optimization: improvements can be made based on the analysis; and (5) Autonomy: self-optimization.

Impuls (Lichtblau et al., 2015)

IMPULS – Industrie 4.0 Readiness framework provides an assessment for mechanical engineering and manufacturing enterprises in six dimensions including 18 items to indicate readiness in a 5-level Likert scale.

In the *strategy and organization* dimension, the aim is to assess the capabilities to develop new business models based on digital technologies. It questions the implementation of I4.0 strategy and usage of indicators, usage of different I4.0 technologies, I4.0 investments and management of innovation among different departments of the company. *Smart Factory* dimension is measuring the level of cross-enterprise collaboration between production systems, information systems, and people. Machine-to-machine communication, human-machine interaction, and data collection of machines and processes are examined with the existence of information systems. Production and production planning are assessed in the *smart operations* dimension; the level of vertical and horizontal integration of the company, existence of autonomous production processes and their data flow, data security applications, and cloud services usage are measured. Flexible, smart and effective products are the outcomes of the smart factory applications and are examined under *smart product* dimension. Technological functionalities like product memory, identification, localization, and monitoring are measured. Another major keystone of I4.0 is *data-driven services* as the data collected through different processes of production can be used for new business opportunities. The organizational aspect of the I4.0 competences are measured under *employees* dimension. Technological skills like data analytics, IT infrastructure, data security, and automation collaboration software as well as non-technical skills like system thinking and process understanding are evaluated.

Overall comparison of maturity models

Based on the attributes provided in Table 1, an overall comparison can be provided. The studies differ from each other in the way they conceive the assessment framework among DX stages. The toolboxes of Wang et al. (2016) are proposed to be used during the Analysis and Idea Generation stages of general DX processes. Likewise, Ganzarain and Errasti (2016) position their assessment model in the Enable 4.0 Roadmap stage of DX. Jung et al. (2016) place their framework in Profiling the Current Stage of the DX process. Lee et al. (2017) and Lichtblau et al. (2015) focus only on the assessment of I4.0 competencies without an overall view of DX.

In general, the DX frameworks include a Roadmap stage in which the assessment outputs are transformed into precise steps for DX. Wang et al. (2016), Ganzarain and Errasti (2016), and Jung et al. (2016) propose their assessment models to act as the basis for the generation of a roadmap which includes the implementation guidelines of DX specific to the enterprise. Lee et al. (2017) do not specify a roadmap. Lichtblau et al. (2015) identify action items for improvement.

Frameworks can be compared with respect to the evaluation dimensions they include. Digitalization levels in product design, production process, and intralogistics are the areas from which the idea of I4.0 emerged, so they appear in almost all assessment approaches. Organizational perspectives, leadership and strategy, and employees criteria appear in the recent versions of these studies by noting that the success of DX highly depends on these aspects. Business models, value network, and collaboration culture reflect the disruptive effects of DX in the way of doing business, and they are recognized in the recent works of Wang et al. (2018a), and Ganzarain and Errasti (2016). Some studies consider information connectivity and data-driven services separately in addition to the above areas (Jung et al., 2016; Lichtblau et al., 2015). Finally, IT security appears as one of the most critical areas of DX in the recent study by Wang et al. (2017).

The frameworks are quite similar in their scorings. However, considering the drawbacks in the organizational culture and employee capabilities of SMEs, the digital assessment requires consultancy support. Nevertheless, this is not easy for SMEs considering their financial limitations (Mittal et al., 2018). Furthermore, finding the right consultant is a challenge as SMEs are not close to research institutes or consultancy firms. One way of tackling these problems is to generate self-assessment tools for SMEs. Wang et al. (2016) provide a practical self-assessment tool that helps companies to assess their current status in company workshops. Lichtblau et al. (2015) generate a practical online tool for SMEs to assess themselves and compare with others.

It is not very surprising to find that all frameworks are focused on the manufacturing industry, since I4.0 concepts emerged from the idea of vertical integration in manufacturing enterprises. However, the advances in ICT extend connectivity to end-to-end integration to create collaborative business models with suppliers and customers. Wider integration and industry options are considered in (Wang et al., 2018a) and (Ganzarain and Errasti, 2016).

Finally, we explore how these studies incorporate SME characteristics into their frameworks. Mittal et al. (2018) classify the special characteristics of SMEs and state that none of the existing frameworks includes all. We further explore this issue by matching the SME characteristics with the assessment dimensions to create awareness of the significance of these characteristics on the performance of SMEs in the dimensions involved. First of all, noting that all SMEs have improved their capabilities of product customization, the digitalization level of the product is expected to be high. Secondly, the fact that financial and technical limitations induce obstacles should be recognized in the evaluations for product design, production, assembly, automation, intralogistics, operations, engineering, as well as IT maturity, connectivity, performance maturity, and data-driven services. Furthermore, SME drawbacks in organizational culture, employee participation, and collaboration should affect the analysis and evaluation in the dimensions for business models, market, value network, organizational maturity, leadership, strategy, and employees. Finally, it should be recognized that limitations on standard considerations and lack of alliances with research institutions induce obstacles for digital improvements in all areas including products, production, operations, IT security, performance management, connectivity, and data-driven services.

Comparison of maturity models based on the Procedure Model of Becker et al. (2009)

Becker et al. (2009) define eight requirements based on the design science description of Hevner, March, Park, and Ram (2004). Their eight-step procedure includes i) comparison with existing maturity models, ii) development with an iterative procedure by proposing, refining, evaluating, and enhancing solutions, iii) evaluation of the usefulness, quality, and effectiveness of the model, iv) use of thoroughly adapted and well-grounded research methods for the development of the model, v) identification of problem relevance to researchers and practitioners, vi) problem definition, vii) targeted presentation of results based on the application conditions and target users, and viii) providing scientific documents for the development process.

The GMPI4.0 framework of Wang et al. (2016) is one of the earliest and most comprehensive studies. The model is generated iteratively by improving the earlier versions of the assessment framework. They first published the product and production toolboxes and improved these by adding new ones, i.e., intralogistics, assembly, engineering, IT security, and business models. The framework was presented in several workshops and conferences, and the progresses were published as academic papers which proved that the models were developed by appropriate research methods. The models were validated with several project and workshop formats.

The development process in (Ganzarain & Errasti, 2016) is not stated explicitly; no comparisons are made with the existing studies, and the methodology is not clear. A pilot study supported by the government is stated to take place to verify and validate the model. Documentations and publications still need to be completed.

Jung et al. (2016) generate the SMSRL index by comparing it with the existing indices like technology readiness level, manufacturing readiness level, and supply chain readiness level. The model is based on the reference activity model developed by Jung et al. (2017). Although the iterative development of the model is not clearly stated, the validation of the framework as well as the methodologies used are explicitly explained. The study is presented in conferences and published as an academic paper.

Lee et al. (2017) provide a detailed comparison of their approach with the existing studies that include the IMPULS model (Lichtblau et al., 2015), the Korean Productivity Center, and the European Foundation for Quality Management. The iterative model development procedure is clearly explained by stating how the criteria network is constructed and how the criteria weights of the ANP methodology are calculated. A case study is made among 20 SMEs to test the effectiveness of the model. It is presented and published as an academic paper.

The IMPULS model by Lichtblau et al. (2015) is developed iteratively by conducting workshops with companies and by using the expertise of the project partners, based on a survey conducted with 431 companies. The framework is validated with empirical studies. The model is published as an online self-assessment tool for SMEs.

The frameworks can be evaluated as design science artifacts if the models include formal documentation that provides the information for the basic requirements in (Becker et al., 2009). In many cases, either the comparison with the existing studies is not sufficient, or the iterative procedure is not explicitly stated, or the evaluation of the performance of the methodology is unclear. Presentations in academic conferences and documentations in the form of academic papers should be accompanied by professional meetings and detailed tool documents. Nevertheless, the intension to incorporate the SME characteristics into the assessment framework should be explicitly stated in the problem definition. Accordingly, the GMPI4.0 (Wang et al., 2016) and IMPULS (Lichtblau et al., 2015) should be rated higher than the other studies.

Conclusions

Our research study shows that comprehensive digital maturity models have been developed for SMEs that include DX dimensions ranging from product and process to organizational culture, to IT security and new business models. However, SMEs have special characteristics that still need to be reflected in the existing digital maturity models. These characteristics should be interpreted as limitations on the maximum performance expectations from SMEs. Research studies should generate new ideas for providing reasonable guidance to SMEs in developing their specific DX roadmaps and to help them overcome these limitations. In our study, we provide a matching of the SME characteristics with the evaluation dimensions in which they have significant impacts.

Noting the critical role of SMEs in the success of the DX of the supply chain, we highlight the need for practical online self-assessment tools for SMEs. Moreover, the evaluation frameworks should be applicable on wider integration levels and on a broader range of industries where the SMEs are taking roles.

Finally, let us note our concerns on the arbitrariness of the framework developments. Based on the requirements in (Becker et al., 2009), we argue that design science principles should be successfully implemented during the development of digital maturity models for SMEs so that these frameworks can serve as design science artifacts.

Acknowledgements

This study has been carried out by the Industry 4.0 Platform at Bogazici University as part of a research project supported by Istanbul Development Agency (Grant# TR10-18-YMP-0171).

References

Becker, J., Knackstedt, R., & Pöppelbuß, J. (2009). Developing maturity models for IT management. *Business & Information Systems Engineering*, *1*(3), 213–222.

Dyerson, R., Spinelli, R., & Harindranath, G. (2016). Revisiting IT readiness: An approach for small firms. *Industrial Management & Data Systems*, *116*(3), 546–563.

Gabriel, M., & Pessl, E. (2016). Analysis of environmental potential by implementing industry 4.0. International Scientific Journal "Industry 4.0", *1*(2), 141-144.

Ganzarain, J., & Errasti, N. (2016). Three stage maturity model in SME's toward industry 4.0. *Journal of Industrial Engineering and Management*, *9*(5), 1119–1128.

Hevner, A. R., March, S. T., Park, J., & Ram, S. (2004). Design science in information systems research. *MIS Quarterly*, *28*(1), 75–105.

Jung, K., Choi, S., Kulvatunyou, B., Cho, H., & Morris, K. C. (2017). A reference activity model for smart factory design and improvement. *Production planning & control*, 28(2), 108–122.

Jung, K., Kulvatunyou, B., Choi, S., & Brundage, M. P. (2016). An overview of a smart manufacturing system readiness assessment. In *IFIP International Conference on Advances in Production Management Systems*, Springer, *Cham*, 705–712.

Kavis, M. J. (2014). *Architecting the cloud: design decisions for cloud computing service models (SaaS, PaaS, and IaaS)*, John Wiley & Sons, New Jersey, USA.

Kennedy, J., & Hyland, P. (2003). A comparison of manufacturing technology adoption in SMEs and large companies. In *Proceedings of 16th Annual Conference of Small Enterprise Association of Australia and New Zealand*, 1–10.

Kumar, M., Khurshid, K. K., & Waddell, D. (2014). Status of quality management practices in manufacturing SMEs: a comparative study between Australia and the UK. *International Journal of Production Research*, *52*(21), 6482–6495.

Lee, J., Jun, S., Chang, T. W., & Park, J. (2017). A smartness assessment framework for smart factories using analytic network process. *Sustainability*, *9*(5), 794.

Lichtblau, K., Stich, V., Bertenrath, R., Blum, M., Bleider, M., Millack, A., Schmitt, K., Schmitz, E., & Schröter, M. (2015). *IMPULS – Industrie 4.0 Readiness*. Project Report Impuls – VDMA, Aachen-Kölns.

Mittal, S., Khan, M. A., Romero, D., & Wuest, T. (2018). A critical review of smart manufacturing & industry 4.0 maturity models: implications for small and medium-sized enterprises (SMEs). *Journal of Manufacturing Systems*, *49*, 194–214.

Müller, J., Dotzauer, V., & Voigt, K. I.(2017). Industry 4.0 and its impact on reshoring decisions of German manufacturing enterprises. In: Bode, C., Bogaschewsky, R., Eßig, M., Lasch, R., Stölzle, W.(eds.) Supply Management Research(pp. 165–179). Springer Gabler, Wiesbaden.

Schumacher, A., Erol, S., & Sihn, W. (2016). A maturity model for assessing Industry 4.0 readiness and maturity of manufacturing enterprises. *Changeable, Agile, Reconfigurable & Virtual Production*, *52*, 161–166.

SME 4.0 (2019). SME 4.0 Smart manufacturing and logistics for SMEs in an X-to-order and mass customization environment. Retrieved on September 17, 2019, from http://www.sme40.eu.

Terziovski, M. (2010). Innovation practice and its performance implications in small and medium enterprises (SMEs) in the manufacturing sector: a resource-based view. *Strategic Management Journal*, *31*(8), 892–902.

Vasudevan, H., & Chawan, A. (2014). Demystifying knowledge management in Indian manufacturing SMEs. *Procedia Engineering*, *97*, 1724–1734.

Wang, Y., Fakhry, R., & Anderl, R. (2017). Combined secure process and data model for IT-Security in Industrie 4.0. In *Proceedings of the International MultiConference of Engineers and Computer Scientists 2017 (Vol. 2).*

Wang, Y., Tran, T., & Anderl, R. (2018a). Toolbox approach for the development of new business models in Industrie 4.0. In *Proceedings of the World Congress on Engineering and Computer Science (Vol. 2).*

Wang, Y., Wang, G., & Anderl, R. (2016). Generic procedure model to introduce Industrie 4.0 in small and medium-sized enterprises. In *Proceed of the World Congress on Engineering and Computer Science (Vol. 2).*

Wang, Y., Faath, A., Goerne, T., & Anderl, R. (2018b). Development of a toolbox for engineering in project teams for Industrie 4.0. In *Proceedings of the International MultiConference of Engineers and Computer Scientists (Vol. 2).*

Wuest, T., Thoben, K. D. (2012). Information management for manufacturing SMEs. In: Frick J., Laugen B. T. (eds.) Advances in Production Management Systems. Value Networks: Innovation, Technologies, and Management. APMS 2011. *IFIP Advances in Information and Communication Technology, Vol 384.* Springer, Berlin, Heidelberg.

Zezulka, F., Marcon, P., Bradac, Z., Arm, J., Benesl, T., & Vesely, I. (2018). Communication systems for Industry 4.0 and the IIoT. In *15th IFAC Conference on Programmable Devices and Embedded Systems PDES*, Ostrava, Czech Republic, May 2018.

Esin Bozyazı

Digital Transformation and Social Sustainability

Abstract: Digital transformation promises new business models, increasing profits through enhanced efficiency, and numerous simplifications in our everyday lives. Besides the many opportunities, there are also challenges that must be taken seriously. Those challenges are typically non-technical, concerning social implications of living with advanced digital technologies, artificial intelligence, and the hidden rules of algorithms (Daugherty, 2018). The increasingly fast evolution of algorithms taking over human decision-making, which run everything from search engines to marketing displays, raise questions that we should discuss: What role should humans play in the future world? Is everything that is feasible also desirable? Is it justifiable? Do we have to re-define society and intellectual property protection for our lives with algorithms and throw all the traditional principles of human intelligence and logic overboard? The aim of this argumentative essay is to show the social dimension of challenges through digital transformation by working out a roadmap based on previous research results. The essay will try to find the "right questions for the next step in digital transformation" that we can use in our decision processes, and that we can consider social aspects. What work process suits humans or machines? How can they collaborate with each other? The social sustainability to be considered here is the human view and the human fears that are neglected in the business world. The additional questions evolving from the change of perspective shall help managers to have a better foundation for future decisions in order to use digital transformation properly to develop solutions that are more socially acceptable and macroeconomicly sustainable.

Keywords: Social sustainability, human digital transformation, human-centered, human-machine collaboration, sustainable digital transformation, business with social impact

Introduction

In terms of digitization or digital transformation, we often feel a strong sense of uncertainty. Part of it is called "fear", combined with an "urgency of action" in politics, in science and especially in the economy

– in every part of our social life and in us as people.

What is digitization? What awaits us? What do we have to do first? What are the future perspectives for us as human beings, as persons in our environment and in our relationships, e.g., in a family, in a business, in an economy, in a state, in politics, in the world? Parents feel overwhelmed by the digital natives, companies question everything and do not know how or what they should start with: processes, employees, organization, with everything.

We define "social sustainability" as a good relationship of people to themselves, others and their environment (land, politics and nature). The question is how we can achieve the best possible human relationships with ourselves and others in this new kind of environment: the totally unexplored and also exciting new digital land. How can we make digital transformation socially sustainable? How can people (managers, employees, suppliers, customers) feel comfortable and work on digital transformation with as little concern as possible? How can we take away people's concerns and provide them with the best working and decision-making conditions for successfully implementing digital transformation?

Today we are dealing with these questions and issues relating to the digital transformation worldwide in different contexts. This essay also deals with this topic and takes particular account of the social aspects of digital transformation. We focus on humans because we believe that digital transformation is also human transformation and because we are striving for a human digital transformation.

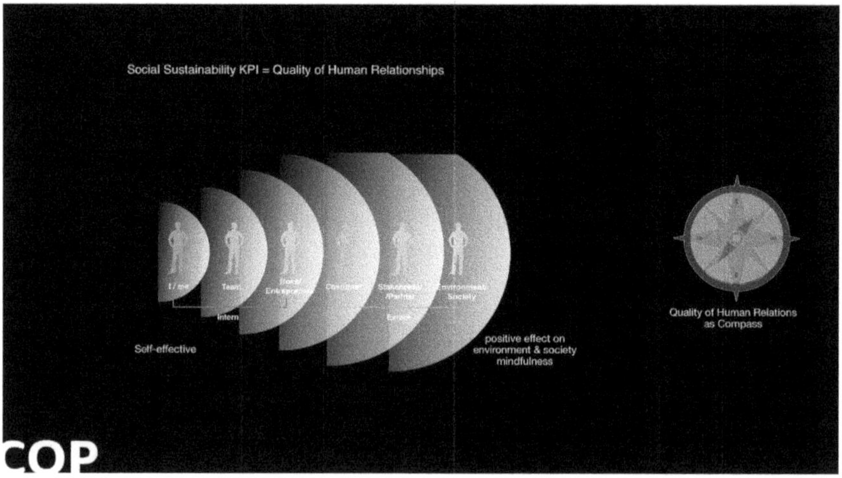

Figure 1: Quality of Human Relations as a Social Sustainability Compass (Bozyazi, 2019).

Even though everybody is aware of that we have to do something, a big question mark is about the best way how to successfully put it into practice. There is no advice or a clear approach. Our pursuit is to find a solution for a more human-centered process. Therefore, we can use the compass for social sustainability (quality of human relationships) as a guide to the right direction in the jungle of digital transformation (Figure 1). In this complex world, there is no perfect answer to all questions, but we can use a human-centered perspective to design the right questions for the future. Thus, we can give Business Leaders an approach how to deal with future challenges.

The purpose of this argumentative essay is to highlight the social dimensions of challenges posed by digital transformation and to develop a roadmap based on previous research. The essay will seek to find "the right questions for the next step in digital transformation". We can use these in our decision-making processes to consider social issues.

Digital Transformation and Social Sustainability

"*Any Big Problem is a Big Opportunity*" (Khosla, 2002).

Digital transformation is a cultural and social change. So we have a change problem (also an opportunity). Kubler-Ross's change management approach can be transferred to digital transformation in order to better understand the development. In his model, he describes the seven phases of change. These phases of change are shown as the Kubler-Ross Curve in Figure 2.

The Kubler-Ross Model also holds true when it comes to business, work or employment. Every organization needs to bring about changes in its management and policies. But besides the improvement of systems, there must be a change in the people or employees as well. If even bringing about several changes in systems and processes the employees of your company persist in their old ways, thousands of dollars invested will go waste. This is why, it is important for the employees too to adapt and change accordingly. Only when the workforce of an organization makes personal changes or transitions can the company move ahead and reap the benefits.

Every organization needs to support the employees in the process of making transitions or changes. These individual transformations can be traumatic and may involve a lot of power loss and prestige issues. The easier it is for the employees to move along on their journey, the easier will it be for the organization to move toward success. Thus, this impacts the success rate and overall profits experienced by the company. The Change Curve in business is thus a powerful model that can help one understand and deal with changes and personal transitions. It helps to fathom how one will react to change and how to provide support during the process of change. (Cleverism, 2015).

If we transfer the phases of change in the sense of digital transformation to the German economy, we are usually in the fourth phase. The experience with our clients and several studies confirm this assumption. We have now almost

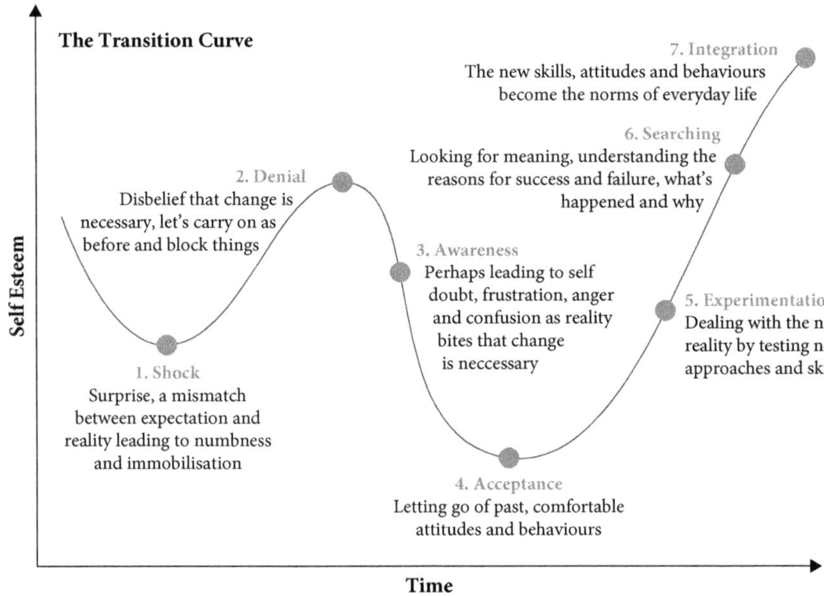

Figure 2: Kubler-Ross Change Curve (Brenig-Jones, 2018).

reached the fourth level of acceptance in Germany (in Figure 2). This also means that German companies let go of old attitudes and behaviors. The next step is to experiment and explore the new reality by testing new approaches and capabilities. It takes time to go to the next step in the change circle. However, it is much quicker to reach the final phases compared to phases one to four.

In the special study by bearinPoint.com about Digital Transformation (257 Companies in 3 Countries D, A, CH) in 2018 with 5,000 interviews, there is still a need to catch up in areas such as *corporate culture, HR and agile organization.* These areas will be discussed below. (Bearing Point, n.d.)

Agility and competitiveness

The classic form of organization in almost all companies is a pyramid, consisting of an upper and lower area, a left and a right. As a result, the divisions are separated from each other, and it amounts to Silo mentality and internal competition. In addition, there are sluggish decision-making processes due to overburdened and under-informed decision makers. The insight that performance and added value can only emerge as an overall product and that everyone has to make their contribution is lost or even absent. The result is that all are 100% busy, but only work 50% or less. Paradox? Not when work is defined as a direct contribution to value creation and is understood as meeting customer needs or increasing competitiveness. Everything else is employment. The principles of such organizations are: instruction and control, rules and regulations, formal hierarchies, planning and control, etc. (Bozyazi, 2017).

If agile tools such as Scrum or Design Thinking are introduced in such classic organizational structures, success can only be minimal or even negative because these tools follow very different principles: self-organization rather than control, feedback and iterative improvement rather than control, principles rather than rules, changing leadership through reputation rather than formal hierarchy, preparation rather than planning, just to name a few. We call organizations that follow such principles agile or dynamic robust. Teams are functionally organized: everything needed for business activities is present in the cell (Herbert, 2017).

The cells have direct contact with the "market": customers and competitors. If something changes, it can react quickly. In this case, the market, the customers and the activities of the competitors "control" the organization, not the center.

If information or support is required for the business, e.g., from the Controlling, IT, Purchasing or HR department, these are requested. The so-called Info- or Orga-shops can make recommendations, but the decision is up to the cells. So if daily business is done by the cells, what exactly do business managers and owners do? Quite simply, you have the big picture in mind and make sure that the organization can obtain enough new impetus from outside to stay connected and respond adequately to medium to long-term change. They determine what fits in with the business model and what does not and thus they fundamentally guide the course of the company.

> *Success formula for agile transformation: urgency x vision x know-how x mindset = successful transformation* (Bozyazi, 2017, p. 66-76):

Communicate urgency The Digital Revolution does not change the landscape like the railroad did. And it is not loud and nor does it pollute the air like factories. It is quieter, faster and less obtrusive than the Industrial Revolution was, so it is underestimated by too many. It is essential to ensure that the employees are aware of this and also that every change always opens up new opportunities.

Vison: what exactly? Is it worth abandoning paths that have been made and questioning previous thinking and actions? What would be the alternative? Create a worthwhile picture of the future of work, your vision in which:

- free time and working hours no longer have to be distinguished between but rather the meaningful use of life,

- occupational health management is as unnecessary as works councils and trade unions,
- compatibility of family and work is no longer a topic worthy of discussion,
- everyone can develop their individual talents and use them for their own life,
- work is fun again.

Address the needs of people: simplicity, autonomy, freedom of design, security, acceptance, etc. This creates a personal connection to the agile transformation and generates motivation and commitment. Employees will act voluntarily.

Know-how: Agile, but how? Quite simple: we have to stop managing. That would provide 0% of power with 50% agility. The rest is know-how: what laws do teams follow when they suddenly have to organize themselves? How do you deal with conflicts as a leader? Which alternatives are available for budgeting and measuring individual performance? What is meant by Consensus Individual Decisions, Sociocratic Consensus or Systemic Consensus? When do you use which of these decision-making procedures? Why can corporate culture not be changed directly, and where else can you start? What is the difference between working on and working in the system? Why can Agile Transformation not work as a rollout according to the waterfall model? And how does roll-in work? Anyone who demands lifelong learning from his employees should not make an exception for himself (Bozyazi, 2017).

Principles – important part of the know-how. When it comes to digitization and agility, most think of tools and methods. Few have dealt with the underlying principles, without which a successful launch of Kanban, Scrum and Design Thinking and Co. is not possible.

Mindset and personal maturity: The hardest-to-describe factor concerns social sustainability. What helps to develop the necessary mindset? Systemic-constructivist training, for example. At the very least, this is confirmed by executives who have furthered their education in this area or, rather, have developed further. The will and the ability to self-reflect, combined with the knowledge that you have virtually nothing under control. Curiosity and openness to everything that is different and thinks differently. The permanent questioning of the principles and assumptions behind our thoughts and actions. The study of philosophy, sociology and system theory in order to lead a few scientific disciplines in the field. Not least respect for oneself, all other forms of life and the awareness of one's own finitude. The list goes on.

Also, Digital transformation requires a change in corporate culture (special mindset and personal maturity) and society. Change is the only constant in human history. So, the changes in our DNA are present and in no case is the implementation of the changes hopeless, even if some change experiences provide counterexamples. It takes time for the change to be internalized. This can be shortened by targeted measures and by global influences, for example. How can you design the changes in the company, and how can we consider human perspective and ensure social sustainability? For this, we first define and introduce the base principles of social sustainability.

Definition of Social Sustainability according to the UN Global Sustainability Goals: "Social sustainability is about identifying and managing business impacts, both positive and negative, on people. The quality of a company's relationships and engagement with its stakeholders is critical. Directly or indirectly, companies affect what happens to employees, workers in the value chain, customers and local communities, and it is important to manage impacts proactively" (United Nations Global Compact, n.d.).

Figure 3: Sustainable Development Goals (SGD) (UN Global Compact, n.d.).

The first six of the UN Global Compact's principles focus on this social dimension of corporate sustainability, of which human rights is the cornerstone and covers the human rights of specific groups: labor, women's empowerment and gender equality, children, indigenous peoples, people with disabilities, as well as people-centered approaches to business impacts on poverty. As well as covering groups of those with rights, social sustainability encompasses issues that affect them, for example, education and health.

Businesspeople should undertake to avoid harming human rights and to address any adverse impacts on human rights that may be related to their activities.

They should contribute in other ways to improving the lives of the people they affect, such as by creating decent jobs, goods and services that help meet basic needs and more inclusive value chains.

In the business world, actions to achieve social sustainability may unlock new markets, help retain and attract business partners, or be the source of innovation for new product or service lines. Internal morale and employee engagement may rise, while productivity, risk management and company-community conflict improve (Bozyazi, 2018).

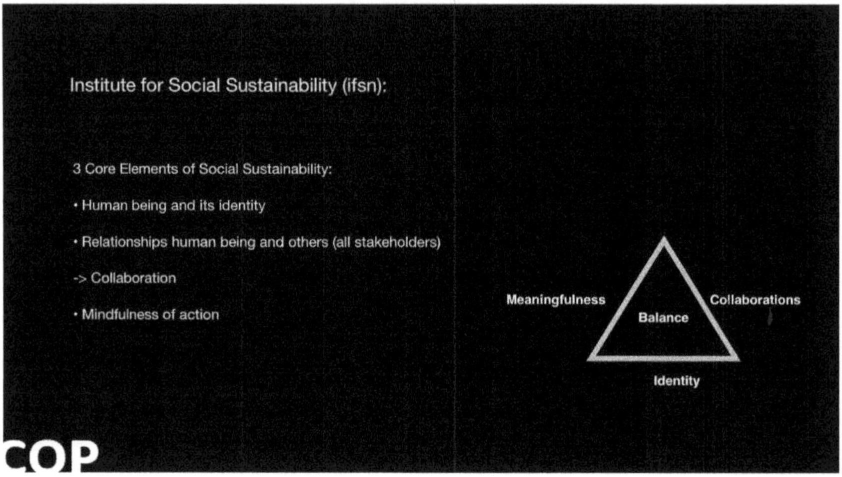

Figure 4: Action Levels of Social Sustainability – Based on Three Core Elements of Social Sustainability (Bozyazı, 2019).

A society whose members do not cultivate relationships with each other can hardly be imagined as a socially sustainable society that can be sustained as a society.

Relationships grow into a community that, in a way, holds together and is capable of reciprocity, solidarity, and common sense. But only good relationships are building blocks for social cohesion, as they are an international relations basis for coexistence, peace or even partnership.

What makes good relationships? In the latest release by James Ritchie Dunham "Ecosynomics: the science of abundance" distinguishes five relationships: the "self" (ego), the "other" (you), the "group" (us), the "nature" and the "spirit" (Dunham, 2014, p.5). In these various dimensions, Ritchie Dunham has different states that describe poorer or better relationship qualities.

Institute for Social Sustainability (ifsn) defines three core elements of social sustainability and three levels of action (Figure 4). People have many more as well as diverse relationships – this essay focuses especially on three relations of human, partially summarized. These are relations between (Castellucci, 2016, pp. 6):

1. Identity – person and relationship to himself
2. Collaboration – person and relationship to others (including groups, teams, business partners, managers, bosses, employees and within virtual teams) and
3. Meaningfulness of work (including relationship to nature)

In addition, a balance between action levels must be achieved to enable social sustainability. All three levels play an important role in the understanding of humanity at least in the value system of today's Europe. Therefore, the balance must be based on human dignity and its social and ideal needs. The actions are based consequently on a human-centered approach.

Challenge Question:

How can we achieve the balance between the three illustrated action levels to enable social sustainability?

Identity of person and relationship to himself

When we – as an individual – act self-confidently in the world, when we participate and share fully, we are self-effective. In this stage, we experience great strength and happiness that embraces all people around us (cf. Ritchie-Dunham, 2014, p. 5). Thus, we should draw attention to the spectrum of possibilities how we can reach such a stage and how we can be self-effective in the business world.

Of course, it depends on the level of personal development of those affected. However, companies can create the framework for further development. The Philosophy and Vision of companies can be extended with Ethikcodex (in USA, e.g., BCorp (B-Corporation/ see https://bcorporation.net)), which describes the frameworks of good cooperation. These could include the following values:

- Social values
- Human values
- Values of pluralism and Diversity

In addition, further training measures as well as personal coaching and activities to promote these values could help to build and extend the required qualities in the company, which on the one hand further humanity in the company and on the other hand support the change through digital transformation:

- Open mindedness
- Empathy
- Lifetime learning
- WE-Q (=Team-intelligence) instead IQ (=Individual-intelligence)
- Networking
- Creativity

For both measures, a suitable good communication concept is unavoidable. Transparency and compliance are also an important part of the communication concept. Especially it needs orientation, learning and new habits of handling a whole new digital toolset.

Depending on the size of the company, the Golden Rule can be experienced through implemented role models or through binding rules for individuals, regardless of the hierarchy:

"Treat others as you would like to be treated by them". In other words, the more robust Silver Rule says: "Do not treat others the way you do not want to be treated by them" (Taleb, 2018). The framework conditions for personal development and personal happiness will then be exemplarily illustrated in the following chapters under two selected aspects of social sustainability (diversity & participation/education).

Challenge Question:

How can we be self-effective in the business world?

Collaboration as mindset – between all stakeholders

Society as a whole can quite probably be interpreted in the global world as a "network society". So, in a networked world, relationships are important. However, it is not just the purely quantitative relationships in the network; it is the quality of the relationships that needs to be considered. Anne-Marie Slaughter wrote in 2009 in "Americas edge" about "Power in a networked world" saying, "In this world, the measure of power is connectedness."

In the context of social sustainability in this chapter, it is collaboration and not cooperation between stakeholders (customers, employees, the state, institutions, business partners and competitors), as collaboration is considered a principle of good relations. The difference between the two terms shown in the excursus (s. excurses).

In practical work with networks, three levels of action have proven to be critical to success, matching the dimensions of relationships shown.

The main focus in working with networks is on good collaboration. Above all, good communication is crucial for this. The second area of successful networking, however, involves the identities and self-esteem of the individual participants. In short, those who do not have their own safe stance, have fluctuating self-esteem (also in the sense of being self-aware, that is, who I am or want to be) or lack self-esteem, are also an unstable factor in collaboration.

The third limiting factor to successful joint work is about common orientations. This can be achieved through an agenda of common goals and priorities or the overall sense of value creation. However, the frequently occurring and often deep-seated problems of cooperation tend to result less from how the collaboration is organized. The commonality of basic orientations in the form of values or goals is already more difficult to elaborate or keep upright. It also plays a role that the values and goals of an organization are not necessarily shared by all their relatives. Discontinuities on the personal level can mean breaks and twists. Surprisingly, however, the basic preoccupation with the "why" is missing. (Castellucci, 2016).

Excurses into the deeper understanding of Co-Laboration vs. Co-Operation:

> "*When collaborating, people work together (co-labor) on a single shared goal.*
> *Like an orchestra which follows a script everyone has agreed upon and each musician plays their part not for its own sake but to help make something bigger.*
> *When cooperating, people perform together (co-operate) while working on selfish yet common goals.*
> *The logic here is "If you help me, I'll help you" and it allows for the spontaneous kind of participation that fuels peer-to-peer systems and distributed networks. If an orchestra is the sound of collaboration, then a drum circle is the sound of cooperation.*
> *For centuries collaboration has powered most of our society's institutions.*
> *This is true of everything from our schools to our governments where we have worked together through consensus to build systems of increasing complexity.*
> *But today, cooperation is fueling most of the disruptive innovations of our time.*
> *In virtually every aspect of our culture, the old guard is being replaced by cooperative, self-organizing, distributed systems.*" ("collectives", n.d.)

Challenge Question:

How do we design the good relations in our business in digital work environments?

Meaningful work – the why?

Meaningful work is something we all want. It is a topic in the field of psychology, management studies, sociology and ethics. The psychiatrist Viktor Frankl famously described how the innate human quest for meaning is so strong that, even in the direst circumstances, people seek out their purpose in life. During a review of the literature on meaningful work, we define meaningful work as *"when an individual perceives an authentic connection between work and a broader transcendent life purpose beyond the self. More recently, researchers have shown meaningfulness to be more important to employees than any other aspect of work, including pay and rewards, opportunities for promotion, or working conditions."* (Bailey & Madden, 2016). Meaningful work can be highly motivational, leading to improved performance, commitment and satisfaction.

In 2016, Bailey and Madden interviewed 135 people in UK working in 10 very different occupations and asked them to tell stories about incidents or times when they found their work to be meaningful and, conversely, times when they asked themselves, "What's the point of doing this job?" They found that meaningfulness tended to be intensely personal and individual; it was often revealed to employees as they reflected in their work and its wider contribution to society in ways that mattered to them as individuals. The research showed that quality of leadership was virtually not mentioned when people described meaningful moments at work, but poor management was the top destroyer of meaningfulness (Bailey & Madden, 2016).

The study found that meaningfulness appeared to be increased and decreased by different factors, whereas the interviewees tended to find meaningfulness for themselves rather than it being mandated by their managers. The study discovered that if employers want to destroy that sense of meaningfulness, it was far more easily achieved. The feeling of "Why am I bothering to do this?" strikes people as the instant a meaningless moment arises, and it strikes people hard. Avoiding the destruction of meaningful work while nurturing an ecosystem generating (or-regenerating) feelings of meaningfulness emerged as the key leadership challenge (Bailey & Madden, 2016).

The seven deadly sins when it comes to meaningful work

What factors serve to destroy the fragile sense of meaningfulness that individuals find in their work? Interestingly, the factors that seem to drive a sense of meaninglessness and futility around work were very different from those one might at a first glance associate with meaningfulness. The experiences that actively led people to ask, "Why am I doing this?" were generally a function of how people were treated by managers and leaders. Interviewees noted seven things that leaders did to create a feeling of meaninglessness (listed in order from most to least grievous) (Bailey & Madden.2016):

1. Disconnect people from their values.
2. Take your employees for granted.
3. Give people pointless work to do.

4. Treat people unfairly.
5. Override people's better judgment.
6. Disconnect people from supportive relationships.
7. Put people at risk of physical or emotional harm.

We have to take care of the people in their values and prepare an ecosystem to secure this, especially in a change process of digital transformation. Digital transformation is making it happen – frequent change, increased demands and always-connected expectations that can take its toll on humans. The quantitative proof is accumulating as well. According to Gallup's 2017 State of the Global Workplace report, an overwhelming majority of employees (85%) reported being either not engaged or actively disengaged at work – in which Gallup estimates costs companies $7 trillion a year in lost productivity (Overby, n.d.).

Meanwhile, the Yale Center for Emotional Intelligence found that one out of five highly engaged employees said their burnout levels were also high – and researchers uncovered even higher turnover rates among this group than disengaged workers.

> *"We're constantly bombarded by information from our devices, but when you constantly react to every buzz and bing, you end up in a state of overwhelm"* said Peter Bostelmann, director of SAP's Global Mindfulness Practice, in an interview with CMO by Adobe. *"It's the reality of the global economy, and we have to find ways to cope with it."* (Machmeier, 2018).

Challenge Question:

How can we create an ecosystem for feelings of meaningfulness?

Balance and dependency between three action levels

The three considered action levels (1) good relationships with oneself, (2) Joint work with others, and (3) the meaningfulness of work are the framework within which we can develop social sustainability. In a socially sustainable society, individuals develop their full potential, build resilient relationships and collaboration (which is deeper than co-operation), and it also creates a healthy orientation on a meaningful whole which is both: An incentive to us and a motivation!. All three areas depend on each other and, in the best case, support and stimulate each other (Castellucci, 2016).

Conclusion: How to Meet the Challenges of Digital Transformation with a Clear Concept of Social Sustainability

This essay provides a sketch of a more human-centered perspective on digital transformation processes. It illuminates blind spots that can occur from a narrow implementation that emphasizes mainly the technical challenges of digital transformation. To promote the idea of a more holistic approach, it stresses the deficits from a social sustainability point of view and suggests spheres of activity as well as factors of success that focus mainly on the people that have to deal with the challenges of digital transformation in their daily business. Thus, this chapter is an attempt to build awareness for the requirements and human needs within the process of digital transformation. With the goal to integrate social sustainability into this massive change of economic habits, it can give a framework for spheres of activity and a broader understanding of the factors of success. With the vision to harmonize this transformation toward digitalization with human needs and shape a digital revolution that it is integrating and serving social sustainability, this essay focuses on good relationships as the core of social sustainability within the digital transformation. Because as Wilhelm von Humboldt said, *"Basically, it's always the connections with people who give life its value"* (Humboldt, n.d.). And improving quality of life and securing and developing a future worth living in should be the higher goal of all our economic actions.

References

Bailey, C. and Madden A. (2016). *What Makes Work Meaningful — Or Meaningless* Retrieved November 4, 2019 from https://sloanreview.mit.edu/article/what-makes-work-meaningful-or-meaningless/.

Bearing Point (n.d.). *Lost in Digitalization – Digitalisierungsmonitor 2018.* Retrieved November 4, 2019 from https://www.bearingpoint.com/de-de/unser-erfolg/insights/digitalisierungsmonitor-2018/?gclid=CjwKCAjwiZnnBRBQEiwAcWKfYusKIXWaiGJMn3lsTeSedta13qhuXcYGBbCsb050FcxNGMrOND0FUhoCElwQAvD_BwE.

Bozyazi, E. (2017). *Business Design Workshops. Inspiration für Innovatoren und Start-ups.* Schäffer-Poeschel- Verlag, Stuttgart.

Bozyazi, E. (2018). *Soziale Nachhaltigkeit. Was ist das überhaupt?. Keynote-Presentation.* Reallabor STADT-RAUM-BILDUNG. On 11. 10. 2018. in Heidelberg.

Bozyazi, E. (2019). *Digital Transformation and Social Sustainability.* Presentation in 1st Annual Business Administration Conference on Digital Transformation in Business (theory/practice), Turkish-German University, Istanbul, Turkey on 15.11.2019.

Brenig-Jones, M. (2018). *Brexit: The Challenge of Accepting Change.* Retrieved November 4, 2019 from https://www.catalystconsulting.co.uk/brexit-challenge-accepting-change/.

Castellucci, L. (2016). *Nachhaltigkeit vom Menschen her gedacht. Die soziale Dimension als Schlüssel zurnachhaltigen Entwicklung*. Discussion Paper Series No.1. Mannheim.

Cleverism (2015). *Understanding the Kubler-Ross Change Kurve*. 24.06.2015. Retrieved October 4, 2019 from https://www.cleverism.com/understanding-kubler-ross-change-curve/ June 2015.

Daugherty, P. R., Wilson, J. (2018). *Human + Machine. Reimagining Work in the Age of AI*. Accenture Global Solutions Limited. Harvard Business Review Press, Boston, Massachusetts (Audible).

Herbert, L. (2017). *Digital Transformation. Build Your Organization's Future for the Innovation Age*. (Audible). Bloomsbury Business Publishing, London.

Humboldt, W. von (n.d.). Im Grunde sind es immer die Verbindungen mit Menschen, die dem Leben seinenWert geben. https://gutezitate.com/autor/wilhelm-von-humboldt Retrieved October 4, 2019 from https://gutezitate.com/autor/wilhelm-von-humboldt.

Khosla, V. (2002). *Any Big Problem is a Big Opportunity*. In Kleiner, Perkins (April,2002). Retrieved November 4, 2019 from https://www.youtube.com/watch?v=p2FMQQ_VaKc., by Stanford eCorner.

Machmeier, C. (2018). *Mastering Digital Transformation with Mindfulness*. Retrieved October 10, 2019 from https://news.sap.com/2018/09/mindfulness-training-master-digital-transformation/.

Overby, S. (2019). *Mindfulness And The Importance Of Digital Disengagement*. Retrieved October 4, 2019 from https://cmo.adobe.com/articles/2018/2/mindfulness-in-the-digital-age.html#gs.88gb1g.

Ritchie-Dunham, J. (2014). *Ecosynomics*. Vibrancy Publishing, USA.

Slaughter, A. (2009). *America´s edge. Power in the networked century*. Foreign Affers, Vol. 88, 1, January/February 2009: 94–113.

Taleb, N. (2018). *Skin in the Game*. (Audible). Penguin. Munich.

United Nations Global Compact (n.d.). *Social Sustainability*. Retrieved October 4, 2019 from https://www.unglobalcompact.org/what-is-gc/our-work/social.

"collectives" (n.d.). *Cooperation vs Collaboration*. Retrieved November 4, 2019 from http://cloudhead.headmine.net/post/3279118157/cooperation-vs-collaboration.

Çiydem Çatak

Digital Transformation in Finance: Robo-Advisors vs. Human Financial Advisors

Abstract: Robo-advisors are financial advisory tools that help investors to make appropriate investment decisions. These digital services protect investors through professional asset management based on their time horizon, risk tolerance and investment preferences. Robo-advisors quickly spread around the world and begin to compete with human advisors. This study makes a comparison between robo and human advisors. The future of robo-advisors was discussed, and the potential of this digital consulting service was investigated. While innovative robo-advisors are seen as competitors to traditional human consultants, this study shows that robo-advisors are not suitable for dedicated, self-managed investors and for investors seeking a high level of personal service. On the other hand, it is concluded that the development of new algorithms, models and personalized services will help drive digital asset management.

Keywords: Robo-advisors, traditional human advisors, risk profiling, portfolio optimization

Introduction

Digitalization is today an indispensable necessity and no longer a choice. As in all other areas, digitalization has also an important place in finance. Banks, investment and insurance companies have been strongly influenced by digitalization and have undergone a radical transformation process in recent years. Both in Turkey and also in the financial industry around the world, everyone has recently experienced innovative digital applications. Robo-advisors are one of these digital services that provide an automated investment with minimal human intervention. With more than 200 robo-advisors, the USA is the market leader (Abraham, Schmukler & Tessada, 2019). On the other hand, with a total of 31 robo-advisors, Germany has the largest share in Europe (Burnmark, 2017). According to Statista's report, in 2019, robo-advisors manage approximately $980.541 million assets and are expected to have an annual growth of 27%. In addition, the number of robo-advisor users is estimated to be 147.018 by 2023. On the other hand, if we look at the situation in Turkey, even though robo-advisors are only just beginning to enter our lives, assets under management in the robo-advisor sector stand at $22 million in 2019, and it is supposed to have an annual growth rate of 47% between 2019 and 2023 resulting in total amount of $102 million by 2023. The number of users is estimated to reach to 17.5 thousand by 2023 (Statista, 2019).

In a certain phase of life, for small investments, investments for the future of the children or for the car loans, everyone needs financial advice. Banks often offer an investment solution for these situations, or there are companies that give investment recommendations. According to Georgarakos and Inderst (2011), taking financial advice is an essential factor in households' willingness to invest. For this reason, traditional human financial advisors entered our lives years ago and were generally preferred by people who want to get professional help. The process of investment is actually not easy for everyone especially for the people who do not have financial skills and who are afraid to invest. In general, they get nervous when they make their own investment decisions (Kahneman & Riepe, 1998). It seems too risky. They want someone else to do it for them, but they do not want to pay high fees for this service. This is where robo-advisors came in; one of the strongest trends in the financial service industry. A robo-advisor is an online platform set up by a bank, brokerage firm or company to help people invest the right portfolios (KPMG, 2015). Customers connect to a system as online, complete detailed questionnaire for the purpose of determining their risk profile, investment objectives and time horizon. There's nothing more to do, robo-advisors do everything else. They create and manage the ideal portfolio for clients whose risk profile is determined. Clients' money is automatically invested in a well-diversified portfolio with the right mix of stocks, bonds, real estate, etc. These digital financial advisors, which enable customers to create and invest in the right portfolio according to their investment goals and risk profile, also manage the portfolios they create for their customers. Above all, they offer a time-saving, cost-effective and long-term meaningful investment strategy. The investment strategies of robo-advisors are based on algorithms. They observe the financial markets at any time and make adjustments if there is a need to achieve the highest possible long-term return (Deloitte, 2016).

The aim of this study is to describe the emergence of robo-advisors, the similarities and differences to traditional human advisors and the future potential of robo-advisors. The chapter is structured as follows. First, the risk profile is presented in detail, and models for creating an optimal portfolio are explained. Robo-advisors are then introduced, and the differences between human advisors are mentioned. Finally, the study is summarized and some future suggestions are made.

Determination of the Optimal Portfolio on the Basis of the Risk Profile

The robo-advisors offer the right portfolios depending on the risk profile of the investors. The term "risk profile" is used to classify investors' risk appetite as the basis for investment recommendations. It is a process for identifying the ideal degree of investment risk by balancing three key components of the risk, which are required risk, risk capacity and risk tolerance. Risk tolerance is the psychological willingness to take risk. Besides that, the risk capacity is the financial ability to take risk, and required risk is the need to take risk (Ramudzuli, 2016). It is impossible to recommend suitable investments unless the exact risk profile of the investor is understood. It is well known that the "buyer beware" philosophy has harmed too many investors in the history (Klement, 2015).

The individual risk profile is influenced by a number of factors, including personal risk appetite and the investor's life and financial situation. Therefore, we can say that risk profiles are not static. Basic life events such as marital status, educational status, the continuity of the investor's income, experiences, habits and motives, cultural background and expectations can have a lasting influence on the risk profile (Chavali & Mohanraj, 2016). Today, the risk profile can be determined using three methods. The first method is to create a risk profile based on customers' demographic characteristics. The risk profile of an investor is determined by age, gender, number of children and occupation. The second method is to look at the past investment decisions of the investors and create a new risk profile. As the last method, a survey can be used to determine the risk profile of the investor. There are scenario-based questions and clear questions such as: Can you estimate your risk tolerance from one to ten? (ten is the highest). On the other hand, scenario-based questions explain a particular situation and try to learn from these scenarios how investors behave when they are in the same situation. With the answers they receive, they try to create an appropriate risk profile (Anbar & Eker, 2009).

The next step after determining the risk profile is to create an optimal portfolio according to the risk position of the people. The traditional portfolio selection model developed by Harry Markowitz states that an optimal portfolio can be achieved with diversification. The investor can diversify his portfolio and achieve maximum return at a risk level by selecting a variety of financial instruments. Based on very simple assumptions, Markowitz Portfolio model is the basis for many other models developed to solve the problem of portfolio optimization.

But it is a known fact that the Markowitz Portfolio Theory Framework has major problems such as extremely high input sensitivity, estimation error maximization and highly concentrated portfolios (Beketov, Lehmann & Wittke, 2018). Today, due to these problems, many complex models are being used in addition to the traditional portfolio theory to create an optimal portfolio. Black and Litterman, VaR and CVaR are some of these models.

The portfolios created according to the methods described above can be adapted to changes in the market and the lives of investors. As they are very sensitive to changes in the financial markets, some critics argue that robo-advisors remain below expectations during periods of instability and that their investment tactics will be insufficient. However, some argue that robo-advisors are not day traders and that too much emphasis on market movements already leads to negative trading decisions for long-term investors. If a buy-and-hold approach goes beyond that, robo-advisors should work well in times of uncertainty (Kaya, 2017).

Robo-Advisory vs. Human Advisory

Robo-advisors target younger generations, who tend to maintain digital services, value speed and ease of use (CH&Co, 2018). The key characteristics of robo-advisors are determining an automated customer profiling, leading an automated investment process and creating a passive investment product (Jung et al. 2018). Current robo-advisory functions can be specified as follows (Accenture, 2015):

1. Understand customer needs: Collecting customer information, understanding customer needs and preferences, evaluating risk appetite, considering outside accounts,
2. Propose solutions: Preparation of a financial plan, selection of asset allocation, choice of securities model, creation of proposals,
3. Implement solutions: open accounts, transfer assets,
4. Monitor results and adjust strategy: quarterly or annual performance evaluations, dashboards and progress reports, market updates and searches.

The workflow of a robo-advisor begins with investor profile identification. After that comes asset selection. Most of the robo advisors use EFTs because of being less risky. Once the risk profile has been defined, asset allocation and portfolio optimization phase comes. The next phase is monitoring and re-balancing based on the daily and calendar check. The last stage is performance review and reporting. It offers control and monitoring options over the website, smartphone app and e-mail (Beketov, Lehmann & Wittke, 2018).

People have been using traditional human advisors for advice-based wealth management for many years. The workflow of a human advisor is no different

Table 1: Robo-Advisors vs. Human Financial Advisors

Robo-Advisors	**Human Advisors**
Low cost for financial advice	Preferred by wealthy people
No minimum volume requirements for opening an account	Work only with very large investment portfolios
Fully automated investment service	Robust automated capabilities
Online questionnaire	In-depth conversations
Limited capabilities for providing commentary that is customized to each client's situation	More customized goal plan
A new generation of clients	Traditional generation not good with technology
No need of "in depth" market knowledge	Need to know the market well
Risk-return preference is static	Risk-return preference is dynamic

from that of a robo-advisor. The biggest difference between robo-advisor and traditional human advisor is assessing customer risk profile. Human advisors specify the risk profiles through conversations. With better identifying customer interests, human advisors can recommend more customized investment goal plans. On the other hand, the features that make robo-advisors more advantageous is lower fees, and there are not any limit requirements. This also enables people with small wealth to invest. Table 1 compares robo-advisors and human-advisors in detail.

Actually, investors should consider some aspects when choosing a financial advisor. The most important aspect is to consider their financial situation. If their situation is simple and they feel themselves comfortable with online transactions, then a robo-advisor could be better. If they have more complicated financial problems, then a traditional human advisor may be more suitable. Another important issue is interaction. If customers prefer the option of using an online tool instead of a human touch, robo-advisors are better suited for them. Another point concerns fees. This is essential for both traditional and online advisors. People who want to manage their wealth should pay attention to how much they value this service. With the arrival of robo-advisors, this service has become much cheaper. The low costs of robo-advisors have attracted the investors that are young and feel comfortable with online transactions and have low level of wealth. Of course, robo's innovation in financial advisory sector is not limited to these. Robo-advisors rightly question traditional financial advisors about their transparency (Renaux, Rudnicki, Beniere & Lorain, 2019).

Another reason why robo-advisors have recently become more attractive than human advisors is their transparency and objectivity. The wage system for human consultants is usually commission-based, which leads to conflicts of interest between the advisors and the clients and is a major obstacle to transparency (Better Finance, 2017). No "in-depth" financial and market knowledge is required to get advice from robo-advisors. However, in order to receive financial advice from human advisors, a certain amount of knowledge is required to analyze the accuracy of the recommendations. Robo advisors are not suitable for investors who have advanced financial knowledge and wish to change their portfolio according to their wishes. On the other hand, detailed discussions with personal consultants and jointly created portfolios can increase the attractiveness of human resources advisors. It is expected that the robo-advisors will renew themselves day by day and respond more closely to customer needs. The ability to track and test based on experience, synthesize customized solutions, explain complex and confusing issues and guide customers through difficult markets are the expected future capabilities of robo-advisors (Accenture, 2015).

Conclusion

Robo-advisors target mainly younger generations. However, being young and prone to technology does not necessarily mean that they will take robo-advisors into their lives. Robo-advisors will not work for committed self-directed investors. Investors who prefer a high degree of personal service would not find robo-advisors attractive. The robo-advisory industry is still at an early stage, and there is not much information about its true effects on the financial system. As robo-advisor industry grows and more knowledge about them gets to hand, additional understanding of this topic would help better identify their true capabilities and drawbacks.

Instead of looking at robots and humans separately, the combination of both systems would be a good option for the people who want to get investment advice. So they can take advantage of both robo-advisors and traditional human advisors. In the future, the best investment companies will combine customer-oriented technology with the advantages of human consulting.

References

Abraham, F., Schmukler, S. L. & Tessada, J. (2019). Using Big Data to Expand Financial Services: Benefits and Risks, *Research & Policy Briefs from the World Bank Chile Center*, No. 26, Malaysia Hub, and Seoul Center.

Accenture (2015). The Rise of Robo-Advice Changing the Concept of Wealth Management. Retrieved October 20, 2019 from https://www.accenture.com/_acnmedia/pdf-2/accenture-wealth-management-rise-of-robo-advice.pdf.

Anbar, A. & Eker, M. (2009). Bireysel Yatırımcıların Finansal Risk Algılamalarını Etkileyen Demografik ve Sosyoekonomik Faktörler, *ZKÜ Sosyal Bilimler Dergisi*, 5(9), 129–150.

Beketov, M., Lehmann, K. & Witthe, M. (2018). Robo Advisors: Quantitative Methods Inside the Robots, J Asset Management, https://doi.org/10.1057/s41260-018-0092-9.

Better Finance (2017). Robo-Investing: Cyborgs vs Robots: Competing to Attract European Cıtızens' Money. Retrieved October 22, 2019 from https://betterfinance.eu/fileadmin/user_upload/documents/Research_Reports/en/Robo_Investing_Report_070617.pdf.

Burnmark (2017). Digital Wealth Report

Chavali, K. & Mohanraj, M. P. (2016). Impact of Demographic Variables and Risk Tolerance on Investment Decisions: An Empirical Analysis, *International Journal of Economics and Financial Issues*, 6(1), 169–175

CH & CO (2018). Robo-Advisors: New Reality for Wealth and Asset Management. Retrieved November 5, 2019 from https://www.chappuishalder.com/wp-content/uploads/2019/05/8.-CHCO-Fintech-Article_Robo-Advisors.pdf.

Deloitte (2016). The Expansion of Robo-Advisory in Wealth Management. Retrieved November 1, 2019 from https://www2.deloitte.com/content/dam/Deloitte/de/Documents/financial-services/Deloitte-Robo-safe.pdf.

Georgarakos, D. & Inderst, R. (2011). Financial Advice and Stock Market Participation, *European Central Bank (ECB) Research Paper Series - Working Papers*, No. 1296.

Jung, D., Dorner, V., Glaser, F. & Morana, S. (2018). Robo-Advisory: Digitalization and Automation of Financial Advisory, https://www.researchgate.net/publication/322643071_Robo-Advisory_Digitalization_and_Automation_of_Financial_Advisory/link/5a67299fa6fdcc72a589cd2d/download.

Kahneman, D. & Riepe, M. W. (1998). Aspects of Investor Psychology Beliefs, Preferences, and Biases Investment Advisors Should Know About, Journal of Portfolio Management, 24(4), 67–91.

Kaya, O. (2017). Robo-Advice – A True Innovation in Asset Management, *Deutsche Bank Research, EU Monitor Global financial markets.*

Klement, J. (2015). Investor Risk Profiling: An Overview, *The CFA Institute Research Foundation Briefs*, 1(1).

KPMG (2015). Robo Advising: Catching up and Getting Ahead, *DealBook Conference*. Retrieved November 5, 2019 from https://assets.kpmg/content/dam/kpmg/pdf/2016/07/Robo-Advising-Catching-Up-And-Getting-Ahead.pdf.

Ramudzuli, P. M. (2016). Subjective Financial Risk Tolerance among Students at Selected South African Universities: A Comparative Analysis of Different Fields of Studies, https://repository.nwu.ac.za/bitstream/handle/10394/25432/Ramudzuli_PM.pdf?sequence=1&isAllowed=y.

Renaux, M. C., Rudnichi, M., Beniere, A. & Lorain, F. (2019). How Will Robo-Advisors Reshape Asset Management?, *Initio Group*. Retrieved November 5, 2019 from https://www.aixigo.com/fileadmin/user_upload/Ueber_uns/News_und_Presse/Dokumente/INITIO_White_Paper_Robo_Advisors_incl._Interview_CFR.pdf.

Statista Report (2019). https://www.statista.com/outlook/337/100/robo-advisors/worldwide.

www.ingramcontent.com/pod-product-compliance
Ingram Content Group UK Ltd.
Pitfield, Milton Keynes, MK11 3LW, UK
UKHW021833100926
8556IPUK00004B/308

9 783631 817186